PROFESSORS WHO BELIEVE

THE SPIRITUAL JOURNEYS OF CHRISTIAN FACULTY

edited by

PAUL M. ANDERSON

InterVarsity Press
Downers Grove, Illinois

InterVarsity Press
P.O. Box 1400, Downers Grove, IL 60515
World Wide Web: www.ivpress.com
E-mail: mail@ivpress.com

InterVarsity Press® is the book-publishing division of InterVarsity Christian Fellowship/USA®, a student movement active on campus at hundreds of universities, colleges and schools of nursing in the United States of America, and a member movement of the International Fellowship of Evangelical Students. For information about local and regional activities, write Public Relations Dept., InterVarsity Christian Fellowship/USA, 6400 Schroeder Rd., P.O. Box 7895, Madison, WI 53707-7895.

All Scripture quotations, unless otherwise indicated, are taken from the Holy Bible, New International Version®. NIV®. *Copyright ©1973, 1978, 1984 by International Bible Society. Used by permission of Zondervan Publishing House. All rights reserved.*

Chapter 5, "Three Heavens—Our Home," adapted from a lay sermon presented at the Macedonia United Methodist Church, Hockley, Texas, October 13, 1996.

Chapter 16, "Down by the Cross," ©1998 by Patricia Raybon.

Chapter 17, "Marxism and Me," reprinted and edited by permission from The American Enterprise, *July/August 1995.*

Cover illustration: Roberta Polfus

ISBN 0-8308-1599-6

Printed in the United States of America ⊖

Library of Congress Cataloging-in-Publication Data

Professors who believe : the spiritual journeys of Christian faculty /
edited by Paul M. Anderson.
    p.   cm.
   Includes bibliographical references.
   ISBN 0-8308-1599-6 (paper : alk. paper)
    1. Christian biography—United States.   2. Christian college
teachers—United States—Biography.   I. Anderson, Paul M., 1938- .
BR569.P76 1998
270'.088'372—dc21
[B]
                                                      98-27832
                                                          CIP

15	14	13	12	11	10	9	8	7	6	5	4	3
09	08	07	06	05	04	03						

To Carol
and to
Elmer and Eileen

Acknowledgments

Professors Glenn Tinder and Gene Ashby provided affirmation and encouragement when I asked them whether or not a book such as this one might be of value—I wish to express my thanks and appreciation to them. As I began the project, a colleague warned me about the difficulties inherent in putting together a collection of original essays. I interpreted that warning in the context of a friend's observation that obtaining the cooperation of university faculty in meeting deadlines is like herding cats. The project did take longer than I had anticipated, but not because of those who contributed to this volume. I wish to express my sincere thanks to all of the authors, not only for their timeliness in submitting their essays but also for their kind words of support and encouragement and for their acceptance of this work as a shared project.

Many individuals contributed to the process that led to the final selection of authors, including Terry Morrison, director of faculty ministries for InterVarsity Christian Fellowship, and Mike Duggins, national director of Christian Leadership Ministries, as well as their staffs. Their assistance and their encouragement are gratefully acknowledged. I was fortunate to have had expert professional advice and encouragement throughout the project from James Sire, who, along with Cam Anderson, was instrumental in bringing this collection to the attention of InterVarsity Press. Finally, I wish to express my gratitude to my wife, Carol—a wonderfully patient and faithful encourager.

Introduction

This We Proclaim

Consider the following excerpt from a letter that was written nearly two thousand years ago: "We proclaim to you what we have seen and heard, so that you also may have fellowship with us. And our fellowship is with the Father and with his Son, Jesus Christ. We write this to make our [some Greek manuscripts have 'your'] joy complete" (1 John 1:3). The author of this letter, a Jewish man named John, was apparently writing to several new church fellowship groups near the city of Ephesus (in western Turkey). He had been a witness to the life, the teaching, the death and the resurrection of someone named Jesus. This proclamation was made based on the conviction of John and others that this Jesus was from God and, in fact, was God. Jesus had entered into history in order to restore the broken relationship that existed between humankind and God as well as to model for people, as individuals and as a society, a much better way to live. A way of life that includes joy, no less! This was a rather audacious proclamation! Equally audacious is a similar statement in another letter written at about the same time: "My purpose is that they may be encouraged in heart and united in love, so that they may have the full riches of complete understanding, in order that they may know the mystery of God, namely, Christ [Jesus], in whom are hidden all the treasures of wisdom and knowledge" (Colossians 2:2).

Many modern university faculty members, whose honorable and legitimate business is (as it has been for centuries) exercising the mind to seek truth and knowledge and to teach about it, view the message of these writers, written two thousand years ago, as implausible and irrelevant. From a secular point of view this is perhaps understandable. Condoleeza Rice, provost at Stanford University, addressing a group of businesspersons said, "I believe that God gave us a brain and intends for us to use it. I believe that it is a part of his plan that we know more about the universe today than the disciples who walked with Jesus knew about their universe. That, I believe, is a part of the growth of humanity. So I don't see knowledge and understanding and science and exploration and progress as threats to my faith. Nonetheless, have you ever tried to explain why you believe what you do about God? It is very hard, frightening, sometimes unrewarding because the story of our Lord must just sound incredible to people who don't believe."[1] Yet the fact is that many scholars in the university community today share these views and proclaim them, as the essays in this book attest. In a sense, the authors of these essays share a kinship with the ancient writer: "this same message we proclaim."

Those of us who work at universities are profoundly aware that our youth are maturing in a culture that increasingly views moral and ethical values as relative. Individualism is the predominant influence. Rationalism and naturalism tend to deny the existence of a Creator God, and religious faith is viewed as irrelevant.[2] Are these trends inevitable? Do they reflect a natural, evolutionary consequence of a more knowledgeable, a more scientifically and academically sophisticated, a more complex society? The essays in this book suggest otherwise, asserting that there is a Creator God who can be known, that there are foundational ethical values to guide the behavior of individuals and society, that "good" exists, including a common good that transcends the individual. The essays in this volume demonstrate the contemporary relevance of religious faith and of the message proclaimed by writers living two thousand years ago.

The authors of these essays are members of the faculty at major secular research universities and are accomplished and respected in their profession. They have wrestled with these issues of life in our increasingly secular and complex world, and they have found meaning and purpose and value, the essence of life, in their Christian faith. Each essay is an account of an aspect of the author's own experience of Christian faith and its relevance to the academic enterprise, life in general and his or her own life. These essays are not theological treatises. Other scholars—Christians—at secular universities have recently addressed issues of faith in books that are similar to this collection of essays but have a different focus.[3]

Glenn Tinder, a contributor to this volume, in the preface of *The Political Meaning of Christianity* expresses the hope that people of all persuasions will read the book in the same sense "that non-Marxists should read and learn from Marxist writings; people who reject the atheism and materialism of Freud readily consult the writings of Freud and his followers. It seems arbitrary and hazardous to be less openminded toward Christianity. I believe," Tinder writes, "that Christian ideas are properly of concern to people who are not Christians and even to people who are entirely closed to the possibility of becoming Christians. This is simply because of the wisdom—the deep and credible good sense concerning life, as distinguished from the revealed truth concerning God—that those ideas contain."[4] It is our hope that readers will approach the essays in this book in this same spirit and will read these essays as invitations to explore the possibility that the "good news" proclaimed by writers living two thousand years ago is, in fact, "revealed truth" and is valid and relevant today for individuals and for society.[5]

Notes

[1]From an address delivered to Straight Talk, a ministry of Menlo Park Presbyterian Church, on November 11, 1995. A tape of the address can be ordered from Virginia Woodson, Menlo Park Presbyterian Church, 950 Santa Cruz Avenue, Menlo Park, CA 94025.

[2]See, for example, Robert Bellah et al., *Habits of the Heart: Individualism and Commitment in American Life* (New York: Harper & Row, 1985); Bellah et al., *The Good Society* (New York: Alfred A. Knopf, 1991); Stephen L. Carter, *The Culture of Disbelief: How American Law and Politics Trivialize Religious Devotion* (New York: BasicBooks, 1993); Stephen L. Carter, *Integrity* (New York: BasicBooks, 1996); Phillip E. Johnson, *Reason in the Balance: The Case Against Naturalism in Science, Law and Education* (Downers Grove, Ill.: InterVarsity Press, 1995).

[3]See, for example, Kelly Monroe, ed., *Finding God at Harvard: Spiritual Journeys of Christian Thinkers* (Grand Rapids, Mich.: Zondervan, 1996); Kelly James Clark, ed., *Philosophers Who Believe: The Spiritual Journeys of Eleven Leading Thinkers* (Downers Grove, Ill.: InterVarsity Press, 1993); Morris V. Thomas, ed., *God and the Philosophers: The Reconciliation of Faith and Reason* (New York: Oxford University Press, 1994); D. John Lee, ed., *Storying Ourselves: A Narrative Perspective on Christians in Psychology* (Grand Rapids, Mich.: Baker, 1993); Robert James Berry, ed., *Real Science, Real Faith* (Eastbourne, U.K.: Monarch, 1991).

[4]Glenn Tinder, *The Political Meaning of Christianity: The Prophetic Stance, an Interpretation* (New York: HarperCollins, 1991).

[5]The following two books are recommended for a more comprehensive exploration of the basic tenets of the Christian faith: C. S. Lewis, *Mere Christianity* (Riverside, N.J.: Macmillan, 1975); John R. W. Stott, *Basic Christianity* (Downers Grove, Ill.: InterVarsity Press, 1976).

1

A Common Thread

PAUL M. ANDERSON

Biochemistry &
Molecular Biology

University of Minnesota, Duluth

Christ Åsmen

Will-power does not change men.
Time does not change men. Christ does.
—HENRY DRUMMOND

The authors in this book represent a wide range of circumstances, disciplines, ethnic and educational backgrounds,
university affiliations, and academic accomplishments. The
essays reflect a broad spectrum of focus and experiences.
Nevertheless, all of the essays are woven together by a thread of
common spiritual experience. For me, one of the thrills of the Christian
life is recognizing this common thread in another person's story, which
leads to celebration and fellowship. Those who are connected by this
common thread desire to share this joyous fellowship with all. They
recognize both their personal inadequacy and, ironically, their
profound value to God. They have received a gift from God that they
could never have earned through their own effort. The operative word
is *love*, a caring that is unconditional and may involve suffering and
foregoing personal rights. In this essay I describe my own experiences

and understanding of Christian faith in the context of my profession as a scientist and try to clearly identify this "common thread" of recognition that I share with others in the Christian faith.

Several years ago I participated in an educational exchange with a medical school at a university in Russia. During the visit I was invited to give a lecture on the topic of science and faith. I began by suggesting that those in the audience might share the perception that science and faith are antithetical, that a scientist is a person who accepts the basic principles of science and must therefore reject faith in God. Indeed, there are scientists who take this stance, just as there are many nonscientists who do also. But there are many scientists whose faith in God gives meaning and purpose to their lives and to their work. I am one of them.

Some argue that science and faith are antithetical because religion (1) involves no experiments, (2) tests no hypotheses and (3) is committed beforehand to a set of beliefs.[1] I have not found such arguments convincing. First, science is a process that people use to understand the world, whereas religion addresses questions of purpose and meaning. Both science and religion are interested in truth. Science represents human efforts. Religion, especially the Christian faith, looks to revelation—i.e., God's initiative. Galileo Galilei, considered the father of modern scientific inquiry, captured the essence of this distinction when he stated that "the Bible tells us how to get to Heaven, not how the Heavens go."[2]

Second, it seems to me that some of the postulates of religion can, in fact, be tested for relevance or plausibility. For example, Jesus Christ said, "If you obey my commands, you will remain in my love, just as I have obeyed my Father's commands and remain in his love. I have told you this so that my joy may be in you and that your joy may be complete. My command is this: Love each other as I have loved you" (John 15:10-12). Such a statement begs the question: Is there joy for those who believe and follow?

Natasha Gorelova came to faith by testing a premise of the teachings of Jesus. Natasha is a scientist working in the area of applied mathematics at Akademogorodok, a community of some twenty different research institutes of the former Soviet Academy of Sciences, near Novosibirsk, Siberia. As a student at the University in Moscow, she received the Lenin Prize in 1971, and then pursued doctoral work in cybernetics at Akademogorodok. She soon became depressed about her life, feeling as though she could not survive her current state. She had always believed in God, but as she has pointed out, there is a big difference between believing in God and "coming to Christ." When she was twenty-five, Natalya read a book about cybernetics in which the author explained positive and negative feedback by referring to Christ's statement about turning the other cheek. Christ's words made sense to her mathematically—if someone hits you and you hit back, you merely increase the amount of evil. To reduce the amount of evil you must refuse to repeat evil actions.

She found it easy to test this thesis. "You know our buses and how crowded they are. When someone shoved me or put his foot on mine, I didn't say something offensive, only 'Please, how about sitting here,' without sarcasm, in a kind voice. I saw how the tension in the bus immediately went down. I understood from my experiments that you can reduce the stress in a line or a crowd by refusing to respond to aggression with more aggression, but instead responding with kindness. That was my first step to Christ. I began to think of the Gospel of Christ as a very wise book. The Resurrection of Christ, however, was something that I couldn't understand. Christ said, 'Knock and the door will be opened, seek and you will find, ask and it will be given.' I decided to knock on the door until it opened." Her test worked. The door to understanding opened, and her life was changed. Meaning and purpose came into her life and into the lives of many of her colleagues, who started participating with her in regular church services. Jesus said, "Peace I leave with you; my peace I give you" (John 14:27). Natasha Gorelova experienced that peace.[3]

Third, such arguments ascribe to science a purity and an objectivity that may not be real. Science is generally viewed as an objective form of inquiry. A hypothesis is stated to explain a set of observations, and experiments are then designed and conducted to test that hypothesis. Science is thought to be careful scholarship that is free from prior commitment to a particular answer or belief system. However, anyone with a few years of experience in science knows that science is, in fact, often strongly influenced by preexisting expectations. Paleontologist David Raup of the University of Chicago addressed this issue in his insightful book about science *The Nemesis Affair: A Story of the Death of Dinosaurs and the Ways of Science.*[1]

Raup reviews what was at one time an exciting controversy over the hypothesis (now an accepted paradigm) that had been proposed to explain why the dinosaurs suddenly became extinct sixty million years ago. The hypothesis proposes that a large meteor about ten kilometers in diameter struck the earth. This resulted in massive global fires and a huge quantity of soot and debris being ejected into the upper atmosphere, so much that sunlight was cut off for several months. Raup tells about receiving the original manuscript describing the evidence for the hypothesis, which the editor of the prestigious journal *Science* sent to him for peer review. Initially he rejected the hypothesis, as did many scientists. Their view was conditioned, Raup argues, by the previously existing belief that major terrestrial events take place gradually in geologic time and are not produced by cataclysmic extraterrestrial events. This is one example of how faith in a current paradigm influences science.

It is important to remember that science is practiced by human beings who make mistakes and sometimes pursue a scientific objective with ulterior motives, possibly power or fame. Nevertheless, science is a legitimate and powerful exercise in the search for truth and certainly is essential to our technological society as we address problems in areas such as the environment, health and our food supply.

The word *physics* is derived from the Greek word *physis*. *Physis* represents the early Greek philosophy that science (natural processes), philosophy and religion are all one. The Greek philosophers aimed to discover the essential nature, or *physis*, of all things. The roots of Western science lie in this philosophy. By the fourth century B.C. the belief in a unity of all things had given way to dualism, which separates spirit and matter. The Greek philosopher Aristotle embraced a dualist philosophy that served as the basis of the Western view of the world for nearly two thousand years. These early philosophers, including Aristotle, believed that questions concerning the human spirit, or soul, were far more important than investigations of the material world. This emphasis on the ethical and the spiritual went essentially unchallenged until the Renaissance, when it was determined that it is possible to (1) ask a rational question, (2) objectively analyze natural processes and thereby (3) learn about the material world. Galileo, for example, invited his critics to look through his telescope and see for themselves. Modern science was born in the seventeenth century, along with a strengthened view of dualism in the philosophy of René Descartes. This "Cartesian," or mechanistic, view of the world has dominated modern science ever since. It divides nature into two separate and independent realms—mind and matter —and views the material world as a huge machine composed of different objects that are separate from the mind.

Some scientists, particularly physicists, have in recent years questioned this dualistic view of the world in their search for unity in the universe. Efforts to understand the implications of the "new physics" (issues such as general relativity, quantum mechanics, black holes, the origin of the universe, space and time relationships) have led some to speculate about relationships between matter and mind and to consider the question of the existence of God or the nature of God. Some, such as physicist Fritjof Capra in his book *The Tao of Physics*, have drawn parallels between modern high-energy physics and Eastern philosophies (mysticism or New Age religion).[4] A number of interesting philosophies or systems have been proposed in well-intentioned efforts to bridge the dualistic chasm between mind and matter, between the physical world as perceived by science and the spiritual dimension of life or the spiritual essence perceived to be lying behind the workings of nature.[5]

It seems to me, however, that such humanistic views of the unity of the universe are limiting because they are just that—merely humanistic. Each individual has attempted to construct a view of the universe, and of humanity's place in the universe, within the framework of his or her own experience, academic field or personal objectives. A missing consideration is the possibility of the existence of God—a Creator with purpose and intent, a God who exists independently of what people might like him to be, a God who is involved in his creation. The possibility of "revelation" (knowledge that originates apart from human effort) is not usually addressed in these philosophies. (The use of masculine pronouns in reference to God does not imply that God has gender; God is "spirit" and is gender neutral—see for example John 4:24.)

In his book *The Galileo Connection: Resolving Conflicts Between Science and the Bible* Charles E. Hummel writes that, despite the predominant dualistic view of the world, for such early giants of modern science as Copernicus, Galileo, Kepler and Newton the search for truth in the natural world was closely linked to spiritual faith.[2] Hummel notes, for example, that Newton wrote more about theological issues than about science and mathematics. These early scientist-philosophers saw two paths to truth: (1) the study of nature through human inquiry (science) and (2) special revelation. It was their view that science and revelation would be found in agreement. Religious faith and science were not considered mutually exclusive; in fact, each supported the other. I embrace such consistency between revelation and science not as a point of theology, a scientific argument or philosophical reasoning but because my own life experiences confirm it.

My first serious spiritual encounter occurred while I was in graduate school at the University of Minnesota. A renowned carbohydrate biochemist, Fred Smith, challenged me to consider my relationship with God. A few years later, my family and I were living in Indiana. By most standards my life would have been considered a success story. I had a wonderful wife and family, a new home and a successful career. I thoroughly enjoyed science and felt fortunate to have a career in that field. Yet I felt an emptiness, a lack of purpose and meaning. Neither my job nor my money nor my success filled this void. Was this all there was to life? The beauty, order and design evident in the world I observed as a scientist only whetted my desire for spiritual understanding. It was my view that there was a Creator and meaning and purpose behind the design of the natural world and behind human existence.

Although I accepted the idea of God intellectually, the person of Jesus made no sense to me. I had many friendly discussions and intellectual arguments about all of this, but I neglected to follow an important principle of open scientific investigation, which is to consider the data and information about a subject before drawing conclusions. I had never really read the Bible and had little knowledge about it. It occurred to me that if God, a Creator, exists, he must be who he says he is, not who I say he is. The God I had based my arguments on was a God of my imagination. And if God exists, is it not reasonable to assume that he would communicate with his creation?

During the one year we lived in Indiana we became friends with a man who had a strong faith in God. He pointed me toward an understanding of God through Jesus Christ. Like Natasha Gorelova, I was seeking truth, and like Natasha Gorelova, I found it. Or, more accurately, it found me. Coming into this relationship with God was not something I accomplished on my own—it was a gift that God gave me. I did not receive this gift all at once but over a period of several months, perhaps years. However, I do recall one evening reading a statement made by the nineteenth-century professor of natural sciences Henry Drummond: "Will-power does not change men. Time does not change men. Christ does."[6] I was somewhat startled—and excited—to realize that I understood its meaning.

Subsequently I bought a New Testament and read most of it in about three weeks. It amazed me. Here was a blueprint for living and a description and explanation of the sense of separation from God that I had been experiencing. The consistency that exists between Old and New Testaments spoke to the character, purposes and promises of God, particularly the promise of a plan for reconciling human beings to himself. I was particularly impressed by the vivid authenticity of the biblical stories. The dark side of the human race is recognized along with the good side. The struggles, failures and weaknesses of great leaders are evident, as well as obedience to God. I came to understand that one of the ways God communicates to us is through the writings of godly people as collected in the Bible and that understanding its message is also a gift (see 1 Corinthians 1:21-25).

During our first year at the University of Minnesota, Duluth, I became involved with InterVarsity Christian Fellowship, a nondenominational student organization. I was asked to serve as faculty adviser—a role for which I was hardly qualified having arrived at UMD only six months after the seed of faith had taken root! This was fortuitous, however, since the Bible studies with students and IVCF staff, leadership training experiences and times of prayer and thoughtful book discussions were wonderfully helpful as I began to understand a little of the deeper nature and the implications of this "faith." My wife and I began hosting a weekly Bible study fellowship for medical students (and many of their friends) in our home. This Bible study lasted fourteen years and was a defining experience in helping me come to a fuller understanding of my faith. I am enormously grateful for these experiences with students—many of whom were my teachers.

Somewhat later in my Christian experience I became puzzled about why I was not particularly interested in or concerned about some of the public controversies between science and faith (for example, biological evolution and the "big bang" origin of the universe as guiding paradigms). Several years ago a group of friends and I decided to take turns sharing our thoughts about how our professions impact our faith, and vice versa. This was a significant exercise for me. As I struggled with my own thoughts on this matter, I came to realize that science had propelled me in the direction of faith. Why then should I find the two to be in discord? Certainly there are important issues to address in the relation between science and faith, but the Christian faith has provided me with a foundation from which to answer questions that science does not answer, such as What is the meaning of life? Why are we here? How is life to be lived? and Where do the values and morals which guide a peaceful society come from? As noted by brilliant theoretical physicist Stephen W. Hawking in *A Brief History of Time: From the Big Bang to Black Holes*, "Even if there is only one possible unified theory (explaining the physical laws of the universe), it is just a set of rules and equations. What is it that breathes fire into the equations and makes a universe for them to describe?"[7]

What is it that brings an individual to (Christian) faith? What specifically does the believer have faith in? What does that mean? I suppose that it is an aptitude for science that causes me to think about this in terms of plausibility or logic—others may think about it in different but equally valid ways. Indeed, to me this "faith" is plausible and logical, but not, as I have noted above, because it follows from any fundamental laws of nature established by scientific inquiry or any provable theorem of science. For me, it confirms, and is confirmed by, life's experiences. I think of this as the "logic of the gospel of Jesus Christ."

No one becomes a believer by joining a church or by belonging to a particular family, race, political party or country, or by trying to obey a set of rules or memorizing religious literature. However, based on my understanding of (1) my own experiences, (2) the transmitted written and oral experiences of many others and (3) the main themes of the Bible, being or becoming a believer does include the following.

1. Desiring to know God, reflecting an awareness that there may be a Creator and that there may be a better way to live than we may be experiencing. An awareness that a foundational standard of moral and ethical values for individuals to follow is necessary if society is to function well. We may arrive at this point out of distress, for example, despair over failure or loss of a loved one, loneliness, rejection, illness or (as I experienced) a need for a sense of meaning and purpose in life.

2. Recognizing that we act on our own pride and selfish desires and fail to follow God's precepts for living, that is, we are alienated from God. The ecclesiastical word for this is *sin*, that is, we violate the boundaries of God's directives, we miss the mark in our created and intended relationship with God. We have the gift of free will and may certainly choose to live this way, but there are practical consequences (not punitive, but simply the result of not living the kind of life we were created to live) and there are eternal consequences (the glory of eternal life with God versus the eternal agony of separation from God), since God promises that we are all accountable for our deeds, whether good or evil. We may not like the idea of a Creator who promises perfect judgment and wrath in response to our sin, but consider the consequences of the alternative—a Creator who is indifferent to good and evil.

3. Understanding that God loves all people individually and desires the relationship that God intended when he created us and that all people have eternal life, but failing to live in accordance with God's standards results in a broken relationship with our Creator.

4. Realizing that we cannot earn eternal life or a restored relation-

ship with God through our own efforts. To do so would require us to be perfect in our relationship to God, and that just isn't going to happen, one of the important messages of the Bible.

5. Learning that God took it upon himself to restore this broken relationship, something that we were incapable of doing. At a particular time in history Jesus Christ (God manifested, the "Son") came and lived as a human person. He experienced all the trials, temptations, difficulties and emotions that we experience in everyday life. He taught with uniquely powerful authority. He healed the sick, cared for the poor and loved people of all social strata, especially the poor. He was obedient to God (the Father). He endured unjust treatment at the hands of religious authorities. Although he did no wrong, he was accused of wrongdoing by the leaders, with the support of the people. He was killed in a very painful way, by being nailed to a wooden cross.

As painful as Jesus' death was, it was God's great plan from the beginning for restoring the broken relationship between himself and us. Jesus came to live the perfect life that we cannot live, to suffer the consequences of our sins. He did not demand justice for himself—for our sake. He gave up his prerogative to be God—for our sake. This is the essence of love—the love of God. He never wavered from the path of obedience—the path of love. But Jesus also overcame death and returned to his place with God and offers to everyone, today, the gift of eternal life and a restored relationship with God (mediated by God, the "Spirit"). What is offered is a gift. We cannot add to it and we are incapable of earning it. This gift is referred to as the grace of God.

6. Accepting the gift of eternal life and forgiveness by faith, trusting in Jesus Christ alone for restoring our relationship with God, repudiating our sins and desiring to turn our lives in the direction of God's purposes. Faith itself is a gift—we can reject it or we can accept it and live by it. A friend once gave an illustration of this. A man was practicing on a tightrope about three feet off the ground for a walk on a rope across Niagara Falls pushing a wheelbarrow. He asked a neighbor who was watching him practice, "Do you think that I can accomplish this feat?"

The neighbor replied, "I have faith that you can do it."

"Well then," the man said, "get in the wheelbarrow and go with me."

7. The result of receiving this gift is a new life, an eternal life, which is manifested by a deep and genuine desire to love God and all people, seeking forgiveness for the inevitable failures, asking for God's help and giving thanks to God, not letting the world "squeeze us into its mold" (Romans 12:2 Phillips), but seeking to serve Jesus and follow his example of how to live, experiencing the truth that to love as Jesus loved is the real source of peace and joy.

This is the essence of my understanding and experience of the Christian faith. This is the "common thread" that runs through all of these essays. It is a disarmingly inclusive thread, pulling together fabric of all designs and colors and histories and qualities. It weaves its way into lives from all angles and starting points, from the profound to the simple. The cloth may be worn and frayed, even on the edge of extinction or despair, yet when it is mended by this thread, all becomes new and unique and accepted by God. We need not understand how this thread mends our lives; indeed, there is a great mystery here that is beyond our comprehension. This mended relationship with God and other believers does not make me or any believer perfect and certainly does not make problems go away, but it does provide the same strength, the same encouragement, the same hope and the same guidance that has helped and fulfilled Christian believers for centuries.

We cannot fully comprehend God in this life, as the Bible acknowledges (see 1 Corinthians 13:12). But we can look at the life of Jesus and catch a glimpse of the nature of God and an example of how life is meant to be lived (see, for example, Philippians 2:5-11 and 1 Peter 2:20-25). Jesus taught that if we want to be "great," we must become servants (Mark 10:43), and that our joy will be complete only when we love as he loves us (John 15:11-12). Again, the operative word is *love*, as exemplified by the life of Jesus. The gift of understanding and acceptance is exhilarating and joyful. But along with it comes a conflicting emotion—a sense of unworthiness and a profound awareness of one's sinful nature. Yet we are commanded to practice this kind of love. It is laid out as the highest standard of the Christian life. Why? This is the secret of precisely how we can experience joy and completeness. It is as if God says, "I realize that from your perspective in the world this may not make sense, but trust me."

The implications of following a life patterned after Jesus' life, with God's help, are profound for individuals and, consequently, for society. For example, those in political leadership find themselves speaking for justice for those who have no voice, even if it is dangerous or unpopular to do so. Whatever form the government may take, be it socialist or capitalist, the minority defers peacefully to the majority by trust, and the majority recognizes its responsibility to the welfare of the minority. Those who have great ability or possess material goods discover a willingness to share with those who are in great need, even though they are not their friends. One marriage partner says to the other, "You are a very important person, and I am going to honor, respect and encourage you" (without waiting for the other partner to make a similar declaration). Individuals in positions of authority are led to make decisions that benefit those under them, even if it means a loss of their authority. It is expressions of love and servanthood such as these that bring a measure of joy, peace and hope, to an individual[8] and to a society. Such was the result of Natasha's act of kindness on a Russian bus.

Notes

[1]David Raup, *The Nemesis Affair: A Story of the Death of Dinosaurs and the Ways of Science* (New York: W. W. Norton, 1986).

[2]Charles E. Hummel, *The Galileo Connection: Resolving Conflicts Between Science and the Bible* (Downers Grove, Ill.: InterVarsity Press, 1986). Galileo made this statement while defending his claim, based on physical observations, that the earth is not the center of the universe.

[3]Gorelova's story is summarized here from Jim Forrest, "Siberian Christianity," *One World* 165 (May 1991).

[4]Fritjof Capra, *The Tao of Physics: An Exploration of the Parallels Between Modern Physics and Eastern Mysticism,* 3rd ed. (London: Flamingo, 1992).

[5]Renee Weber, *Dialogues with Scientists and Sages: The Search for Unity* (New York: Routledge & Kegan Paul, 1986).

[6]Henry Drummond, "The Greatest Thing in the World," address given in England, 1887. It is available from a number of publishers.

[7]Stephen W. Hawking, *A Brief History of Time: From the Big Bang to Black Holes* (New York: Bantam Books, 1988).

[8]Bill Hybels and Rob Wilkins, *Descending into Greatness* (Grand Rapids, Mich.: Zondervan, 1993).

2

The Necessity of Trust

JOHN PATRICK

Clinical Nutrition
& Biochemistry

University of Ottawa

The only safe place is inside a story.
—ATHOL FUGARD

He's a hedonist at heart. All those fasts and vigils and stakes and crosses are only a facade. Or only like foam on the seashore. Out at sea, out in His sea, there is pleasure, and more pleasure. He makes no secret of it; at his right hand are 'pleasures for evermore.'"[1] Thus Screwtape explains to Wormwood the reality of God's plans for us and the difference between immediate perception and ultimate reality. The alternative belief, that the truth is indistinguishable from our perceptions, leads to constant anxiety, which some people defend as the necessary motive force for production. As one of my mentors put it, "Anxiety makes the world go round." Only grimly determined endurance brings results. For academic scholars, this means neurotically driven research with an inevitable deterioration in quality and the current epidemic of data fabrication, as well as destruction to personal relationships. This essay describes how I came to believe Screwtape. I had to learn to ask what is right rather than what is practical. Then I had to trust God's guidance.

What resulted is an odyssey that led through clinical medicine, laboratory research and field work in Jamaica and Africa, university teaching in Canada and now apologetics teaching in a variety of places. This essay is structured around a series of lessons that I learned, lessons that formed and established my faith and my intellect. The first lesson was that God is faithful and hears and answers prayer.

My Christian story dates from the early 1920s. At that time my grandfather was a trade union organizer, a Marxist and an excellent toolmaker. He would get fired because of his ideology and then would get hired because of his skills. When my mother received a scholarship to continue her education, he refused to let her accept it because he could not give the same to all eight of his children. Despite my mother's unhappiness at this turn of events, God was at work. She found herself employed as a seamstress next to a Christian woman who invited her to listen to some missionaries from the Belgian Congo. Their stories centered around their commitment to prayer—they were faith missionaries with the Worldwide Evangelisation Crusade. They had no regular salary, although the mission sent what was given for them. Thus they understood prayer in a very practical way.

My mother went back to hear them several times, and that was the beginning of her Christian life. Thereafter she wrote regularly to Herbert and Annie English, who were stationed in the heart of the Ituri forest. When my mother married and became pregnant, the Englishes prayed daily that I would become a Christian doctor who would go to the Belgian Congo (now Zaire). They prayed this prayer until they passed away thirty years later. I grew up in industrial Birmingham in England and lived on a street that had some four hundred houses. Only four boys went to university between 1930 and 1970; only one became a doctor. I did not learn about these prayers until 1987, when I told my father I was going to Zaire. He replied that he had waited forty-seven years for that prayer to be answered.

Thus I have good reason to be in awe of God's grace and faithfulness in answering faithful prayer. No aspect of faith moves me more than the sheer grace of God's entrance into our lives. We are utterly dependent on grace to begin the Christian life; yet God does this without humiliating us. The habit of acknowledging the reality of grace by active remembrance is an important Christian discipline, exemplified poetically in many psalms. The psalmist in the midst of trouble and despair cries out to God, and then the Spirit of God causes him to review his own and Israel's history. Usually the result is a calming of his spirit and a renewed reliance on God. We continue in the faith not because of our experiences but because we believe them to be true and because Christ has the "words of eternal life" (John 6:68). The habits of the heart, in remembering, keep us true to the story as a whole. Learning the importance of a commitment to truth was the second great lesson in my Christian maturation.

I cannot remember a time when I did not believe. It was telling the truth to say that God was the source of everything, and the years have only confirmed that initial childlike belief. I believe now, as I did implicitly then (sophisticated arguments came later), that the argument from design is strong. And I believe that molecular biology will make it stronger. The philosophical argument for the necessity of someone with the properties of eternal self-existence is compellingly powerful.

In the beginning, what? Certainly not our cosmos. But something was there before us. How did our cosmos come to be? Chance, say many. But the cosmos knows of nothing that is made by chance. Chance is only a word for a statistical means of dealing with our ignorance. No coin flipped into the air comes down by chance; it comes down as it does because of a complex array of interacting forces that are sufficiently random as to allow the use of probability theory. The theory describes; it does not cause. Evolution does not proceed by chance but by a series of discrete chemical changes that we can only describe in statistical terms. Polanyi's comment on the honest misuse of statistics because of a conceptual error, even by one as eminent as R. A. Fisher, is worth considerable meditation.[2]

If chance does not serve as a sufficient cause, what does? The only other possibility, apart from someone like God, is a self-creating universe. But that is illogical, and since I need logic to do science, I am necessarily committed to, at least, deism. (A self-creating universe is illogical because to be self-creating is to be present before creation.) Why are so many professors unwilling to be truthful about these things, even making dogmatic claims to universal knowledge by saying that God does not exist? Do they really mean that they understand the universe? Of course not. In the words of James Joyce they scream, "I will not serve." The truth is that we are creatures. It is a truth that is liberating because we are incapable of being responsible for the universe and, as creatures, we are not responsible for it.

On to my third lesson: How am I to understand myself? I am a creature, but what sort of creature am I? Like everyone else, I am constrained not to do certain things, which could benefit me, because I "know" them to be wrong. But when temptation comes, I frequently yield and do what I acknowledge to be evil. How can this be? What evolutionary benefit could possibly accrue from the experience of guilt? Dostoevsky was right when he said, "If God does not exist, everything is permissible." The fact that we all know that everything is not permissible, that we are all, mercifully, constrained from the worse excesses of self-indulgence, is totally unexplained by evolutionary theory but totally explained by the Christian story. The two things that caused Kant to wonder are the same for me: the starry sky above (as well as the molecular world that is hidden) and the moral law within. Chesterton's description of how this understanding changed his life is far better than anything I could ever write. Chapter five of *Orthodoxy* ought to be read as a whole, but a few sentences from the last two paragraphs must serve to whet your appetite:

> And then followed an experience impossible to describe. . . . I had found this hole in the world: the fact that one must somehow find a way of loving the world without trusting it; somehow one must love the world without being worldly. I found this projecting feature of Christian theology, like a sort of hard spike, the dogmatic insistence that God was personal, and that he had made a world separate from Himself. The spike of dogma fitted exactly into the hole in the world—it had evidently been meant to go there—and then strange things began to happen. When once these two parts of the two machines came together, one after another, all the other parts fell in and fitted with an eerie exactitude. . . . Instinct after instinct was answered by doctrine after

doctrine. . . . My sense that happiness hung on the crazy thread of a condition did mean something. . . . It meant the whole doctrine of the Fall (of man away from God). . . . My haunting instinct that somehow good was not merely a tool to be used but a relic to be guarded, like the goods from Crusoe's ship—even that had been the wild whisper of something originally wise, for, according to Christianity, we were indeed the survivors of a wreck, the crew of a golden ship which had gone down at the beginning of the world.

Christian optimism is based on the fact that we do not fit in to the world. I had tried to be happy by telling myself that man is an animal, like any other. . . . But now I really was happy, for I had learnt that man is a monstrosity. I had been right in feeling all things as odd, for it dwelt in the unnaturalness of everything in the light of the supernatural. The modern philosopher had told me that I was in the right place, and I had felt depressed even in acquiescence. But I had heard that I was in the wrong place and my soul sang for joy. . . . I knew now . . . why I could feel homesick at home.[3]

Moral truth, my own sinfulness, and the strange loneliness described by Chesterton are confronted and resolved in the life, death and resurrection of Jesus. Ultimately coming to terms with the historical Jesus defines the core commitment of Christianity. For me this has never been an issue of fact, only one of commitment. Lewis describes the classical argument and its correlate with consummate lucidity in *Mere Christianity:*

> Christ says that He is "humble and meek" and we believe Him; not noticing that, if He were merely a man, humility and meekness are the very last characteristics we could attribute to some of His sayings. I am trying here to prevent anyone saying the really foolish thing that people often say about Him: "I'm ready to accept Jesus as a great moral teacher, but I don't accept His claim to be God." That is the one thing that we must not say. A man who was merely a man and said the sort of things Jesus said would not be a great moral teacher. He would either be a lunatic . . . or else he would be the Devil of Hell. You must make your choice. Either this man was, and is, the Son of God: or else a madman or something worse. You can shut Him up for a fool, you can spit at Him and kill Him as a demon; or you can fall at His feet and call Him Lord and God. But let us not come with any patronising nonsense about His

being a great human teacher. He has not left that open to us. He did not intend to.[4]

This seems to me to confront anyone who has intellectual integrity with a major problem. It can only be avoided by commencing with the prejudice that God could not be incarnate. Who are we to say what God can and cannot do?

This brings me to the next lesson: the question of witnesses and role models. Throughout my education I have had Christian role models of high ability and great integrity who served to encourage my faith when it was under siege. An engineering professor at Birmingham University, W. G. Ainslie, was my first major influence during my undergraduate studies, followed by Donald Mackay, the x-ray crystallographer turned brain physiologist and theologian, during my undergraduate time. Dr. Martyn Lloyd-Jones filled a similar role during my clinical years. I did not know these men personally in any depth, but I watched, I listened and I was influenced. I did not see a similar depth of intellectual integrity elsewhere. The temptation for academics is always to intellectual arrogance, to "outgrow" Christianity. But I was confronted with high ability combined with faith. It should have humbled me, but I nevertheless remained extremely arrogant.

Benedict's first three virtues—humility, humility and humility—were and are a necessity for me, although I did not know it then and have only mastered the introductory lessons now. I needed particularly to learn real respect for good people, for those who were wise and holy, without respect to their social or intellectual status. And such people were my next teachers. Faith allows us to pass through the valley of the shadow of death without fear, but one needs to witness that reality.

Soon after I was qualified as a doctor, I was taught an abiding lesson about God's faithfulness by one ordinary family from blue-collar London, whose name I, sadly, do not remember. There were two children who were about eight and ten years of age. Their mother was my patient. She was complaining of excessive tiredness and a little nausea, nothing serious she was sure, but her doctor sent her to the hospital. When I examined her, I could find only a modest anemia. But the lab results showed her to be in kidney failure and to have hardly

Out growing Christianity

any function left. In those days before dialysis we could make her comfortable, but we could do nothing to prevent the inevitable death. I noticed a Bible by her bed and so discovered that we had a shared faith, of which she knew far more than I.

After a few days she asked me why her improvement was so slow. I hedged a little and said I would prefer to speak to her husband first. She corrected that error then and there, and I spoke to them together! Tearfully, they informed the children. Over the next few weeks I witnessed a lesson about dying in the faith. For some years afterward father and children sent me Christmas cards to tell me they were managing well. Coming to terms with death can only be meaningful if there is life after death and can only be rationally peaceful if God is known and is known to be love. I now tell medical students, "Watch how your patients die and think about it honestly." All honest physicians confront the reality of faith if they are present at the end of their patient's lives. Many, however, have not come to terms with their own mortality. Diane Komp has collected end-of-life stories in a lovely book called *A Window on Heaven*,[5] in which she recounts how she was humbled and brought back to faith by her child patients. The first time she sat with a dying child, the little girl sat up and said, "Mummy, can you see the angels, can you hear their singing?" And then she died. Diane Komp was left wondering what to do with this real event. After a struggle she bent the knee and acknowledged that God was God and she was a creature. Teachers are all around if we will but look.

The next lesson has been to learn the continuing importance of hospitality and care in the nurturing of faith. This is a duty that we can all do and in so doing we may well entertain angels unaware. Life as a student and young physician was busy and interesting. I did not give much attention to faith. My Christian disciplines faded and I was in danger. Fortunately, others with the gift of hospitality paid attention to me and thereby rescued me from many of the worse excesses of self-indulgence. I was undoubtedly arrogant, flippant and well on the way to cynicism, but God gave one couple the capacity to see beyond that veneer and to love me—simply and nonjudgmentally. Just as my life was about to go badly wrong, God brought me my wife and thereby edged me back on track.

I did a Ph.D. ("M.D. by thesis" in British terms) in cell physiology, in part because I wanted to see more of my children. During the process of learning to do research I had meningitis. Eighteen months had passed without a significant result from my research, so I had reason to be neurotic. But during the recovery from that illness, I had another lesson to learn about being open to God's ways. Because of the illness, I had gotten to know one of our neighbors, David, rather better than I would otherwise have done. During convalescence I was often sitting in the communal garden when he returned from college where he was doing an M.Sc. in nuclear engineering, and we began to play chess together.

I learned that he had left school at age fifteen because his father didn't believe in higher education. He started as an apprentice electrician at Rolls Royce. Fortunately, Rolls recognized his talent. When I met him he was head of the heat flux program in the nuclear engine division, having completed an external degree in mathematics from London University in half the normal time. Everything he did turned to gold, but, unknown to me, he was deeply discontented. I was to relearn the wonders of the mercy of God through David and our humble but wonderful role as witnesses. One afternoon, whilst playing chess, I developed a severe headache and went into the house to lie down. I had been reading a commentary on Habakkuk by Martyn Lloyd-Jones. It was called *From Fear to Faith*.[6] Inadvertently I left it in the garden; David picked it up and read it that night. The next day he asked whether I had any other books like that. I gave him *Mere Christianity*, and on Sunday he came to church with us. In just a few days his life was totally reoriented. He had found peace from a commentary on Habakkuk! More important, when he returned home after the course he noticed things of which he had been previously unaware, such as the lack of a youth group in his village, so he remedied the deficiency. The whole process was dependent on the tiny link of friendship and my willingness to be known as a Christian.

David was a good man before he became a Christian. He was a better man afterward. Goodness in those without faith is a problem. During my doctoral research I worked with a man of the highest integrity who believes in God but not in personal salvation. People who lack a personal faith but practice the highest ethics have crossed my path many times. They challenge the easy standards of so many Christians. Real virtue is found in many people who do not have a deep personal faith, and evangelicals need to think about that. More on this later.

The next lesson was somewhat cynically contrived from my perspective, but in the larger picture it was to be the beginning of my realization that I was required to be ready to give reasons for the faith that is within me. My wife and I wanted to travel, so I searched for an application of my skills in the developing world. I found one in the problem of infantile malnutrition. My research had been concerned with the mechanism of transport of sodium and potassium into and out of cells and particularly with the disorders of these mechanisms in disease. Malnourished children clearly had such a disorder, which had never been studied. So I applied for a fellowship from the Wellcome Trust, and in due course we arrived in Jamaica. In this way the plight of malnourished children entered my world. In Jamaica I was introduced to the extraordinary and immensely satisfying phenomenon of resuscitating these children and watching a ten-pound two-year-old doubling its weight in six weeks. We went for two years and stayed for five.

Students from smaller islands came to the university in Jamaica. When they got off the plane and traveled to the university campus, the unacceptable face of capitalism was revealed to them. On the right, on Long Mountain, are mansions whose foundations cost $100,000; on the left, shacks with ten to the room. By the time they reached campus, any with a touch of uninformed idealism were like ripe fruit waiting to be picked by the Marxists (remember, this was the seventies). Their churches had never mentioned social justice. The gospel had been preached in simplistic formulas, and by the grace of God the foolishness of preaching had done its divine work. But working out the meaning of salvation was almost unknown territory.

My background was replete with horror stories of social injustice from my grandfather, but I also knew about the behavior of Stalin and his sacrifice of thirty million to the greater good of communism. I had intuitively understood the importance of the doctrine of the Fall—

according to Chesterton, the one doctrine that needed no proof—but I needed to apply it more thoroughly. Many times I sat down with students to point out that the communist formula was based on an untrue premise: we are not reliably altruistic. Lenin understood this when he wrote almost immediately after the Bolshevik revolution, "It is necessary to legalize terror." The people never got their utopia. Our own democratic traditions are fragile flowers, which amongst other things need to be rooted in individual, self-imposed civic restraint. That is only logical if the doctrine of the Fall is true. The widespread assumption that humankind is basically good makes restraint nonsense, so it is not surprising that is has become a diminishing asset in these days of libertarianism.

One of the most penetrating analyses of our problem is this one, whose author I will identify later.

> Do not imagine that it was by force of arms that our ancestors made a great nation out of a small community. If that were true, we should today have a far more glorious nation. In allies, in our own citizens, in armaments . . . we have greater resources than they enjoyed. But it was other causes that made them great, causes that have ceased to exist: energy in our own land; a rule of justice outside our borders; in forming policy a mind that is free because it is not at the mercy of criminal passions. Instead of these we have self-indulgence and greed, public poverty, and private opulence. We praise riches, we pursue a course of sloth. No distinction is made between good men and bad: the intrigues of ambition win the prizes due to merit. No wonder when each of you thinks only of his private interest, when at home you are slaves to your appetites, and to money and to influence in your public life. The consequence is that an attack is being launched on a republic left without defense.[7]

Private opulence and public poverty surely describe us. But this quotation is from Cato, quoted by Augustine in *The City of God*. Thus I began to appreciate that Paul's insight in the book of Romans in the Bible must be the starting point for any proper understanding of myself and for any rational public policy. "The evil that I would not, that I do" is not a preconversion reality instantly washed away by grace; it is an ongoing battle. The glorious difference is that I am no longer necessarily under the power of Satan; if I choose to obey Christ and use the means of grace in a disciplined fashion, the power of evil can be defeated. If this description of the human predicament is true, then it follows that education must lead; one cannot expect that merely following our natural inclinations will be sufficient to educate us. Yet in our educational system we deny the intrinsic bent to evil and create victim categories to explain those who fail to perform or even those who do ill. Yeats's prescient poem is now fulfilled: "The best lack all conviction, while the worst are full of passionate intensity."[8]

It is dishonest to assert that although there is a bent to evil in our nature, we are capable of responsibility. We will self-destruct if we do not repent. John Steinbeck in a letter to Adlai Stevenson put it something like this:

> Mainly my dear Adlai I am concerned about the cynical immorality of our nation. Strange creatures we are; we can stand all that God and nature send upon us save only plenty. If I wished to destroy a nation I would make it rich and powerful and self interested and it will destroy itself.[9]

The whole edifice of education based on the notion that we are basically good and construct our own values needs to be deconstructed, not because the perpetrators did not know but because it is untrue.

Finally, what have I learned about faith from my academic work with malnutrition? Several persistent, deeply challenging questions have forced me back to my primary understanding of the world. Why does nutrition education not work in many cultural groups? Why does malnutrition persist in the presence of food? We have known how to prevent and correct malnutrition very effectively since the mid-seventies, yet its prevalence is unchanged in many places despite intensive educational efforts. Following World War II there was much malnutrition in Europe, but once the war stopped it disappeared in a few months, before any significant economic recovery. It has also diminished steadily in some places like Chile, but not in sub-Saharan Africa. It was this question that took our family to Africa in 1987. Now, some ten years later, I think I understand. That understanding is rooted in another lesson first taught by Moses to the children of Israel as recorded in the Bible: the necessity to continue to teach our children the stories that enable us to make sense of our lives.

The part of Africa where we have been privileged to learn has been evangelized for a short time; there are no third-generation and few second-generation Christians. The gospel was readily accepted as a solution to animist fear and guilt, and the joy that accompanied the initial arrival of the gospel is still remembered. But the idea that the gospel should change the way people think and the way they live is not understood in some critical and practical areas. Church services are long and largely musical. Content and teaching are minimal. Ethical systems and thought patterns are still dominantly animistic and fatalistic. Efforts to teach nutrition after the laughable manner of a modern Western university, through lecturing and questioning, have not succeeded in changing people's behavior. Even nurses have children who die of malnutrition in the presence of food.

Where the world is conceived of in magical or, indeed, miraculous terms, consequence and responsibility get lost. In a world where most children die before maturity, where crops fail apparently at random, the idea of a God of consistent character and the correlate of causality that is reliable does not grow easily. The long story of God's dealing with Israel and the Christian church was necessary for the idea of consequence, both moral and physical, to enter into our thinking. Only then can nutrition education be expected to work. There are plenty of signs of the reemergence of pagan-animistic-fatalistic thinking in the West, from the trivial, such as the growing interest in horoscopes and divination, to serious changes in belief patterns, such as the various New Age philosophies and even the anti-intellectualism of some sectors of the Christian church. Even the increasing importance of music and the diminishing role of biblical exposition can easily be understood in terms of the reemergence of paganism.

In politics the idea of truth is being displaced by the worship of power. Politicians are more interested in manipulating the public than in practicing rational persuasion; hence their obsession with opinion polls. They follow opinion instead of making it. Phrases that sound good but are devoid of meaning, such as "the politics of meaning," are characteristic of our society. Ends are forgotten and means and process are all.

One other vital lesson arises here: the importance of family. Orthodox Jews recognize that the survival of their culture has depended on its ability to withstand the hedonistic appeal of paganism, which has depended, to a very large extent, on obedience to the injunctions in Deuteronomy 6. The Jews had an overwhelming encounter with the presence of God at Sinai. They then promised to keep the commandments, but they broke the first three immediately. The experience of God did not make them virtuous, and neither does conversion make a modern Christian virtuous. It does make the beginning of real virtue possible. Moses explains that virtue is necessary for the survival of the Jews and that it is produced by teaching one's children diligently all that God has done. The human need for meaning and purpose is to be found in the stories of God's dealings with his people. Allan Bloom understood this when he wrote:

> My grandparents were ignorant people by our standards, and my grandfather held only lowly jobs. But their home was spiritually rich because all the things done in it, not only what was specifically ritual, found their origin in the Bible's commandments, and their explanation in the Bible's stories and the commentaries on them, and had their imaginative counterparts in the deeds of the myriad of exemplary heroes. My grandparents found reasons for the existence of their family and the fulfillment of their duties in serious writings, and they interpreted their special sufferings with respect to a great and ennobling past. Their simple faith and practices linked them to great scholars and thinkers who dealt with the same material, not from outside or from an alien perspective, but believing as they did, while simply going deeper and providing guidance. There was a respect for real learning, because it had a felt connection with their lives. This is what a community and a history mean, a common experience inviting high and low into a single body of belief.[10]

He went on to say that his Ph.D. cousins had no comparable wisdom. What they had lost was the knowledge of their own cultural history and the stories that give them reasons for "fulfillment of their duties." This essay should have brought to the mind of the educated reader at least eight passages of Scripture. A generation ago they would have been recognized, but in a biblical metaphor recognition test that I use, current students score 20 percent or less. We, the current generation of senior professors, have presided over the progressive dismantling of a culture by the denial of its informative story and the emptying of meaning from its metaphors. Unless the biblical story is taught to our children, they will become even more alienated than at present. My survival has depended on those stories, which provided the grist for the mill of moral decision. Often their effect was so deep as to be almost subconscious. "Thy word have I hid in mine heart, that I might not sin against thee" said David (Psalm 119:11 KJV). Perhaps my greatest debt is to those who put God's Word into my heart, because it has guided and kept. Those stories give a foundation that allows a child to do what is right and trust God for the outcome. Even a phrase as short as "but if not" can import a whole affirming story into the mind of those who have hidden God's Word in their hearts. Such a phrase and its story affirm the truth that if we do what is right, God will be vindicated and we will rejoice in his incomparable capacity to write stories beyond all that we can ask or imagine.

Notes

[1]C. S. Lewis, *The Screwtape Letters* (Toronto: Saunders, 1945), p. 112.
[2]Michael Polanyi, *Personal Knowledge* (Chicago: University of Chicago Press), p. 35, note.
[3]G. K. Chesterton, *Orthodoxy* (London: Collins-Fontana, 1967), p. 78.
[4]C. S. Lewis, *Mere Christianity* (New York: Macmillan, 1952), chap. 1.
[5]Diane Komp, *A Window on Heaven* (New York: HarperCollins, 1992).
[6]D. M. Lloyd-Jones, *From Fear to Faith* (Leicester, U.K.: InterVarsity Press, 1979).
[7]Augustine, *The City of God* (London: Penguin Books, 1987), p. 200.
[8]W. B. Yeats, "The Second Coming," in *The New Oxford Book of English Verse* (Oxford: Clarendon, 1972), p. 820.
[9]J. I. Steinbeck had this comment in a notebook, but I have never been able to trace it to its source.
[10]Allan Bloom, *The Closing of the American Mind* (London: Penguin Books, 1988), p. 60.

3

To God Alone
Be the Glory

JAMES N. BEMILLER

Whistler Center for
Carbohydrate Research

Purdue University

Beautiful are the things we see,
More beautiful those we understand,
Most beautiful those we do not comprehend.
—NIELS STEENSEN

Writing this essay has forced me to examine the totality of my faith—its meaning for all aspects of my life. Everything I think and do, wherever I am, in whatever role, should be governed by my faith. But is it? No. I am human. If my faith were perfect, I would put my entire life in God's hands in whatever I was called to do, wherever that calling led me. But I am not perfect. Sin is a part of who I am. Considering who and what I am in this way brings me to the realization that my identity should be a reflection of Christ in me. So I encourage all who read this essay to think through their faith in a similar way for themselves. Here's how I did it.

I am a carbohydrate chemist. I have a Ph.D. degree in biochemistry.

Most of my professional life has been devoted to the organic chemistry of carbohydrates and their practical applications. So I could be labeled a bio-organic chemist or a natural products chemist who is involved with food and the industrial uses of carbohydrates.

What do I understand, or think I understand, about the origin of my faith? How I came by my faith is a testimonial to daily growth and strengthening. My faith has been an inherent part of me throughout my conscious life. I truly believe that it was implanted in me at baptism. Then my Spirit-given and Spirit-filled life was nurtured by the same parents who brought me for baptism and were true to the promises they made. Whenever I have tended to stray from my faith, the Holy Spirit has pulled me back and has healed and strengthened me.

What impact does my profession have on my faith? All of us have an innate desire for proof. Even Jesus' disciples asked for proof of his identity and his power. My professional life is centered around learning, discovery, critical thinking and teaching. Do I take the same intellectual approach to my faith? No. My faith is not something I do. It is a gift from God. Being receptive to God and God's Word is neither something that I do nor something that I can control. As stated by Martin Luther in the Small Catechism, "I believe that I cannot by my own reason or strength believe in Jesus Christ, my Lord, or come to him; but the Holy Spirit has called me by the Gospel, enlightened me with His gifts, sanctified and kept me in true faith." This is not easy to accept for persons who rely on their intellect. Professionally, I do not accept a statement about anything that cannot be measured and substantiated with unequivocal data. But in regard to my faith, I know that it is the Holy Spirit within me that shapes and strengthens my belief. It is important for me to remember that my ideas about God are not the ultimate truth. It is God who comes to me, not I who come to God.

The excitement of discovering and then teaching others about what I have learned motivates me as a scientist. Some think that, given enough time, we humans can eventually know everything and do almost anything. That idea is mistaken, as the story of Adam and Eve teaches. As a research scientist, I try to discover as much as I can about the small facet of the universe that I am most interested in and know the most about, which naturally leads me to investigate things that I do not understand and cannot describe in that area. I marvel at the beautifully ordered complexity and diversity of the universe as we know and understand it (from subatomic particles to complex, living, thinking organisms). When I contemplate the many, many marvels of nature (for example, how one of the enzymes involved in starch biosynthesis in both leaves and nonphotosynthetic storage tissue has the same catalytic unit in both tissues but different regulatory units because of different functions of the starch), I must conclude that God —the all-powerful, our Creator—is the greatest scientist of all. I must be open to God's mystery as well as my curiosity. And I must remember that this marvelous universe is insignificant compared to God's love for us. What we will learn from scientific investigation will not bring us any closer to God's grace and God's love, freely given and unrelated to anything we do.

How does my faith influence who I am? Any statement of my beliefs and how they influence my life begins with the question Jesus asked his disciples: "But who do you say that I am?" (Luke 9:20, RSV). Jesus was asking them and us, "In what way do you know me?" My approach to problem solving works one way in research and another way in fixing a leaking faucet at home. My understanding of the persons who make up the Trinity comes from the Holy Spirit, but I am not always aware of how the Spirit working in and through me influences me. I only know that it does and that I cannot use the scientific method to learn God's will for me. Where God is concerned, I cannot develop a hypothesis to be tested. I must be open to what has been and is being revealed to me. I must understand that God comes to me, not the other way around. My relationship with God does not depend on a proper understanding of God, sound theology, proper doctrine or anything else. It only depends on God's love for me and my acceptance of that love, through the action of the Holy Spirit. There is so very much I do not understand about the physical and biological world, let alone God's holiness as compared to our humanness. So I pray continually for a better understanding of God's will, realizing that I must be ready to accept God's response to my prayer. I myself have witnessed the power of prayer in my life and in the lives of others.

How does my faith influence my personal life? It tells me that life is more than biology. It has meaning, joys, sorrows and a oneness with creation. The value of my faith to me, my family, and society is in providing hope and peace in an imperfect world and in giving significance to my life.

How does my faith influence my professional life? Even if I wanted to, I could never escape the power of my baptism. I felt this strongly after my Ph.D. final oral examination. Instead of celebrating in the usual way, I felt a need to give thanks to God. I realize that I have been given certain talents that I must use to the fullest and that I am part of something much bigger than myself. When I first decided on the career path I would take (that is, responded to God's call for me), I realized that God's creation was entrusted to us for our care and use. That realization gives my work a purpose, a purpose that makes serving God and serving humankind inseparable. The power of my baptism makes me aware that (1) my personal commitment is not what it should be, (2) God is constant in love and forgiveness to those who are open and receptive to that love and forgiveness and (3) I have a special calling/opportunity to serve God in this time and place. Others who follow me will build on what I will have contributed scientifically. I would like my legacy to consist of the positive impacts I have made on the lives of those with whom I come into contact.

I learned recently that J. S. Bach ended his musical works with S.D.G. *(Soli Deo Gloria)*—"to God alone be the glory." Because I can comprehend neither the majesty, mystery nor power of God nor God's past and present involvement with and in his creation, including with and in me, nothing says it better, from my perspective. Thus I also close with S.D.G.

4

God Is Faithful

E. C. "Gene" Ashby

Chemistry & Biochemistry
(Emeritus)

Georgia Institute of Technology

> Did I not tell you that if you would
> believe you would see the glory of God?
> —Jesus (John 11:40 RSV)

A few years ago I was asked to give a talk about God's role in my life. I smiled and said that such a talk would be very boring. I have spent my entire life studying, working and helping raise a large family, but in recalling my early life in particular, I see clearly how the hand of God has guided my life through an intricate web of circumstances. Now my incredible journey is almost over, and I can truly say that the most important lesson I have learned in life is that *God is faithful.*

I was born in New Orleans in 1930 to immigrant parents. My mother was born in Sicily in 1903 and came to New Orleans at the age of three. My mother's family came to the United States because they had heard it to be a land of plenty and a land of unusual opportunity. But they soon learned that a fortune in lire (saved from owning a bakery) didn't amount to much in American dollars. Within a year the whole family was destitute. My grandfather made a living by collecting discarded fruit and vegetables from wharves along the Mississippi River. He washed the produce at home and peddled it the next day from a cart that he pulled through neighborhood streets. My mother told me that many nights she went to bed hungry. Her family's financial insecurity played a major role in her life, leading her to remain in an abusive marriage relationship. My most vivid remembrance of the first twenty years of my life, which I lived at home, is that my mom exhibited a lot of inward anger and an unusual lack of love for her children.

My father, on the other hand, was born in Mexico to wealthy European parents. He came to the United States when he was twenty-six years old after the family sugar factory was burned down and the family farmland was confiscated by revolutionaries. My father was well educated and obtained a white-collar job soon after entering this country. He had an accent, but his grammar was impeccable. He was very intelligent and worked hard. In time he became the Argentinian consul general in New Orleans. He was handsome, articulate and charming in his work as a diplomat but was entirely different at home. I realize now that he was emotionally ill and by present-day standards probably would be referred for professional help. My father seemed to be incapable of showing any love or affection to his wife or his children.

My brother, my sister and I were badly scarred by the violence and fear that dominated our family life. We could not bring friends home because of my father's violent outbursts. The three of us lived in a state of constant turmoil, which has had a profound effect on all our lives.

Outwardly I was a happy, somewhat extroverted person who dealt with the unpleasantness of life by repressing it. The bright spots in my life enabled me to survive emotionally. I had a grandmother and two aunts who were wonderful and loving. They realized the strain that we children were under and did everything they could to love us. At age nineteen, as a college senior, I left home to live with one of my aunts because I could no longer endure the constant fighting. After about three weeks my father called and threatened to kill my aunt unless she sent me home, so I returned. Neither my father nor my mother spoke to me when I arrived home or said one word to me about the matter. It was as if I had never left.

At St. Aloysius High School in New Orleans I was popular, a relatively good student and a member of the school tennis team. I was junior class president and did some dating, unbeknownst to my parents, and considered myself a happy person. During these early years, thanks to some inspiring teachers, I came to know God deep down in my heart. I spoke to God constantly in order to get through the turmoil of home life. In spite of everything in my life at that time, God was always faithful to see me through, and we had a strong relationship.

I entered Loyola University in New Orleans when I was sixteen on a work scholarship. In April and May of each year Loyola took me off the work scholarship and put me on a tennis scholarship for the two-month tennis season. I played three years on a highly ranked varsity tennis team at the number six position of a six-man team. The other five players were full scholarship players from out of state. I was very proud to be a member of a team, any team, and I was well accepted by the other players because I won so many matches. This acceptance was very important to me because I desperately needed to be affirmed. Although my father was an avid tennis player throughout his adult life, he never once came to see me play a high school or collegiate match. Once he came to see me play in the finals of the New Orleans boys' tennis championship when I was fifteen. When I lost the first set, he got up and left. His leaving embarrassed me. In the twenty years I lived at home, my father never once told me that he loved me. In fact, he hardly spoke to me.

At Loyola University I struggled to juggle my studies in the chemistry program and a twenty-hour work week. At that time my mother's anger at my father kept her so preoccupied that she seemed oblivious to the fact that she had three children. I don't remember ever receiving a kiss, a hug or a kind word from her. I thought I was a terrible person, but I didn't know why. I realize now that she was under tremendous stress (and I have long since forgiven her). Nevertheless, I was troubled by feelings of insecurity. My parents did not attend a single graduation ceremony, not high school, Loyola, Auburn or Notre

Dame. But God was my strength at this time in my life.

At the beginning of my freshman year at Loyola, I met my first serious girlfriend. Three years later she graduated from nursing school and was expecting an engagement ring. I was nineteen and she was twenty. I had no money and no prospects, since I was still in school. I also knew I wasn't ready to get married. She broke off our relationship and married someone else within a year. Although I was devastated at the time, I have come to realize that what happened was best for both of us.

In the summer of 1950, during my senior year at Loyola, the Korean War began. I was a staff sergeant in the National Guard. It seemed certain that our unit would be called to Korea after our training period that summer. Instead, only soldiers from our unit having special skills were called. By the end of the following year I still had not been called, and my four-year enlistment was up. So I decided to go to graduate school. Several friends from my unit who were called up early in the war were killed.

I enrolled in a graduate program at Auburn University and was delighted to be on my own for the first time in my life. My roommate was a fellow Loyola graduate, and we often attended early morning Mass. I met a student named Carolyn in the basement of St. Mary's Catholic Church after Sunday Mass. Shortly thereafter we began to see each other almost every night, when I walked her from the chemistry building to the dorm. On weekends we would take long walks to see the dogs at the dog kennels or take walks in the woods. We did a lot of talking and found out that we had a lot in common. It was the most beautiful one-year courtship imaginable. We were married in Mobile, Alabama, Carolyn's hometown, and it was a beautiful wedding. We both felt very close to God, and God was an important part of our life together at that time.

Seven children were eventually born to us, first three boys and then four girls. Our son Chris was born at Auburn eleven months after we were married. He was a happy child and we played with him constantly. I received a master's degree in chemistry after the required two years and then stayed an additional year doing contract research in order to save enough money to go to the University of Notre Dame for a doctoral program. Carolyn, Chris and I arrived at Notre Dame in September 1954 and were impressed by its beauty. I worked very long hours and took extra jobs grading papers at the university and bellhopping. Carolyn took in babies during the day for working mothers. Our big night out once a month was going to the neighborhood drive-in. We had very little money, but we were happy. Notre Dame was a special place for Carolyn and me; it had deep spiritual overtones for two young Catholics, and I graduated with a sense of fulfillment and hope for the future.

Since I was unable to secure an academic position, I took a job with the Ethyl Corporation in Baton Rouge, eighty miles from New Orleans, in 1956. Despite my unhappy childhood, I wanted to be close to home. At this stage of my life, God was alive and well in my heart.

At the Ethyl Corporation I was treated very well and was involved in interesting research. In 1958 I made a discovery of commercial interest that led to the building of a chemical plant in Houston, Texas. I became a group leader and was successful in other research projects. However, my main desire was to teach at a major research university. As God would have it, Professor H. C. Brown (1979 Nobel Prize winner in chemistry) was a consultant for the Ethyl Corporation, and he played a major role in my being offered a position at Georgia Tech, starting in the fall of 1963. I was ecstatic to be offered an academic position, even though it paid less than half of what I was making in industry.

Three months after arriving at Georgia Tech, I had a lump removed from my groin that was reported to be malignant with a good possibility of metastasis. This was a very unnerving situation for a young man with a wife and five small children. During the seven days before cancer surgery I went to 6 a.m. Mass every morning before lecturing at Georgia Tech. The church was almost empty, and I poured my heart out to God, saying that I didn't want to leave my family. After the third day, I had peace about the situation and told God that I trusted him and would accept any verdict with respect to my life. The same day a colleague suggested that I get a second opinion on the tumor. The second laboratory called me just before major surgery was scheduled, with the news that the tumor was not malignant. I never did have the surgery. I believe that this was a sovereign act of God, and I am grateful for his mercy toward me and my family.

Within three years I had a research group of ten students working toward their Ph.D. degrees. My students and I were successful in our research efforts, and we published many scientific papers. I was invited to speak at prestigious universities and gave plenary lectures at national and international meetings. But all this success did not bring me satisfaction; in fact, I felt quite empty. I spent about seventy hours a week working and spent only one hour a week with God at church on Sunday. I lost my prayer life, and by the time I was thirty-nine years old I began to question God's existence. I find that relationships that aren't nurtured tend to fade.

About this time, a Catholic colleague invited me to attend a three-day retreat, called a *cursillo*, at a monastery near Atlanta. I heard the salvation message for the first time and a call to total commitment to God. I said yes to Jesus in every aspect of my life, and instantly all doubt and lack of faith disappeared. I felt a profound sense of the presence of God in my life, which to this day has not left. The Bible, which seemed so unintelligible to me before, now came alive. My Sunday-school teaching changed and became more focused on the Bible. In time the priests became concerned about this development and called me to account. Eventually I was labeled a fundamentalist. At age fifty-four I joined a nondenominational, Bible-oriented church. I still love and respect my Catholic friends, but I am happier being part of a church that is more biblically oriented.

Carolyn and I and two of our daughters spent a year at Stanford University on a Guggenheim Fellowship (1978-1979). I learned a lot of chemistry at Stanford and met some terrific people. But while I was at Stanford, my research group decreased from thirteen to four and I had to go back to the building stage. During these travels I had many opportunities to share my Christian faith, but not with much success. I believe that pride keeps many scientists from finding God because becoming a Christian requires humbling yourself before God and becoming vulnerable before men.

I have received a number of awards and medals for which I am grateful. Two chemical plants have been built as a result of discoveries made in my laboratories at the Ethyl Corporation and at Georgia Tech. These events, however significant, have not had a significant impact on my life. A number of things, however, have changed my life. First, I became emotionally involved in the Vietnam War, initially through training provided to me as a prospective consultant for the Department of Defense. The training included briefings at the highest levels: the assistant secretary of state, the chairperson of the Joint Chiefs of Staff, leading figures at the Rand Corporation and the Hudson Institute, and the like. It was never the intention of the United States to win the Vietnam War, thereby precipitating a world war, but simply to confront communism and cause the Soviet Union to continue its military buildup, forcing the expenditure of funds it could not afford to spend. In my opinion all Vietnam veterans are heroes and carry much of the credit for freedom today throughout the world. It has taken a long time to be healed from the emotional wounds caused by the devastating losses of precious American soldiers. Few people know that since the war ended, more than 150,000 Vietnam veterans have committed suicide, over 70 percent are divorced and 40 percent are unemployed.[1] I have broken down on a number of occasions as I have borne the grief of this tragedy, and I still grieve to this day.

In 1988 a rheumatologist diagnosed me with polymyocitis and said that I had approximately three years to live. I learned that polymyocitis is a degenerative muscular disease for which there is no cure. I prayed and asked God to heal me, but I was also ready to go home to him if that was his will. The next Sunday at church, the pastor picked up the bread at Communion and said, "This is the body of Christ that was broken for our sins and our diseases." When the pastor said the word *diseases*, I was instantly healed. The next morning I jumped out of bed, did a vigorous dance and proclaimed the wonders of God. Further blood tests were normal. This was the second time God healed me of a terminal illness.

My parents separated after thirty-two years of marriage. I visited my father about three times a year in New Orleans. I was with him three weeks before he died and witnessed the greatest miracle of all— a calm, peaceful and repentant person. God had answered my most difficult prayer.

My mother lived in our home for six months of each year and spent the other six months with my brother. Life now included hugs and expressions of affection every day. In time my mother became a pleasure to be with. God clearly worked a great healing in her life and in mine. Most important, the chain of misery had been broken. Our children grew up in a family that was more loving than mine had been. As a result they are even better parents toward their children. The outcome with my parents has elicited in us amazement, once again, at the goodness and mercy of God.

In 1990 I, among others, was called to Hanford, Washington, the home of the largest military nuclear facility in the country, to assess the possibility of explosions occurring in high-level nuclear waste tanks. The problem was extremely complex, and it was hard to know where to begin. I recruited three colleagues from Georgia Tech to help study the problem. Together we came up with a reasonable understanding of the source of the problem and how its solution might be approached. When I presented the results of our study at a meeting four months after the initial meeting, we were given a sizable grant to move forward with the proposed study. We hired some postdoctoral assistants, and for three years a group of twelve scientists attacked this problem. We did indeed find many answers to the problem at hand. The people at Hanford, who were under immense pressure to solve this problem, finally had some firm chemical understanding of the problem. At the beginning of this project, I asked God to help us solve a seemingly unsolvable problem. I believe he led us every step of the way.

But three years of long hours, continuous travel and frequent presentations, in addition to teaching and conducting a second research group in single electron transfer chemistry, left me feeling completely burned out. I retired from teaching in 1993 at sixty-two years of age. It turns out that retiring early was the best thing I could have done. I am still involved in chemistry, but now I am able to be involved in other projects as well, particularly working with children. My greatest contribution to society has not been in my scientific achievements but in being the father of seven remarkable children who know God. They are very loving, dedicated people who are reaching out to help a dying world. I could not be more proud. However, it has not been easy. We had our problems, but we never lost our faith in God. Carolyn and I have prayed over the years for seemingly hopeless situations. In spite of tough times, illnesses, parental rejection, the difficulties of raising seven children, the trauma of the Vietnam War, and other painful events and difficult relationships, I would not change anything about my life. In everything God was molding me and shaping me to become the person he wanted me to be. I would not know God today the way I do if I had not suffered through the unique circumstances of my life. Today my sensitivity to suffering enables me to help others.

God had a plan for my life, as I believe he has for anyone who submits to him. I trusted him and realize now that he has met my every need and has indeed been faithful.

Note

[1]For a broader discussion of the postwar struggles of Vietnam veterans see Chuck Dean, *Nam Vet: Making Peace with Your Past* (Portland, Ore.: Multnomah Press, 1990).

5

Three Heavens—
Our Home

PATRICIA H. REIFF

Space Physics & Astronomy

Rice University

The heavens declare the glory of God;
and the firmament showeth his handywork.
—PSALM 19:1 KJV

One of my fondest childhood memories is of a father-daughter astronomy course with my Brownie troop at the Oklahoma City planetarium. I had always been interested in the natural world, and our five-acre home with its pond and animals gave me ample opportunity to observe life and its wonders. Bottle-feeding a lamb was a sheer delight for my sister, Kaethe, and me. Our favorite lamb (named "Georgie" for being born on February 22—Washington's Birthday) would jerk his tail with glee as he downed his bottle. By April he could almost bowl me over with his enthusiasm. I proudly led him in the Easter fashion show at my church—proud, that is, until he made a huge puddle on the ramp! Despite that horrifying experience, I thought that a career as a veterinarian might be in my future—combining medical work and my love of the outdoors.

I often sat in my quiet place in the woods: a flat rock surrounded by trees. The sights and sounds of civilization were nowhere evident. God talked to me in the bird song and the frog chorus. It's no wonder that "In the Garden" is my favorite hymn, then and now. I was very fortunate to grow up in a family that had a deep faith in God. I was the first person baptized in the futuristic new building of the First Christian Church ("The Church of Tomorrow"), with its paraboloid dome and unusual tower, on Easter Day in 1957. Although I was only seven, my immersion sealed my commitment to live for Christ as my personal Savior, and I have tried to keep that commitment ever since.

Space science has made me a high-tech naturalist. Sir Fred Hoyle predicted that when humans left the earth, they would look back and see the planet as being small, fragile and beautiful. He was right. The perspective acquired from space has changed our appreciation of our island home. We have visited all save one of the planets and have viewed all the large and moderate-sized moons without finding evidence of life. Recent evidence suggesting bacteria in early Mars comes from a time when liquid water existed and Mars's magnetic field was capable of protecting life from the ravages of ultraviolet and cosmic rays—protection that is gone now. Shielded from cosmic rays by our magnetic field and from energetic photons by our atmosphere, and nurtured by the ocean, earth is a special place and deserves our careful stewardship. The lower atmosphere, the domain of life and weather, is the first heaven, and we are just now learning how precious and rare is this gift from God. I really didn't appreciate our "heaven on earth" until I learned about the atmosphere of Venus that can melt lead, the sterile expanse of Mercury, the dry dust (and dry frost!) of Mars, the sulfurous volcanoes of Io, the noxious atmosphere of Titan and the frigid geysers of Triton. Pluto, our only unvisited planet, is unlikely to be more hospitable, with the sun appearing only as a rather bright star. The planets that scientists have found around other stars are scarcely inviting—all (so far) have been much too close to their home star for habitability—but it's almost certain that more inviting planets will eventually be found.

This brings us to the second heaven: the realm of the stars and galaxies. That astronomy class that I took with my dad left me with a sense of wonder over the vastness of the universe and its mysteries. When I went to Wellesley College in 1967 to major in math, I signed up for the basic astronomy course. The professors at Wellesley knew that a knowledge of physics is essential to an understanding of astronomy. So the first semester of astronomy there was really Physics 100. Physics opened a new door for me. Here I used my math talent to figure out how things work. I owe my physics professor, Phyllis Fleming, a huge debt for making physics enjoyable and interesting. I had found a new major.

Suffering from culture shock and severely Mexican-food deprived, I left Wellesley after a year and returned to Oklahoma, my cowboy boots and my boyfriend. I graduated with honors from Oklahoma State and was accepted for graduate work in both the physics and the space science departments at Rice University. When I learned that I could get a summer job analyzing data from the Apollo 14 mission to the moon, my choice was clear. The drama of Apollo 13 was fresh on my mind, and the prospect of working with NASA as more lunar missions were still flying was captivating. Seven years old when the first Sputnik flew, I was a child of the space age. The thrill of learning something that no one ever knew before was far more exciting than merely adding to our knowledge of processes here on earth.

E. W. Maunder, in his book *The Astronomy of the Bible*, says that the Judaic God opened up the possibility for scientific study of the heavens. Contemporary religions had the sun and moon as major gods, and as gods, they were not suitable for study. An eclipse of either struck people with terror. But the Bible teaches that the sun and other heavenly bodies are created objects (Psalm 148), for days and seasons, for weeks and years (Genesis 1:14; Psalm 136), and as such are suitable for study and must not be worshiped (Deuteronomy 4:19). "It cannot be imagined that God would have intervened to hamper [man's] growth in intellectual power by revealing to men facts and methods which it was within their own ability to discover for themselves. Men's mental powers have developed by their exercise; they would have been stunted had men been led to look to revelation rather than to diligent effort for the satisfaction of their curiosity."[1] God encourages us to understand our universe, and many of the great names of science, from Faraday to Newton, have attributed their success to divine inspiration. God is the author of all knowledge, and I give God full credit both for my incremental additions to the field and for the few flashes of special insight that I have had over the years.

How do I reconcile science and Scripture? Although I certainly believe that God could have created the entire universe in six earth days six thousand years ago, it seems unlike God to confuse us with clues that argue for a much older universe. I believe that the Bible is literally true but that it uses figurative language (when the beggar Lazarus died [Luke 16:22], he was not implanted into Abraham's bosom but was joined with Abraham in heaven). Since God is not subject to the limitation of the speed of light, then God's time is completely irrelevant to human time. As the apostle Peter wrote, paraphrasing one of the psalms, "one day is with the Lord as a thousand years, and a thousand years as one day" (2 Peter 3:8 KJV; see also Psalm 90:4).[2]

Reading the book *Flatland* by Edwin Abbott[3] helped me to visualize the difficulty in comprehending a higher-dimensional God. Abbott describes how life appears to two-dimensional beings (triangles, squares and the like) confined to a plane. The flatland folk can see each other's perimeters but cannot see inside each other. They cannot imagine a three-dimensional being; they can only observe the intersection of a 3-D object with their world. If a three-dimensional person sticks three fingers into their plane, the fingers look like three separate circles to them. The 3-D being can see inside them and can even flip them over or turn them inside out, things they cannot do for themselves. Similarly, time is another dimension that God is outside of —try to imagine us on a plane with time as one dimension and space the other. God can look to the left and see us doing things "in the past" and look to the right and see us doing things "in the future"; but it is all "now" to him.

Considering that the Bible was written thousands of years before Newton discovered his laws or Maxwell wrote his equations, the sequence described in Genesis is amazingly correct by current understanding. For example, a common argument used long ago against the Genesis account asked how light could have appeared on the first day, when the sun wasn't created until the fourth day.

We now know that there is no better, simpler description of the big bang than "Light, be!" (see Genesis 1:3). There was a time when all the energy (and mass and space) in the universe existed in the form of an infinitesimally small point of light energy that "spontaneously" arose many billions of years ago. Only when it expanded and cooled were nucleons able to condense out of the formlessness and fill the void. Similarly, the other five days of creation are the other times when God's specific creative power was required to make the habitable world and life.

Day two, in my view, covers the condensation of the galaxy, the solar system, and the planets, which was a miracle in view of the delicacy of the balance between the pull of gravity and the inertia of the explosion. As outlined by Hugh Ross in *The Creator and the Cosmos*,[4] each of the fundamental constants of physics can only exist in an extremely narrow range to allow stars and planets, and even atoms and molecules, to form. In essence, day one was the big bang and the laws of physics; day two says that the fundamental constants and local conditions were just right so that galaxies, and specifically the solar system and its earth, could form. We now understand that our sun is a second-generation star, formed out of the debris of a neighboring supernova. That fact is absolutely critical to life on earth. Without the supernova, we would not have the carbon and the other heavy elements that are essential for life. And without the compression from the supernova's shock wave, the sun would not have condensed as a single star and would have remained a mass of formless gas. A typical nebula needs several solar masses of material to spontaneously condense; the result is a system with two or more stars. Planets in those systems have erratic orbits and wildly varying illumination, which is not conducive for life.

Day three gave earth its unique combination of dry land and water, again, absolutely necessary for intelligent, communicating life. Day three also brought the first life. I really don't care whether this took an eye blink or a billion years—the creation of life from nonlife, even in a single-celled bacterium, is so complicated and unlikely that it has been compared to an explosion in a junkyard resulting in a Boeing 747 jumbo jet. It's also possible that microbial life hitched a ride on an asteroid or comet or arrived on a fragment of Mars. God's hand was involved, of that I am sure. The transition from single-celled to multi-celled life is another incredible change—cells cooperating to form a single entity and, in many cases, single cells dying for the good of the organism. The plant life from day three made a profound change in earth's atmosphere—taking carbon dioxide out of the atmosphere and putting it into soils, limestone and microfossils, creating food and oxygen for the animals to come. Thus the first heaven was given to us.

On the fourth day the clouds parted, allowing the earth to see sun, moon and stars. This was at least partially due to the extraction of carbon dioxide, cooling the atmosphere "just in time" because the sun was heating up. A transparent yet sheltering atmosphere is unique in our solar system. Only earthlings can stand on the ground and observe the wonders of the heavens without being scorched by the sun, blasted by cosmic rays or shrouded by thick layers of clouds. Only earthlings have perfect solar eclipses that allow the sun's gorgeous, ghostly corona to be seen. It is no coincidence that our eyes are sensitive only to the portion of the electromagnetic spectrum that easily penetrates the atmosphere. Alone in the solar system we have a clear, safe view of the wonder-full second heaven.

The fifth day brought forth animal life in abundance, starting from the ocean. Life could exist in oceans alone (hence the evidence for bacteria on Mars and a possibility of life in the subsurface oceans of the Jovian moon Europa). But energy from fire is necessary for the development of technology and thus long-range communication. Dolphins and whales are intelligent creatures, but their ocean home allows communication only through sound waves. The combination of the nurturing ocean and the challenging land gives earth, alone in our solar system, the right conditions for an amazing array of life. The fifth day also brought birds to explore the skies. It seemed odd to me that the description of the leviathans of the sea is followed in the same sentence by birds; however, scientists now suggest that the dinosaurs are most closely related to birds, not lizards!

The sixth day brought land animals and finally humankind. God made man from the dust of the earth and breathed God's own spirit into him. This infusion of God's spirit is perhaps the most significant creative act of all—it changed the human being from an intelligent animal to a creature that has the capability of eternal life. Whether "the dust of the earth" means an actual handful of soil or a walking australopithecine is not crucial to me. Clearly, there is something special about humanity. And sixty million years of primate evolution in South America (after South America separated from Africa) did not bring people to be there—only in God's hand did *Homo sapiens* become humanity. In this way we can be cognizant of the third heaven—the realm of the spirit. But only through the sacrifice of God's Son, Jesus Christ, can the third heaven become accessible to us. Jesus serves as the bridge between the earth and the other dimensions of God.

I am both a scientist and a Christian. God has called me to understand his world and gives me the insight to do it. And yes, I ascribe many of my best ideas to divine inspiration—the "Aha! insight" that Martin Gardner[5] discusses often comes to me in quiet times and dreams. I have felt the Lord leading me, both in my choice of career and in my everyday life. I have rested on a promise found in the Bible: "Trust in the LORD with all thine heart; and lean not unto thine own understanding. In all thy ways acknowledge him, and he shall direct thy paths"(Proverbs 3:5-6 KJV).

I have felt the presence of God in comfort, strength and joy. The joy of the Lord also drives out fear. I fly many thousands of miles each year, but the bumps don't scare me because I always turn the flight over to the Lord. As a child, I had nightmares from time to time. But when I received the Holy Spirit and learned of God's power as well as his grace, I rebuked the prince of this world and banished him from my house by the blood of Jesus. Now my dreams are sweet (Proverbs 3:24). My three children are also learning the peace that comes from the Lord. When a tornado touched down less than a mile from their school one year, they had to "duck and cover" for nearly an hour. Each of my children prayed to God for deliverance for themselves and their school and lost their fear as they did so. When my mother died, she saw angels coming for her. The nurses were amazed at her joy and strength. I was privileged to be with my father while he talked with God the last two nights of his life. He had fallen asleep in a normal manner, but after a while he sat up and talked (audibly but softly), listened and gestured as he carried on a true, animated conversation with God. The next night I heard him say, "I'm ready." He was eager to shed his worn-out shell and be with Jesus. And his desire was fulfilled: he died the next day.

Many similar stories from other believers convince me that the home I have waiting for me far exceeds what I have here on earth. A missionary once returned to New York after several years on the mission field. On the same ocean liner rode the president of the United States, Theodore Roosevelt. When the ship arrived at dock, the ticker tapes flew and the press mobbed the president. The missionary was ignored and later expressed to his wife his bitterness at this slight. She suggested that he take his frustration before the Lord in prayer. He agreed, and after a time of prayer he was comforted by God's response: "You're not home yet."[6] Jesus tells us, "In my Father's house there are many dwelling places. . . . I go to prepare a place for you, . . . so that where I am, there you may be also" (John 14:2-3 NRSV). The heavenly city is a multidimensional place—it is described as a cube in Revelation 21:16. The "many dwelling places" could be just rooms, or they could be dimensions. Who knows the glories that we will see and experience when we join him in our true, eternal home! I know where that eternal home is, and that knowledge gives me peace and joy every day.

This world's worries do not scare me. Cutbacks in federal funding for research may threaten my work, but my Father owns the cattle on a thousand hills (Psalm 50:10) and will provide for me. I have been very fortunate—a scientific mission that I helped conceive (IMAGE) was just selected as the next MIDEX (mid-sized explorer), and we are preparing for a launch near the turn of the millennium. Nobody can outgive God. He asks for 10 percent and then returns us a hundredfold on our investment. If we are faithful to him, our own resources will grow (Luke 6:38; 2 Corinthians 9:6). God's abundant provision for us covers our professional lives and our daily sustenance as well as the health of our eternal spirits. Part of my tithe (and my "time tithe") I give to environmental organizations, including the Citizens' Environmental Coalition, of which I am a trustee. Many of Jesus' illustrations came from the natural world—the lilies of the field, the sower, the sparrow, the vine and the branches, the shepherd and the sheep. We are to occupy ourselves till he comes (Luke 19:13), and we will have to answer to God for what we do with our talents—including our personal abilities as well as our financial resources and our treatment of the world and the people in it. If we hide our talents, they will be taken away, as the servant described in the Gospel of Matthew learned (Matthew 25). I once heard it said that if you are resting on your laurels, you're wearing them on the wrong end.

I am far from perfect. I try to do too much, I leave too much clutter, and I spend too little time with my family. Hoping to slow me down, my husband gave me a copy of *The Type E Woman*[7] for Christmas one year. I never found time to finish it. Although I sin, I have an advocate with the Father, Jesus Christ the righteous. He is the atoning sacrifice for the sins of the whole world (1 John 2:1-2). "If we confess our sins, he is faithful and just to forgive us our sins, and to cleanse us from all unrighteousness" (1 John 1:9 KJV). The hallmark of true faith in God is hope (Hebrews 6:17-20) and the knowledge that God watches over us, forgiving our sins, healing our diseases, judging righteously, leading us into truth and to eternal life (Psalm 103).

Science cannot prove that God exists. If it could, then only scientists could know him. Jesus came to the children and the poor, scorning the haughty intellectuals of his day. He came to show us what God living in you really looks like. He taught with simple parables that all can understand. He died a Lamb for our sins and forever opened the throne of God to humankind. My faith is based on God's Word and on the eyewitness accounts of men and women who were willing to die for their faith, not on cleverly crafted fables (2 Peter 1:16). The Dead Sea Scrolls demonstrate that today's Scripture manuscripts differ little from manuscripts that are two thousand years old. Archaeological discoveries continue to furnish new evidence of the veracity of the places and people spoken of in the Bible. God preserves his Word, and his Word is what speaks of Jesus. The Bible is very old, yet always new. Like an onion, it has many layers. Each time I read it, I go a layer deeper without ever coming to the end. Bible reading is challenging enough for an intellectual but simple enough for a child. Although the material heavens will pass away, the new heaven, God's home for us, is eternal (2 Peter 3:10-13). Until then, my study of the three heavens—the atmosphere, the galaxy, and our eternal home—continues.

Notes

[1]E. W. Maunder, *The Astronomy of the Bible* (London: Hodder & Stoughton, 1909), p. 404.

[2]See Gerald L. Schroeder, *Genesis and the Big Bang: The Discovery of Harmony Between Modern Science and the Bible* (New York: Bantam Books, 1990), for a discussion of relativity and God's time.

[3]Edwin A. Abbott, *Flatland: A Romance of Many Dimensions* (New York: Dover, 1992), p. 83.

[4]Hugh Ross, *The Creator and the Cosmos: How the Greatest Scientific Discoveries of the Century Reveal God*, rev. ed. (Colorado Springs, Colo.: NavPress, 1995), p. 181.

[5]M. Gardner, *Aha! Insight* (New York: Scientific American Press/W. H. Freeman, 1978), p. 179.

[6]Ray C. Stedman, *Talking with My Father: Jesus Teaches on Prayer* (Grand Rapids, Mich.: Discovery House, 1997).

[7]H. B. Braiker, *The Type E Woman: How to Overcome the Stress of Being Everything to Everybody* (New York: Dodd, Mead, 1986).

6

Ordinary Memoir

JOHN SUPPE

Geosciences

Princeton University

In writing poems, the author must use his image
because he sees it or feels it,
not because he can use it to back up some creed.
—EZRA POUND, *GAUDIER BREZESKA: A MEMOIR*

Given the Christian claim that God not only exists but also communicates and establishes personal relationships, it should come as no surprise that accounts of these interactions are at the core of Christian literature. Augustine, for example, in his *Confessions* describes an event leading to his conversion that he interprets as involving specific communication from God to him.[1] Popular Christian literature, including the oral conversion testimonies of ordinary Christians, contain humble and touching claims of God's acting in the lives of humans by the millions. These claims have been received skeptically by many intellectuals. Some claims are worthy of skepticism because where there is wheat there is chaff and there are weeds. But such testimonies of ordinary human experience seem to be an epistemic necessity if Christianity is to be seriously considered. After all, if God doesn't interact in a communicating way, how will there be significant knowledge of God? Thus the autobiographical essay is an especially appropriate form of Christian expression, particularly in our individualistic culture. For this reason I offer a bit of my story.

My cultural inheritance and tradition included lively discussions and debates at the dinner table—summer squalls punctuated by expectant calms as our parents sent us to the encyclopedia to "get your facts straight." I reached a point where I could argue any side of any issue. But by the time I went to college I was tired of debate and became more interested in understanding life and the universe as they actually are. My brother Fred went on to become a philosopher, which I considered to be the logical end of the dinnertime conversations—to me philosophers were intellectual lawyers. Today I take a kinder view of my brother and even of philosophy.[2] But this family inheritance of testing ideas against each other and against any facts that can be brought to bear was a good and rich one. Ours was not a sterile skepticism but a wrestling for the truth combined with a good measure of wrestling for the wrestle.

Church was also our inheritance. We went every Sunday and my experience was generally positive. But when it came time for my confirmation, I didn't know if Christian doctrines were true or false. And I didn't know how to find out. I was given the impression that if you really understood the Apostles' Creed, you just signed your name at the bottom and you were in, faith coming from knowledge and understanding. When people told me that "you just have to have faith," they sounded like the White Queen, telling Alice to take a deep breath and believe the unbelievable.[3] It smacked of self-deception, and I chose instead not to be confirmed, because I did not believe.

I wasn't negative about Christianity, even though I was aware that hypocritical and even evil people had been in the church throughout history. I even recognized that Christian ethics are basically good and right (which is something some modern intellectuals have remarkable difficulty comprehending). But I knew that Christian ethics were not Christianity.

In spite of my ambiguous feelings about Christianity I wasn't attracted to other religions. I realized that religion has a very substantial cultural component; for example, my growing up in Los Angeles rather than Tokyo didn't make Christianity true. But the little I knew of Zen Buddhism struck me as nothing short of weird, in spite of my interest in Japanese art and poetry.

When I was in high school, I encountered Bertrand Russell's essay "Why I Am Not a Christian"[4] as I worked after school shelving books at our city library. Russell went through one by one destroying some classical arguments for the existence of God and the truth of Christianity. Perhaps for a fleeting moment I became an atheist, but I soon decided that atheism took as much faith as belief in God. I went off to college as an agnostic. There I had no contact with Christianity.

Life went on, as it inexorably does. Days add up to years and years to decades. In principle my life didn't differ from a lot of academic lives. I happened into geology, but it could just as well have been something else. I graduated, got married, went to graduate school, was a postdoc, was hired by Princeton, had children, got tenure. I was successful and happy. But there were also times when my story could have taken disastrous turns. I could tell of my encounter with the mountain lion or the fall on a mountain climb that killed my climbing partner and could just as easily have killed me. But that's true of other lives as well: disastrous spouses we could easily have married (or did marry), ruinous conflicts with colleagues and relatives. Life does not inevitably lead to success and happiness. But my life was generally successful and happy.

By saying that I led a reasonably successful academic life, without spelling out the details, I am trying to stand back as far as I possibly can. Everyone has a story. Although each story involves specific events, facts and details that are dear or painful to our own hearts, it's not obvious that they are significant. The details are, of course, necessary for crafting a well-crafted story, but these surficial details may in fact obscure the meaning of the life. Maybe I should go ruffle through the magazine rack and find old issues of the *Princeton Alumni Weekly* or the *New York Times* and clip out appropriate text from the alumni news or obituary sections and paste them into a collage, calling it *Fig. 1* of this paper, a biographical illustration of the meaning of life. Or perhaps a fictional story could be made more true to life; for example,

James Loder[5] tells a hypothetical story of his life that serves my purpose:

> Let's suppose I'm working late in my Princeton home one fall evening, and even though it's 2 a.m. I decide to take a walk to clear my head. Let's also suppose I slip into some heavy boots because of a recent rain and put on a coat still carrying some tools from a recent camping trip. I don't plan a long walk but go down the hill to Carnegie Lake. At 2 a.m., Princeton is very still. There is music from a few dorm parties in the distance, but houses are dark and there are no street lights. Now, let's suppose I trip on a root as I walk along a steep embankment, fall forward, strike my head on a limb, and plunge into the lake. Unconscious, I sink to the bottom; my coat snags on a branch buried in the mud, and I drown.
>
> No one sees me fall or hears the splash. The circles soon disappear into the smooth surface of the water, and all is quiet again. Dark stillness pervades and time passes. About 3 a.m. my wife wakes up, realizes I've not come to bed.

Loder goes on to describe the unsuccessful search and how his family copes with the disappearance of their father and husband, how classes get rescheduled, how a memorial resolution is read at the faculty meeting, how the family moves west to live with the grandparents, how the children grow up and pursue their own lives, and how the event is finally forgotten, even as the ripples dissipate on Carnegie Lake. Loder continues:

> After fifty years almost no one wonders. This book and others gather dust in the library, and silence settles over all the activity I now so vigorously sustain and intensely value. The irony is deep and powerful. All this comes to absolutely nothing. Now this is probably not *how* it will happen. But it *will happen* to me—and to you. There is not the slightest doubt that the two-dimensional world you and I now so intently sustain will come to nothing at all. This is the perfect statistic, one death per person every time in a material universe that is ultimately destined to silence. That, of course, makes our obsession with meaning, and the meanings by which we live, absurd. It seems as if we dare not live with too large a perspective. . . . or we will not want to live at all.

What Loder describes is as natural as going out to Terhune's orchard in late summer to buy freshly picked New Jersey peaches. The delight of aroma and flavor does not last. The peach is as perishable as we are. The end may come through normal aging and decay of flesh or it may involve senseless pain, destruction and natural or human evil. That is the nature of the universe in which we live.

And so I lived, days adding up to years and years to decades in the two-dimensional world described by Loder, sensing but not articulating my dissatisfaction with this combination of success, happiness and an absence of meaning and purpose. It is of course possible to be courageous in the face of hard realities that we cannot change. But I had been face to face with death; I don't think that was my problem. Rather, I think my unarticulated problem was a sense that the combination of delight, beauty and lack of meaning and purpose didn't ring true. I hungered for something more to life, and my hunger made me sense that there might be something to eat.

I was aware of the opportunities for self-deception. If I was looking for meaning in life, then I was also in danger of creating meaning where it did not exist. But my experience in science had shown me the truth of "nothing ventured, nothing gained." And extreme skepticism carries its own dangers. Bas van Fraassen points out that "there is no escape from skepticism in theory; skepticism has no theoretical limits. . . . [Nevertheless,] seeking to remain in the safest position possible, the skeptic's solution, is no more *theoretically* justifiable than any other."[6]

When I get hungry, I start rattling around the kitchen, looking for something to eat. Similarly, my unarticulated hunger for something more to life eventually caused me to take breaks from work on Sunday mornings to walk across campus to the Princeton University Chapel, a building in Gothic style that is a 1928 copy of King's College Chapel, Cambridge. There I was a spectator at the chapel service—watching, not participating. My focus was the sermons, which thankfully didn't violate my intellectual sensibilities the way sermons did at some parish churches with their Christian jargon and flaws in logic. But the chapel sermons didn't speak to me either. Nevertheless, something unidentifiable was satisfying my hunger and kept me coming back. Gradually I began participating more while maintaining my posture as an observer and still clearly recognizing that participation didn't make me a Christian. I had no idea whether this stuff was true or false, and I wasn't convinced that the people I met at the chapel knew either.

One Sunday a chaplain from a college in New England was preaching from the pulpit, which is halfway up the side of a Gothic column. She said something to the effect that "you students have made it to the college of your choice, a top university, and you professors know more about your fields than anyone else in the world, except for maybe ten other people. You people know your business very well. But you have a kindergarten knowledge of Christianity." Her words shot like an arrow through the Gothic arches right into me. She was absolutely right; I knew essentially nothing about Christianity. If I were to find out if there is any truth to Christianity, I had better start looking into it.

So I started reading books about Christianity in my spare time. Eventually I realized that I had to face up to who Jesus was. So I decided to read the Gospel of Mark because I had heard that it may have been the first Gospel to be written. This was the first time I had read any book of the Bible, and the experience was a shock. As I read along I also did surgery, mentally cutting out parts I felt uncomfortable with. Yet my overall impression of the Gospel was a sense that it was truthful and historical, or at least not obviously fictional.

What shocked me most was that Jesus' words and actions, as described in Mark, show that he considered himself God come to earth, not just some wise and good teacher. Before reading Mark, I had never really seriously confronted the importance of the claim that Jesus is God come to earth. Certainly the idea that the universe was created was not an unreasonable possibility. The idea that the universe exists by itself is just as remarkable as its being created. What dawned as a possibility from reading Mark was that a loving Creator might want to communicate with a part of creation. My sudden impression was that if this were true, it would be the most important fact of human existence. To live life without taking part in the implications of this fact would be to miss out on the essence of what it meant to be human. For the first time in my life I considered it an important hypothesis that Jesus might be the Creator of the universe. Yet I did not know how to find out if it were true or not.

I continued to go to the Princeton Chapel, but less as a spectator and more as a participant. One Sunday I took part in a communion service. The dean of the chapel read the following words of Jesus as part of the liturgy:

> Come to me, all you who are weary and burdened, and I will give you rest. Take my yoke upon you and learn from me, for I am gentle and humble in heart, and you will find rest for your souls. For my yoke is easy and my burden is light. (Matthew 11:28-30)

To me this meant that if I took Jesus' yoke upon me, if I gave him control of my life, he would reveal himself to me. I decided it was now or never; I wanted to get to the truth of the matter. So I prayed, quite honestly, "Jesus, I don't know if you even exist, but I'll try you out. I'll give you control of my life and you reveal yourself to me."

Prayer is an interesting phenomenon. It's where the rubber hits the road. Either I am talking with God, which is remarkable, or I am talking to myself, which is embarrassing. Since that first prayer at Princeton Chapel I have had many experiences with prayer and with God. This history of interaction over a number of years has confirmed to me and continues to confirm the reality of the God who acts, communicates and establishes personal relationships with and among us.

I have been convinced by experience. But my experience has not occurred in isolation; my observations and experiences as a Christian are tested and evaluated within the self-correcting Christian community. In an analogous way, my research is not pursued in isolation; I am in a scientific community in which observations, interpretations and theories are tested vigorously. My observations and insights as a geologist are tested against other observations of the earth and solar system and against the experiences and understanding of other scientists. Scientific research is normally a unique experience—very rarely is research repeated—but experienced scientists easily and routinely evaluate the observational claims and interpretations of other scientists because they have had similar research experiences.

In a similar way the church, although not a scholarly analytical enterprise, has a self-correcting role. We expect the Christian experience of an individual to be consistent with biblical experience, church history and Christian experience today. For example, I have met many people with Christian experience analogous to mine. Our experience is analogous to experiences of past Christians that are described in autobiographies such as Augustine's and in the Bible. Millions of people have claimed that Jesus has revealed himself to them in response to actions of honest surrender that are analogous to my own experience. If Christianity is basically on the right track, we expect this to happen.

This is not to say that millions couldn't be self-deceived or couldn't be deceived as a group. Millions could, myself included. People are funny. They make all kinds of religious experiential claims that can't possibly be true. However, if Christianity is basically true, we would expect interaction between God and humans to take place. That is the Christian claim and it is an extremely important claim about the nature of human existence in the universe. If nothing ever happened, then either Jesus doesn't care or Jesus doesn't exist. In that case we need to face the cold reality with a stiff upper lip. It can be done. Millions of people face the starkness of a meaningless universe with courage. But I don't think it's necessary or conforms to the realities of our existence.

Notes

[1]Augustine *Confessions* 8.29.

[2]On my brother Frederick Suppe, see "Becoming Michael," in *Philosophers Who Believe: The Spiritual Journey of Eleven Leading Thinkers*, ed. Kelly James Clark (Downers Grove, Ill.: InterVarsity Press, 1993), pp. 137-78.

[3]In Lewis Carroll's *Through the Looking Glass* the White Queen tells Alice, "'Now I'll give *you* something to believe. I'm just one hundred and one, five months and a day.' 'I can't believe *that!*' said Alice. 'Can't you?' the Queen said in a pitying tone. 'Try again: draw a long breath, and shut your eyes.' Alice laughed. 'There's no use trying,' she said: 'one *can't* believe impossible things.' 'I daresay you haven't had much practice,' said the Queen. 'When I was your age, I always did it for half-an-hour a day. Why sometimes I've believed as many as six impossible things before breakfast.'"

[4]Bertrand Russell, *Why I Am Not a Christian, and Other Essays on Religion and Related Subjects* (New York: Simon & Schuster, 1957). In retrospect, I see the weakness of Russell's traditional antitheistic arguments. These arguments implicitly make the deistic assumption that no interaction or communication is possible between God and humans. This of course has little to do with the central claims of Christianity. The arguments of philosophical theism that Russell and others have rejected at best would —taken by themselves—lead to a generalized theism, not Christianity. Buckley has argued that the adoption of philosophical theism by the church as a mistaken intellectual defense of Christianity led directly to the rise of atheism of the sort that Russell and others adopted (M. J. Buckley, *At the Origins of Modern Atheism* [New Haven, Conn.: Yale University Press, 1987]).

[5]J. E. Loder, *The Transforming Moment*, 2nd ed. (Colorado Springs, Colo.: Helmers & Howard, 1989), pp. 83-84.

[6]B. C. van Fraassen, "The Peculiar Effects of Love and Desire," in *Perspectives on Self-Deception*, ed. B. P. McLaughlin and A. O. Rorty (Berkeley: University of California Press, 1988), pp. 123-56. Van Fraassen's essay is an elegant and delightful contribution to the literature on self-deception.

7

Unseen Realities

J. GARY EDEN

Electrical &
Computer Engineering

University of Illinois, Urbana

Faith is . . . a conviction of unseen realities. . . . By faith we
understand that the universe was created at God's
command, so that what we now see was made out of what
cannot be seen.
—HEBREWS 11:1-3 NEW BERKELEY VERSION

"Believe me," said Horton, "I tell you sincerely . . . I know
there's a person down there." . . . The Wickersham Brothers
came shouting, "What rot! This elephant's talking to Whos
who are not! There aren't any Whos! . . . For almost two
days you've run wild and insisted on chatting with persons
who've never existed."
—DR. SEUSS[1]

—

S cience has left an indisputable imprint on the twentieth century
—quantum mechanics, genetic engineering, the laser, the
transistor and the eradication of smallpox are only a few
examples from a lengthy list of triumphs in physics, chemistry and the
life sciences over a remarkably brief span of time. These accomplishments testify to the ingenuity and tenacity of the individuals involved.
They are also a tribute to the scientific method itself and the principles
on which it rests. It is the latter—the philosophical underpinnings of
scientific investigation that gave rise to an era of unprecedented

productivity—and its implications to which this essay is devoted.

The birth of modern science and the experimental method in particular took place in a cultural and philosophical environment entirely different from the one that prevails today. The profound influence that the Christian worldview exerted on the development of science in the West is discussed at some length by Loren Eiseley in the book *Darwin's Century: Evolution and the Men Who Discovered It*. Eiseley notes that modern scientific principles arose from

> the sheer act of faith that the universe possessed order and could be interpreted by rational minds. . . . The philosophy of experimental science . . . began its discoveries and made use of its method in the faith, not the knowledge, that it was dealing with a rational universe controlled by a Creator who did not act upon whim nor interfere with the forces He had set in operation. The experimental method succeeded beyond man's wildest dreams, but the faith that brought it into being owes something to the Christian conception of the nature of God. It is surely one of the curious paradoxes of history that science, which professionally has little to do with faith, owes its origins to an act of faith that the universe can be rationally interpreted, and that science today is sustained by that assumption.[2]

Eiseley's observation is underscored by Sir Isaac Newton, widely considered one of the greatest scientists the world has ever known. His writings illustrate the critical role of his religious convictions in motivating and guiding his scientific endeavors.

> This most beautiful system of the sun, planets, and comets could only proceed from the counsel and dominion of an intelligent and powerful Being.[3]
>
> Can it be by accident that all birds, beasts, and men have their right side and left side alike shaped (except in their bowels); and just two eyes, and no more, on either side of the face; and just two ears on either side [of] the head; and a nose with two holes; and either two forelegs or two wings or two arms on the shoulders, and two legs on the hips, and no more? Whence arises this uniformity in all their outward shapes but from the counsel and contrivance of an Author? . . . Did blind chance know that there was light and what was its refraction, and fit the eyes of all creatures after the most curious manner to make use of it? These and

suchlike considerations always have and ever will prevail with mankind to believe that there is a Being who made all things and has all things in his power, and who is therefore to be feared.[4]

In the preface to the second edition of Newton's *Principia* (1713) Roger Cotes wrote:

> Without all doubt this world, so diversified with that variety of forms and motions we find in it, could arise from nothing but the perfectly free will of God directing and presiding over all.
>
> From this fountain it is that those laws which we call the laws of Nature have flowed, in which there appear many traces indeed of the most wise contrivance, but not the least shadow of necessity. These, therefore, we must not seek from uncertain conjectures, but learn them from observations and experiments.
>
> Fair and equal judges will therefore give sentence in favor of this most excellent method of philosophy, which is founded on experiments and observations. And it can hardly be said or imagined what light, what splendor, has accrued to that method from this admirable work of our illustrious author, whose happy and sublime genius, resolving the most difficult problems and reaching to discoveries of which the mind of man was thought incapable before, is deservedly admired by all those who are somewhat more than superficially versed in these matters. The gates are now set open, and by the passage he has revealed we may freely enter into the knowledge of the hidden secrets and wonders of natural things. . . . Therefore we may now more nearly behold the beauties of Nature and entertain ourselves with the delightful contemplation, and, which is the best and most valuable fruit of philosophy, be thence incited the more profoundly to reverence and adore the great Maker and Lord of all.[5]

Newton and Cotes (and others) drew a direct relationship between their observations of the physical world and conclusions regarding the origin and sustenance of the cosmos that may logically be drawn from the experiments. In a nutshell, then, the experimental method owes its birth to the presupposition that the order of the universe was established by the will of God, who is himself logical. Consequently, the "wonders of natural things," as Cotes puts it, may be understood by "experiments and observations."

Generations of scientists living both before and since Newton have recognized and marveled at the extraordinary degree of organization that characterizes the natural world. A more contemporary physicist, Albert Einstein, stated of the scientist that "his religious feeling takes the form of a rapturous amazement at the harmony of natural law, which reveals an intelligence of such superiority that, compared with it, all the systematic thinking and acting of human beings is an utterly insignificant reflection."[6] In 1941, Einstein declared that "science can only be created by those who are thoroughly imbued with the aspiration toward truth and understanding. This source of feeling, however, springs from the sphere of religion. To this there also belongs the faith in the possibility that the regulations valid for the world of existence are rational, that is, comprehensible to reason. I cannot conceive of a genuine scientist without that profound faith."[7]

My own experience in science has convinced me that a greater reality does indeed lie beyond the physical existence with which each of us is familiar. After years of experimental research I continue to be amazed by the intricacies, for example, of the structure of atoms and diatomic molecules. As we gain successively deeper levels of understanding, new patterns and phenomena emerge, even in areas that were once considered well understood. Particularly intriguing to me, however, is the contrast that exists between the simplicity and elegance of the underlying physical laws and principles. The overwhelming complexity and beauty of the physical processes and biological organisms that have been studied thus far—to say nothing of worlds yet to be explored—provide a glimpse of a being whose intellect and creativity dwarf our own. The apostle Paul stresses this connection when he states, "From the creation of the world [God's] invisible qualities, such as His eternal power and divine nature, have been made visible and have been understood through His handiwork" (Romans 1:20 New Berkeley Version). Commenting on the wonders of the physical world, Job declares that "these are but the outer fringe of His works; how faint the whisper we hear of Him! Who then can understand the thunder of His power?" (Job 26:14 New Berkeley Version).

The Bible speaks of "unseen realities" that exist as surely as the reality we find ourselves in at the moment. The fact that we are unable to sense it directly by physical means makes it no less real. Rather, such a lack of awareness is more a reflection on our own limitations. Much of the progress that science and technology have made over the past several decades is attributable to the development of an ever expanding array of tools—experimental, theoretical, and computational—with which physical phenomena can be explored. Each new generation of increasingly sophisticated diagnostic methods has exposed deeper and more complex relationships in the physical and biological world. It would be shortsighted, however, to assume that all that exists lies within the reach of the experimental probes and the theoretical constructs that science is able to devise.

It is my growing conviction that the intricacies of nature have been intentionally placed before us by a Supreme Being for the dual purpose of displaying his power and intellect and drawing our attention from the ephemeral to a consideration of himself. This brings us to the second and most crucial link between the two realities (physical and unseen)—Jesus of Nazareth. Before he was born, the Scriptures predicted the details of his life, death and resurrection with extraordinary accuracy, such that no student of the Bible can avoid being struck by the realization that God has left a clear trail of evidence for the inquisitive. Jesus claimed to be the personification of God, and those who knew him documented his teaching and attested to his death and resurrection as having occurred precisely as foretold centuries earlier. Critical corroborating evidence is provided by Roman historians (such as Tacitus and Suetonius) and Pliny the Younger, the government official whose uncle was the renowned naturalist. Christianity rests on several pillars, of which the dominant is the historical, archaeological and textual evidence. Each pillar reinforces the claims of Christ and the Bible. I am certain that anyone willing to invest time in pursuing these subjects will not be disappointed.

The Scriptures know nothing of the irrational leap of faith that is occasionally portrayed in our culture as a prerequisite for becoming a Christian. Rather, it is reasonable to investigate the critical spiritual questions we all face and the philosophical or religious systems that are available in the same manner that physical laws and data are weighed—by examining the evidence. Truth has the inherent characteristic of looking better as it is scrutinized more closely.

I am persuaded by two truths. First, the physical world—which displays a level of complexity and beauty that we can only begin to fathom (much less duplicate)—bears the unmistakable signature of a superior intellect. Second, Christianity provides a rational explanation for life on this planet as it really is, not as we would wish it to be. In light of these truths, I accept the testimony of the apostle Peter, who states emphatically that "when we made known to you the power and coming of our Lord Jesus Christ, we were not following cleverly devised fables. On the contrary, we were eyewitnesses of His majesty" (2 Peter 1:16 New Berkeley Version).

Notes

[1]Dr. Seuss, *Horton Hears a Who* (New York: Random House, 1954).

[2]Loren Eiseley, *Darwin's Century: Evolution and the Men Who Discovered It* (Garden City, N.Y.: Anchor Books, 1961), p. 62.

[3]Isaac Newton, *Principia* bk. 3. Quoted in *Newton's Philosophy of Nature*, ed. H. S. Thayer (New York: Hafner, 1963).

[4]Isaac Newton, *A Short Scheme of the True Religion*. Quoted in *Newton's Philosophy of Nature*.

[5]Roger Cotes, preface to *Principia*, 2nd ed. (1713).

[6]Albert Einstein, *Mein Weltbild* (Amsterdam: Querido Verlag, 1934); see Albert Einstein, *Ideas and Opinions*, ed. Carl Seelig, trans. Sonja Bargmann (New York: Crown, 1954), p. 40.

[7]Albert Einstein, "Science, Philosophy and Religion," address presented before the Conference on Science, Philosophy and Religion in Their Relation to the Democratic Way of Life, New York, 1941; quoted in *Ideas and Opinions* (New York: Bonanza, 1945), p. 46.

8

From Religion to Relationship

JOHN F. WALKUP

Electrical Engineering

Texas Tech University

My weakness enables His strength to be demonstrated.
—2 CORINTHIANS 12:9

What impact does knowing God have on a person's life? During the forty years that I have been a Christian, God has patiently moved me away from a religious belief system and code of ethics and toward a personal relationship with his Son, the Lord Jesus Christ. I have come to learn that I cannot trust in my own strength and wisdom but only in his. As a college professor, I am convinced of this truth: "The fear of the LORD is the beginning of knowledge" (Proverbs 1:7 NASB).

I grew up in a very loving family on the West Coast. As a boy I enjoyed occasional family trips to the Sierra Nevada mountains of California and later to the Cascade mountains of Washington. I was awestruck by the beauty and obvious complexity of the natural world. I had no reason to doubt that God had created everyone and everything I could see. Any further ideas I had about spiritual things, however, were relatively shallow. I thought that being a Christian meant believing intellectually that Jesus was God's Son and trying to live a good life.

In my junior year of high school, I attended a youth retreat on an island in Puget Sound near Seattle. Several speakers talked about God's desire to have a personal relationship with each of us through his Son. One afternoon my cabin counselor took me aside and asked me if I had ever come to know Jesus personally. He explained that we are by nature self-centered and disobedient toward God but Jesus paid the penalty for our disobedience. We can accept Jesus' sacrifice and thereby enter into a right relationship with God. There was no question in my mind that I was less than what God wanted me to be. Without really understanding the implications of all I was doing, I prayed to put my trust in Jesus Christ as Lord and Savior.

Very little in my life changed initially. I belonged to our church youth group, but I do not remember learning much about how to study the Bible or otherwise grow in my newfound Christian life. My immediate objective was college, as I looked forward to broadening myself and searching for truth. I accepted a scholarship to Dartmouth College in New Hampshire. There I chose to major in engineering science, with the intent of applying the scientific principles I learned to solving human needs.

Attending a college three thousand miles from home was a challenging experience. Being away from home forced me to grow up in a number of ways, but I was not growing spiritually. Although I took part in such enjoyable activities as the glee club and intramural sports, I poured most of my energy into my primary goal—academic success. I achieved my goals, but something was missing from my life. Academic success did not bring me the happiness I had anticipated, and my lack of spiritual maturity was becoming obvious. I would have gladly received counsel from a Christian professor had I known one. I definitely needed the Lord to shine his light into my life.

I returned to California to attend graduate school in electrical engineering at Stanford University. That fall I met the love of my life, a wonderful young woman named Patricia Hagbom. Pat had graduated from Wheaton College in Illinois and was a graduate student in mathematics. She had become a Christian through the ministry of Peninsula Bible Church (PBC) in Palo Alto when she was in high school. As I attended PBC with Pat and listened to the expository Bible teaching of pastor Ray Stedman, I felt my eyes being opened to a whole new world. I began studying the Bible and learning to feed myself spiritually. I started to appreciate how the Bible related to every aspect of my life. I could count on God to meet me in its pages. I was also excited to see God's love at work in the lives of my Christian friends.

Until that time I had lived on an emotional roller coaster, which went up or down in response to changing life circumstances. Yet as I read about the life of Jesus, I noticed that his emotional state fluctuated very little. I prayed that God would stabilize my emotions. Subsequently, God allowed me to go through a number of experiences that left me with no choice but to trust God with my future. Pat and I both received our master's degrees and were married in June 1965. We moved into Stanford's married-student housing with no idea that we would spend the next six years there.

Stanford presented major academic challenges. Nearly all of the graduate students in engineering had been at the top of their undergraduate class, and naturally the competition was fierce. Between 1965 and 1969 I changed dissertation topics twice. The antiwar movement brought protests and political turbulence to the Stanford campus, leading to more difficulties in our program. A sit-in protest of Defense Department research projects conducted on campus overtook our laboratory for nine days. Students distributed communist literature from the student office area. Later, fire watches and riot police became common sights on campus. Our laboratory's professional staff decided to leave Stanford. The graduate students affected by this move, including me, were expected to either find new advisers and new research areas or terminate the pursuit of their graduate degrees.

Faced with the prospect of having to change my research area again, I sought God's guidance. I prayed that God would open a door for me to finish my Ph.D. degree but acknowledged that if I needed to leave graduate school without the degree, I was ready to do whatever God's will for my life might involve. I felt a great sense of release as I waited to see what God would do. Within a few months, Dr. Joseph Goodman became my adviser in the area of optical information processing, and I was able to finish my dissertation in less than two years. What appeared to be a devastating situation for me turned out to be a great blessing, for I am very thankful that God moved me into the field of optics.

During that time of uncertainty I sensed God's leading me one day at a time as I gave him control of my life. A passage from the Bible, "I can do all things through Him who strengthens me" (Philippians 4:13 NASB), continually sustained me. The whole experience was a journey in learning how to trust God when I could not see where he was leading me. It also convinced me that my adequacy comes from Christ and not from any human abilities. My weakness enables Christ's strength to be demonstrated. We Christians are designed to be Christ sufficient, not self-sufficient.

When I started looking for faculty positions, I prayed that God would show Pat and me a place where we could serve him. About three weeks later, the chairman of the electrical engineering department at Texas Tech University contacted me. After I was offered a faculty position, we continued to pray that God would make it clear where we should go. He effectively shut every other door, and so we moved to Lubbock, Texas. Leaving both of our families in California as we started a new life in Texas was a step of faith for us and proved to be the beginning of a great adventure.

Over the years we have had many opportunities to see God's faithfulness as we have trusted him. These opportunities have included caring for sick and injured children, buying a home and obtaining research grants needed for a summer salary and graduate student stipends. Through it all I have come to understand in a new way the meaning of the commandment to "seek first His kingdom, and His righteousness; and all these things shall be added to you" (Matthew 6:33 NASB).

As a college professor, I instruct students in the principles and applications of electrical science and engineering. As a researcher, I investigate the frontiers of optical science. The logic and orderliness of science and engineering remind me that the God I serve is a God of order who has created a universe which is governed by physical laws and held together by God's power and love.

My research area of optical information processing deals with the use of light in signal processing, data storage and computation. I have come to see many analogies between humanity's need for physical light and our need for spiritual light. Just as we need light from the sun to see, to live and to grow physically, we also need spiritual light from God's Son to see, to live and to grow spiritually. To provide for our needs God gives us physical light (Genesis 1:3-4, NASB) and spiritual light (Psalms 27:1; John 8:12). Optics research, including my own, has shown that tasks such as vision and interferometry (the measurement of the interference properties of light waves) grow increasingly difficult at low light levels. Ignoring God's spiritual light similarly leads to loss of discernment and spiritual darkness or blindness (John 1:4-5; 3:19-21).

The Bible calls Jesus Christ the true light (John 9:5). When we come to know him, we learn to see our lives as God sees them (John 1:9-10, 12). Only as we come into a personal relationship with Jesus (John 3:16; Revelation 3:20) are we be able to walk in the light that he provides (John 12:35-36; Ephesians 5:8-11, 1 Peter 2:9; 1 John 1:5-7) and be spiritually alive. I have shared these and more technical analogies with scientists in Russia and have found their appeal to be widespread. The enthusiastic reception of such concepts has convinced me that there is a great hunger for God's truth all over the world.

The life of a Christian college professor is filled with exciting opportunities for witness and service to God. At Texas Tech I have sponsored a Christian student organization, taken ministry trips overseas and directed a faculty and staff Christian fellowship for campus outreach which has placed evangelistic ads in our campus newspaper, hosted visiting speakers and shared testimonies with students taking seminars on making better grades.

Professors have many opportunities to informally share their faith with students. I usually spend a few minutes introducing myself in each course I teach. I state that my relationship with Jesus Christ is the most important thing in my life. I let students know that I am available to discuss my faith with them in more depth outside of class if they are interested. Encouraging responses as much as twenty years later have convinced me of the importance of our being identified with Christ in the workplace in order not to hide our light under a bushel (Matthew 5:15-16).

We need to witness to others, both on and off campus. Several years ago another professor and I invited a skeptical colleague to lunch and shared our faith with him. I will never forget his response as he turned to us and said, "If I really believed what you're telling me, I would drop everything I'm doing and go around telling people about Jesus." How can we be serious about our faith if we do not regularly share our faith?

The university scene has undergone many changes over the years. Many students now come from single-parent homes, work twenty to thirty hours a week at jobs and are heavily in debt due to student loans. In addition, students are exposed to many distortions about what constitutes a healthy and moral lifestyle. They often need encouragement and guidance during what is a critical period in their lives. These new challenges highlight the great need for campus ministry.

A majority of faculty and students reject the existence of absolute truth. This spirit of moral relativism is undermining society on every front. As a Christian, I stand firmly against that relativism and for the eternal truths found in God's Word. Students yearn for meaning and significance in their lives and, like all people, need to hear that this can be found in the truths Jesus Christ articulated. Many do not know that Jesus is "the way, and the truth, and the life" (John 14:6 NASB), the only means of reconciliation between God and humanity (Romans 5:11; 1 Timothy 2:5).

As I get to know Jesus better, I understand more deeply that the truth I was seeking when I began college is fully embodied in a person —Jesus Christ. God is calling out a people who are, by God's grace, forgiven and made new. He offers them a close relationship with him. I have learned that my inadequacy to meet life's challenges is not a handicap because God has designed me to find my adequacy in him. It has been a tremendous privilege and joy for me to be able to work with faculty and students searching for truth because I know that Jesus Christ himself is the ultimate source of truth.

9

Confessions of a "Weird Mathematician"

JAMES P. KEENER

Mathematics

University of Utah

→ tell about their book review

> How long, O men, will you turn my glory into shame?
> How long will you love delusions and seek false gods?
> —PSALM 4:2

I made a discovery recently at lunch. I was sitting with the dean of my college, two departmental chairpersons, several key faculty members and a job candidate. We knew each other only casually. Eventually the conversation turned to religion and then to Christianity. The people who expressed their opinions were filled with contempt and scorn for Christianity and for Christians. The consensus opinion held that an intelligent person could not be a Christian. The dean said that he had rejected Christianity at the age of sixteen, upon hearing an evangelist who "had less intelligence in his whole body than I have in my little finger." In his opinion, an intelligent person had no need for anything that Christianity offered. As the dean spoke, he made no effort to show tact or tolerance or consideration for divergent points of view, since it was a foregone conclusion that no one at the table could possibly be a Christian or could possibly have any defense for Christianity. Clearly, in the academic world, Christianity has been ruled out of court. In a world that prides itself on open-mindedness and on giving fair consideration to all ideas, Christianity is not an option. Its dismissal is a fait accompli.

I did not speak up that day. I had no idea where to begin. My views on life, the nature of the human race and the problems of society were so different from the views expressed at the table that to have engaged in a fruitful discussion of the issues would have been impossible. Why am I so different? How is it that so many intelligent people have come to conclusions about life that diverge radically from mine? Who is out of touch with reality here?

Most of those at that lunch, myself included, were mathematicians. Mathematics, considered to be the queen of the sciences, where rationality and clear thinking reign supreme, where hypotheses are clearly stated and conclusions are drawn on the basis of careful and precise argumentation and calculation, where there is no room for sloppiness and all things must be considered before a conclusion is drawn. These rationalists extraordinaire have concluded that Christianity can have no relevance for them. They do not see Christians as simply being a bit odd, somewhat like the Englishman with the world's largest collection of Chinese war apparel, or a bit eclectic, with a charming taste for the unusual. No, their conclusion is that Christianity is irrational and outmoded, in a word, wrong.

So, I ask, who is right? We can't both be right. Indeed, if truth were determined by a vote of my colleagues, I would lose. But since the validity of an idea is not determined by its popularity or by the intelligence of those who accept it, I am not ready to concede.

A student once called me a "weird mathematician." Surely it is redundant to use the word *weird* to modify *mathematician*. After all, mathematicians are not usually known for advanced social skills or scintillating conversation or fascinating leisure activities. Mathematicians are more likely to be characterized as people who wear plastic pocket protectors or rejoice over their latest computer or calculator purchase. Years ago, we were known for carrying slide rules at all times. So when I was told that I was a weird mathematician, I had to find out what that meant. The student explained that I was weird because I was a mathematician and I was also religious—an unusual combination.

I responded that all mathematicians are religious in that they all have a worldview with premises that they accept on faith, they all have an object of worship, and they all have a source of spiritual strength. Indeed, by this definition, everyone is religious, since everyone has a system of beliefs and explanations for things that are predicated on faith, everyone has one or more objects of worship, and everyone has some motivation to keep going, a source of spiritual and emotional strength, of encouragement and hope. People who claim they have no religion simply do not understand this fundamental reality. Most mathematicians would argue that they have no religion and have no need for religion. Perhaps they have not thought about the faith premises of their view of the world, about their objects of worship or about the basis of their spiritual or emotional strength— their source of hope. But they certainly have all of them.

The basic ingredients of any belief system are summarized by the writer of the book of Hebrews: "And without faith it is impossible to please Him, for he who comes to God must believe that He is, and that He is a rewarder of those who seek Him" (Hebrews 11:6 NASB). Any belief system, whether or not it includes God, begins with faith. It goes without saying that mathematicians believe in mathematics. Mathematicians unquestionably believe in mathematical reasoning and deduction, believe that a universal logic and rationality exist and that the conclusions that are drawn using these are valid and reliable. They believe that a statement can be true, that truth exists and that truth can be discovered by systematic investigation. They believe in the existence of an orderliness to things that is describable and unchanging. Every mathematician believes in logic.

Mathematicians also believe that there is a reward for being a mathematician. There is value in getting things right. There is value in knowing how things work, in knowing what the rules are and in knowing how to use the rules to advantage. No mathematician believes that a wrong answer to a calculus problem is just as good as the correct answer. Wrong results are not publishable. No mathematician brags about publishing incorrect theorems, except for a couple that inadvertently managed to slip through without any errors. For a mathematician, the diligent pursuit of the correct answer is valuable and rewarding.

Every religious system has objects of worship. Worship is simply an act that ascribes value. I ascribe value to something when I honor it by giving up something that I value for it. It is an act of worship when I pay extra money to wear a T-shirt bearing the logo of my favorite sports team. It is an act of worship when I cancel an appointment with my boss to take my wife to lunch. It is an act of worship when I enthusiastically describe yesterday's ski run to a friend or when I describe my latest research finding to a colleague in the hallway. To a mathematician, mathematics is an object of worship. Mathematics is more than adding two numbers together or solving some algebraic equation. Mathematics is a body of knowledge and a way of thinking that transcends any specific problem. Mathematics is intrinsically beautiful and praiseworthy. By that I mean that certain ideas and concepts and arguments have an aesthetic beauty, perhaps because of some esoteric structure or complexity or symmetry. This beauty cannot be explained, but it is there and it is universally acknowledged. This beauty is not simply a matter of individual taste. The best seminars are called beautiful, since there is within mathematics a recognizable beauty and elegance that is worthy of honor and respect.

The famous French mathematician Henri Poincaré put it this way: "The scientist does not study nature because it is useful; he studies it because he delights in it, and he delights in it because it is beautiful. If nature were not beautiful, it would not be worth knowing, and if nature were not worth knowing, life would not be worth living."[1] There is an unspoken understanding that mathematics is mysterious and awesome, filled with wonder. There is no concern that we will soon know all there is to know because of the belief that mathematics is both infinite and inexhaustible. Mathematics departments at universities may close down because of insufficient funding or lack of student interest but not because the job is finished and all of mathematics is known.

Mathematics is also useful and serves as a source of strength and power. Mathematics enables us to do useful and important things, like balance a checkbook or know when we are being overcharged at the grocery store. It is also enriching, or so we believe. It is valuable because it teaches us how to think and helps explain the way things work. A person who has mastered mathematical skills should be able to sort through difficult issues with clarity and precision. We want students to study more mathematics because of the belief that it will enrich their lives. Surely, we contend, a mathematically educated person is a better person than an uneducated one. Mathematical research is promoted because in different ways, some tangible but many intangible, society will be better off because of it.

A person who is good at mathematics usually derives pride and self-worth from that ability. Of course, society is telling young men and women that the way to get the best girlfriends or boyfriends is to be a jock or to drink the right beer, not to study calculus. Yet everyone wants to be good at something that has value and significance. Everyone wants to control some realm of life. Mathematicians are no different in this respect than anyone else. They love to be told how smart they are or how clever or inventive or deep or brilliant their latest paper was. We all are looking for ways to make an impression on other people and want to take credit for something of significance. We derive strength from students who admire us and give us good teaching evaluations, or from colleagues who admire our research. I sometimes suspect that the desire for the admiration of others motivates many mathematicians more than the pure pursuit of knowledge. In fact, there are many who have themselves as their number one object of worship.

Everyone wants to be right. The apostle Paul noted that we are constantly accusing or defending (Romans 2:18-20), giving evidence of an internal need to be right. Mathematicians take comfort in the fact that they can prove their assertions. In fact, many brilliantly intelligent people are so impressed by themselves that they sense no need for God.

So the issue is not whether or not mathematicians are religious, but whether or not a mathematician's religion is reliable. Are the premises of belief reasonable and are the conclusions valid? Are the objects of worship truly worthy of honor and respect? Are the sources of strength dependable? Let me point out that the mathematician's worldview is closely akin to that of scientism, or philosophical natural-ism, the religion of many scientists. The one major difference between the two is the scientist's faith in empiricism and the existence of laws of nature instead of rationalism and the laws of logic. But otherwise the two are quite similar, with similar conclusions and consequences.

Having argued that all mathematicians are religious, I must now concede my student's accusation concerning weirdness because I admit that I do not ascribe to the party line. I do not find the consen-sus view to be compelling; I find glaring inadequacies in it. In fact, for all of its claims of rationality, I find it to be blatantly irrational. My faith begins with a belief in the existence of God, the designer, creator and sustainer of the universe, the ultimate cause of all effects, the reason behind reason, the giver of laws both physical and moral, the value behind values, the definer of beauty, the source of all purpose. There is value in knowing God, partly because it makes sense to know and live by the rules of the designer and to fulfill rather than defy his purposes.

I find it impossible to believe that there is no Creator. In all of my experience, in all of science, I have never heard of an effect that had no cause. I have never seen a design that had no designer, a law that had no lawgiver, an order that had not been ordered, information that had no informer. Chance produces nothing. Saying that something happened by chance merely begs the question of the causes that produced the effect. "It just happened" is simply not an acceptable answer. It is an open admission of ignorance.

God is the sole appropriate object of worship. All other things are consequences of God's nature or creative acts. All truth is God's truth. Just as a beautiful painting or a majestic symphony leads me to honor the artist or the composer, so also the laws of nature and the theorems of mathematics magnify my awe and respect for the Creator. I am confident that I will never run out of new things to learn or discover about the Creator and his creation. The implications of createdness are profound. It implies, for example, that we, creatures and not creators, bear some marks, some distinguishing features or signature of our Creator. Scripture says that we bear the image of God. Our rationality is a reflection of God's rationality. But we are much more than rational beings. We are also spiritual beings, and our spirituality is a reflection of our Creator. So the first weakness of mathematicians' or scientists' worldview is that their objects of worship are creations or reflections of the creation rather than the Creator. Mere shadows of a brilliant light rather than the actual source of the light.

But worship of something other than the Creator has allowed a second mistake to persist. Standing in the shadows, we cannot see that we are living under a vast illusion. The focus of our attention has allowed us to believe that we have no need to know the Creator God and to believe that we are self-made and self-sufficient and self-motivated. Even our rationality is an illusion, since we all are less rational than we claim to be. We live in constant denial of the most obvious of all facts: We are not creators, we are creatures. We are not self-determined. We are not in control. We are not the lawgivers. We continually act as if we deserve credit for things over which we have absolutely no control. Furthermore, we expend an enormous amount of energy to support the illusion that we are something that we are not.

No mathematician has anything at all to do with being intelligent. She could just as well have been born without mathematical insight or could have been born into circumstances in which her brilliance went unnoticed or unappreciated. No mathematician has control over his ideas or determines when or if he will have a brilliant insight or inspiration. No mathematician determines how long she will live or what disease she will die from. Life is an incredible mystery, but so is rationality and consciousness and creativity and emotion. All of these have been bestowed upon us through no effort or merit of our own. All can be taken from us just as readily as they were given. Why then, in light of these undeniable realities, do we insist on taking credit for what we have not done? Why do we claim that we have no need for the bestower of these great gifts when our needs are obvious and our dependence is total? We, who are so skilled at recognizing giftedness, cannot recognize that it is the giver of the gift who deserves the credit and not the recipient.

The Bible identifies denying an empirically observable reality as sin. There is within every person this basic irrationality, this drive to act like creators and lawgivers and designers, to be like gods, when we are nothing of the sort. It seems that the most rational are, in fact, the most irrational, the most intelligent are the most ignorant, when it comes to recognizing who and what we really are. Furthermore, there can be no solution to the problems of the world until this most fundamental of all problems is resolved. Our confidence in science or mathematics or technology is ill founded. More mathematical training or scientific discoveries will not improve the lot of humankind unless there is first a change of heart, a softening of our rebellion and a willingness to admit what we are and to live in consistency with the purposes of the creator and designer, instead of as we individually see fit.

What makes me weird, apparently, is deciding that it is futile to rebel against my Creator, pretending to be what I am not, using rationality as a cover for irrationality, intelligence as a cover for ignorance. My goal is to seek humbly to know him and his desire and to submit myself to his plan and purpose, indeed to acknowledge what cannot be denied, to expose what is obvious and cannot be hidden.

It is probably true that my dean is vastly more intelligent than the evangelist he heard years ago. It may also be that the evangelist said nothing that related to what my dean felt he needed at the time. But Christianity proclaims that there is a universal and undeniable need to know the Creator and that through Jesus Christ reconciliation of this estranged relationship is possible. Furthermore, failure to recognize our own inadequacy and to live in denial of this empirically verified fact is an example of being out of touch with reality, a spiritual psychosis, a condition of blindness that afflicts the vast majority of my colleagues.

It is a curious fact that even among mathematicians the truth is not popular.

Notes

[1]Henri Poincaré, "Foundations of Science," in *Science and Method: Book 1, Science and the Scientist,* trans. George Bruce Halsted (New York: Science Press, 1921).

10

A Life Journey
with Jesus

VERNA BENNER CARSON

School of Nursing

University of Maryland

"For I know the plans I have for you," declares the LORD,
"plans to prosper you and not to harm you,
plans to give you hope and a future. Then you will call
upon me and come and pray to me, and I will listen to you.
You will seek me and find me when you seek
me with all your heart."
—JEREMIAH 29:11-13

Before I tell you how my Christian faith, specifically my relationship with Jesus, influences and shapes my role as a university professor, I want to give you some background information about how I came to know Jesus. This essay is a personal account of my spiritual journey. I seldom think about Jesus in religious or theological terms. As far back as I can remember, I have thought of him as my best friend—a big brother who cares for me and protects me no matter what I do. I have never doubted his existence. I know him as I know my own children. I even imagine him in my mind sitting beside me on a garden bench attentively listening and giving me advice. I know his voice; I talk to him throughout the day. I wake up with a prayer to him on my lips.

I remember how much I loved Jesus as a young child. He was my comforter. He listened when I was lonely or hurt. He helped me in school. He was with me all the time. I can't remember how I came to know him or how our relationship grew. I don't remember not knowing him. As far back as I can recall he was there.

I was born into a Roman Catholic family. My father was a convert to the faith and loved the Lord with his whole heart. My mom also approached Jesus from a perspective of love. There was no religious legalism in our home, but much in the way of a Christian walk—caring for others, kindness, tolerance for differences and gentleness coupled with strength. I am sure that I learned about Jesus from my parents. But exactly how I learned about him is not clear in my memory. Sometimes I think that he reached out to me and initiated the relationship and I merely responded. In any event, he remained my best friend and confidant until my college years. During those four years I was surrounded by people who professed no definite beliefs in Jesus. I don't remember people displaying open hostility to him, just indifference. My own heart grew cold and I moved away from my best friend. I stayed away for many years. Even into the early years of my marriage I kept my back turned toward him. Sometimes I felt a tug at my heart and I knew that the tug was from him. He was calling me back. I continued to resist until my first son was born. My pregnancy and the subsequent birth of my son Adam were spiritually rich experiences. I was very much aware of being a cocreator with God. I found myself thanking Jesus and thinking about him again.

Shortly after Adam was born, my husband and I went to see a priest in the parish where we lived. We wanted to have Adam baptized. In order to do so we needed to comply with the requirements of the Roman Catholic Church, which included being interviewed by the parish priest and attending classes designed to impress parents with the importance of their role in transmitting the faith to their children. The priest asked us why we wanted Adam baptized, and we were unable to give a good answer. We replied with some nonsense that Adam's baptism was important to each of our families, but we were clearly not committed to the church or to a religious education. We professed what we thought was an enlightened view—we intended to allow Adam to choose what he wanted in regard to religion.

The priest, who was rather young, was also incredibly wise. He did not challenge us directly but asked us to look at whether we wanted the world to have free rein with our son. Did we intend to stand back and let the world fill the void that would exist in Adam's heart if we did not teach him values and morals? And if indeed we wanted our child to have the freedom to choose, didn't it make sense that he needed a sound foundation against which he could compare the values espoused by the world? Our drive home from the parish rectory was quiet and reflective. The priest had touched a sensitive chord in my heart. I was flooded with memories of my best friend and how faithful he had always been. Incredible sadness filled me because I had turned away from him. I knew that I couldn't deprive Adam of the opportunity to know and love Jesus as I had known and loved him. I knew that to do so would be terribly irresponsible and unloving as a parent, and I wanted more than anything to be a good mother. As I look back, I can see how the Lord used Adam's birth to catch my attention and draw me back.

We had Adam baptized and I began to attend Sunday Mass. I look back on the months immediately following Adam's birth, and I am impressed with the number of charismatic Catholics that I met. These were individuals who were on fire with their love for Jesus and were not afraid to show it. Many were facing life difficulties that could shatter some people's faith, but their faces reflected peace and joy. As I got to know them, I could see that they possessed qualities that I knew I was missing. I had gone back to church but not back to my friend.

During that same time a former schoolmate called to share an experience she had at a Catholic charismatic prayer meeting. She described the meeting as strange, powerful, deeply spiritual and compelling. She invited me to attend one of the prayer meetings with her. I agreed to go and convinced my sister-in-law Adele to come along with us. The experience proved to be everything that my friend had described. People were praying out loud, raising their hands and arms in praise of the Lord, talking in what sounded like a foreign language, swaying to the music and appearing to be in absolute ecstasy. Obviously I spent a lot of time looking around and soaking up the sights and sounds. I was somewhat frightened by what I saw and heard, yet at the same time curiously intrigued by the sheer abandon of the pray-ers. Believe me when I say that this was not normal Catholic behavior.

Many Catholic congregations are reserved in their singing and private in their prayers and worship. At the end of the prayer meeting my companions commented on the strangeness of the experience. They were sure that they would never go back. Although I agreed with their conclusion that this had been an unusual experience, I knew with certainty that this experience held something for me and that I would go back. Interestingly, both my companions continued to accompany me!

The prayer group offered a seven-week seminar for people who wanted a deeper relationship with Jesus. The seminar explored what that commitment meant; the focus was on studying God's love letter to us, the Sacred Scriptures, and discovering the depth of his love for us and what he wants from us. All three of us signed up for the seminar. As we studied and prepared to commit our lives to Jesus, the most compelling Scripture passage for me was "For God so loved the world that he gave his one and only Son, that whoever believes in him shall not perish but have eternal life" (John 3:16). I read that passage over and over, substituting my name for "the world." It filled me with awe that God could love me this much. As a new mother, I knew that if God asked me to sacrifice my only son for the greater good, I would certainly decline the request. Yet God had done just that for me—and for you! Wow! That was and continues to be my articulate and scholarly response to God's love. At the end of the fifth week of the seminar, each of us made a personal commitment to Jesus. We professed that he was Lord of our lives and we asked him to transform us. I don't think that any of us really appreciated how mighty the transformation would be.

One of the first changes that I experienced was a sense of peace that was independent of external circumstances, a quality that I had envied in my charismatic Catholic friends. I had a heightened appreciation for the gift of my life, and I became increasingly aware of a multitude of blessings that I had previously taken for granted. My desire to pray was probably the most dramatic change—it wasn't just private prayer that I desired, but I experienced a strong desire to pray with anyone who would let me. This was particularly noteworthy considering that I had always been quiet and shy and actively avoided drawing attention to myself.

One story that illustrates my evangelistic behavior occurred several months after I accepted Jesus as Lord. I used to purchase gas for my car at a service station owned by a Christian who put Scripture quotes on a marquee at the edge of the station lot. One winter day (it was snowing and very cold) I stopped for gas. The attendant, John, had a terrible cold. Without hesitation, I rolled down the window of the car and asked John if he wanted me to pray for his healing. What a picture we must have made—John standing at my car door, holding my hands through the opened window, snow coming down in blizzard proportions, while I prayed for his physical healing. *Zealous* doesn't even begin to describe my approach to praying with other people. I was filled with enthusiasm and an evangelizing spirit. I still have those qualities, but today they are more attuned to God's leading than to my own desires to change the world.

Another area of change occurred in the way that I looked at my work with student nurses. I began to see nursing not just as a profession but as a ministry that afforded nurses the privilege of participating in God's healing. As a teacher of nurses, I began to reflect on my responsibility to incorporate spiritual truths in my teaching so that students understood not only why we care for others but how we should give that care. I worked with a team of wonderful nurse faculty who lovingly tolerated my zeal and enthusiasm as a newly "born again" Christian. They were open to examining what we were doing as faculty in light of my suggestion that we needed to incorporate spirituality. They even agreed to add prayer to our faculty roles. We began to pray before we conducted team meetings and before we made decisions that had an impact on students. We even prayed when we evaluated students. It was a most blessed time!

In my efforts to change my own nursing practice to include the spiritual component, I felt driven to share these convictions with the larger nursing community. I decided to write an article about the importance of spiritual care. The first step included a literature search to see what had already been written about spirituality in nursing. I found that prior to 1960 most schools of nursing were based in religiously supported hospitals, and the mission of the hospital and the nursing school was to provide Christ-centered care. However, by the mid-1970s more schools of nursing were affiliating with public universities and colleges. Spiritual concerns and care were becoming an afterthought, at best. That first article I wrote on the importance of spirituality to nursing was never published. Fortunately, the Lord did not let me give up.

As my Christian growth continued, it increasingly spilled over into my faculty role. Because I taught in a state-supported university, I was careful not to evangelize students, but the Lord helped me to find other ways to let students know that I was a Christian. For instance, I asked each clinical group if we could start our day with prayer—either silent or spoken, whichever form group members were more comfortable with. In twenty years only one student expressed discomfort with prayer. When I responded that I did not want to make her ill at ease and that I would eliminate the prayer, she replied that it would be unfair to deprive her peers of something that was important to them and asked me to continue while she stepped out of the room.

The preclinical prayers were real supports to the students who brought to the Lord both their personal concerns and their professional concerns about patients. If I forgot to pray, the students would invariably remind me, "What about our prayer?" The prayers helped break down the barriers that so often stand between faculty and students. I was looked upon as someone who really cared about students, not just someone whose job it was to evaluate them. Consequently, many students sought me out for both personal and spiritual counsel.

I continued to write about spirituality in nursing, and my work began to appear in nursing journals. I submitted several articles to *The Lamp*, a Nurses Christian Fellowship (NCF) publication. The nurse leaders in NCF invited me to participate in several task forces that developed resource materials for nursing faculty interested in bringing Christ into their teaching. My participation in these early task forces allowed me to meet wonderful Christian nurses who have become my sisters and brothers in the Lord. These nurses have enriched my spiritual life by sharing with me their ways of incorporating Jesus into their daily contact with students. These relationships, begun in the early 1980s, have continued to grow and flourish.

Also in the 1980s I felt that the Lord wanted me to start a weekly NCF prayer group, which still meets. It was open to students, faculty and staff members at the university. The first year that I held the group was a real challenge because I had never led a Bible study and I felt inadequate to the task. At first the participants came to the meetings on an irregular basis. I tried to convince myself that this was a sign that perhaps I had misunderstood Jesus when I felt led to start such a group. But deep down in my heart that quiet but persistent voice of the Lord called me to wait. Some weeks I would sit and pray by myself when no one else came to the meeting. Finally some students began to attend with regularity. By the end of that first year there were about eight students who remained faithful to the group. These students and I were blessed beyond measure through our dedication to this shared time. God sent answers to prayers and we provided support to one another. The group was a place to fellowship and connect with other Christians. Because students in the group frequently voiced a need for direction on how to provide spiritual care, I became convinced that I should develop a course that addressed spiritual care.

I was filled with anxiety as I submitted a proposal for a course entitled Spiritual Dimensions of Nursing Practice to the curriculum committee. I had serious doubts about whether the committee would approve it. When it was accepted with minor revisions and a stipulation excluding proselytizing, I was delighted. However, I was also challenged. How could I be true to Jesus while meeting the school's requirements that the course not be "Christian"? After prayerful consideration, I arrived at a strategy that allowed me to communicate my Christian faith, remain within the school's guidelines and respect student differences. The approach I used then has continued to serve me well over subsequent years.

I always begin the course by telling students that I am a Christian. I also explain that I value God's gift of free will. Because of that gift, I am not free to force or cajole anyone to accept my beliefs. I encourage them to explore the wide variety of approaches to spirituality. I recognize that all students are on their own spiritual journey and that the course in some small way may help them discern their own spiritual direction. Feedback from students has confirmed the effectiveness of this approach. They frequently comment that they respect my ability to state my beliefs in a noncoercive manner. They feel respected for who they are, and they feel free to investigate any and all spiritual paths that may interest them. Many students have asked me questions about my faith outside of class. The first year the elective was offered, over fifty students enrolled—the largest enrollment of any elective. I continue to revise, modify and update the course, and students continue to enroll in record numbers. What this tells me is that students are hungry for this information and truly appreciate the opportunity to examine the impact of spirituality on their professional and personal lives.

The course provided the impetus for a textbook, *Spiritual Dimensions of Nursing Practice*.[1] As I was returning home from an NCF task force in New Jersey one day, the whole outline for the book came to mind. I pulled over to the side of the road then and there and wrote out the outline. It was clear to me that the vision for the book was a gift from Jesus. Not only did he provide the vision but he guided the process every step of the way, even changing the heart of the nursing editor who initially turned down the project. I have never had a moment's doubt that the book belongs to Jesus. The only credit that I deserve is for being willing to follow his lead.

As a faculty member I participate on many committees. This has afforded me additional opportunities to integrate my Christian spirituality into the university setting. For instance, I participated in a task force that was charged with updating the philosophical framework for the curriculum. I lobbied hard to change our mission statement from a focus on "biopsychosocial issues" to "biopsychosocial and spiritual issues." This change may seem minor. But once spirituality was delineated as part of our faculty mission, the next step was to examine how spirituality was integrated into course offerings.

Over the years I acquired responsibility for coordinating the courses that I teach (the privilege of age!). Once our philosophy was changed to include spirituality, I was free to add spirituality to the undergraduate psychiatric nursing course as well as the graduate courses. Spiritual content was included in lectures and clinical assessment tools. I firmly believe that if something is important for student learning, then the faculty must do more than pay lip service to that importance; it must be communicated in multiple ways, including assignments.

One of the most difficult challenges of being a Christian professor in a university setting is reconciling the university's priorities with the Lord's priorities. The demands of the university could easily be consuming, depressing and even demoralizing in that no achievement is ever enough. There is always the implicit (and sometimes explicit) question, "What have you done lately?" My relationship with Jesus keeps me focused on a different set of priorities. Jesus doesn't count the number of articles I have published in refereed journals or the number of local, regional, national or international presentations I have given. My worth does not come from the university. It comes from God. This truth is simple but can easily be distorted by the world and specifically the work setting.

The Lord calls me first to be an excellent teacher. He expects me to teach and model nursing as a ministry. The importance of teaching is also affirmed by the citizens of the state of Maryland who pay me to contribute to the education of future nurses. My teaching must be competent as well as caring. I must be present for students, just as Jesus was present to everyone he taught and just as he is present to us today. Sometimes I must put aside a planned discussion topic and listen, respond to and even advocate for student concerns.

Another priority in the academic setting is to support the school through course development, committee work and my attitudinal impact. Responding to this priority in a Christian manner allows me to contribute to a culture of caring that must be nurtured in order for students (as well as staff) to blossom. Jesus calls me to be a good employee, and so I try to do my best regardless of the assignment. I consciously avoid negativism and gossip. Finding kind things to say to other faculty members and staff and remembering them in prayer, as well as sharing their joys and disappointments, remind me that I am part of a faculty body that needs care.

Another priority concerns scholarly activities. The Lord has shown me repeatedly that I must make choices in this area. I cannot do everything that the university would like me to do. The university has a voracious appetite for achievements, just like a flower in the play *The Little Shop of Horrors*[2] that incessantly demands, "Feed me, feed me." The Lord has clearly directed my energies to writing, which I love to do. He has led me to concentrate on writing about spirituality.

Sometimes I find myself engaging in scholarly activity that is not valued by the school but is valued by the Lord, for example, a recently completed textbook that I coedited with Dr. Elizabeth Arnold. In 1996 our psychiatric nursing text, *Mental Health Nursing: The Nurse-Patient Journey,*[3] was published. The text grew out of our dissatisfaction with existing psychiatric textbooks that make no mention of spiritual issues and the importance of these issues to the psychiatric patient. The textbook is written from a theistic worldview. We state clearly that we believe in a personal Creator God who loves and cares for us. We knew that in writing this textbook we were opening ourselves up to ridicule and criticism from psychiatric colleagues in the university and throughout the country. But in our hearts we knew that the Lord wants nursing students to view their profession as an extension of his command "to believe in the name of his Son, Jesus Christ, and to love one another as he commanded us" (1 John 3:23).

When I accepted Jesus as my personal Savior in the fall of 1975, I never dreamed of the opportunities and challenges that lay ahead of me. Many of those opportunities came to me specifically as a professor of nursing in a large university setting. When I look at my own personal characteristics—somewhat shy, certainly not bold, a person who likes to please and tries to avoid rocking the boat—I marvel at the things that the Lord has allowed me to do. I have been privileged to teach nurses across the country the importance of spiritual care and the essential role that Jesus plays in that care, to boldly proclaim that

Jesus is Lord in public forums, to write on the integration of spirituality and nursing and to take unpopular stands at the university based
on my faith convictions. I was an unlikely candidate for these opportunities, yet I have never forgotten something a student told me years
ago: "He doesn't call the prepared, he prepares those that he calls."
The recognition of the Lord's role in what I accomplish keeps me
humble and keeps me on my knees.

I sometimes marvel at the freedom that I have experienced as a
Christian faculty member in a secular university. Part of that freedom
stems from the value that the university places on diversity. It tolerates
all beliefs and practices, including Christian ones. But this tolerance
means nothing if we fail to act on it. I continually pray for boldness in
my faith so that I may express my beliefs, act in a manner consistent
with those beliefs, and communicate respect and love for people who
do not share my Christian faith. I have learned the value of expressing
what I believe instead of telling others what they should believe. I
have learned to build bridges with love, bridges that have the power
to transform the hardest hearts. Finally, I am convinced that our
colleges and universities desperately need Christian faculty to shine
the light of Christ into the darkness that envelops many campuses. In
these settings where science, knowledge, technology, power and influence substitute for God in the hearts of some of our most intellectually
gifted, to be a fool for Christ is to offer real hope to searching students
and faculty.

Notes

[1]Verna Benner, *Spiritual Dimensions of Nursing Practice* (Philadelphia: W. B. Saunders,
1989).

[2]Alan Menken, *The Little Shop of Horrors: A New Musical* (Garden City, N.Y.: Doubleday,
1982).

[3]V. B. Carson and E. N. Arnold, *Mental Health Nursing: The Nurse-Patient Journey*
(Philadelphia: W. S. Saunders, 1996).

11

Christ the Anchor, Christ the Servant

KENNETH G. ELZINGA

Economics

University of Virginia

The saying is sure and worthy of full acceptance,
that Christ Jesus came into the world to save sinners.
And I am the foremost of sinners.
—1 TIMOTHY 1:15 RSV

*I*t was not your typical University of Virginia T-shirt. The design
was right—dark blue with a large orange V on the back. But the
back of the shirt spelled out in bold, white letters four words: *Ask
Me About Jesus.*

Walking home in the snow that night, I thought hard about the shirt.
A Christian student group had just given it to me for speaking at a
meeting. As a chaired professor with some twenty-five years of
employment at the University of Virginia, I considered myself too
respectable to wear such a shirt—the sartorial equivalent of a "honk if
you love Jesus" bumper sticker.

About halfway to my destination I remembered two verses from the
Bible: "For I am not ashamed of the gospel: it is the power of God for

salvation to every one who has faith, to the Jew first and also to the Greek" (Romans 1:16 RSV) and "Always be prepared to make a defense to any one who calls you to account for the hope that is in you, yet do it with gentleness and reverence" (1 Peter 3:15 RSV). My perspective on the T-shirt changed.

The gospel of Jesus Christ first made its claims on me in a way that I do not fully understand. I was blessed with a mother who was committed to the Christian faith. But my father was hostile to it. My mother took me to church religiously (in both meanings of the term). My father responded by being unusually moody on Sundays. For some reason my mother's influence on me trumped my dad's. I'm glad it wasn't the other way around.

I never denied the existence of God and rarely doubted that Jesus was his Son. But I never knew what to do with these propositional truths about God, even though I was not prone to question them.

My mother died when I was young and my father proceeded to make a mess of his life.[1] While I was in graduate school, adhering to the Sunday worship practice my mother had instilled in me, I found two churches in which people talked about a personal relationship with Jesus Christ. The expression *a personal relationship with Christ* caught my attention. I was also fascinated by the two churches. In one of them distinguished professors from my university worshiped next to blue-collar guys who made Oldsmobiles. At the other church I met students wearing white bonnets (later I learned they were Plymouth Brethren) and preppy-looking students from high-church backgrounds. A personal relationship with Jesus seemed to be the defining element common to all these people.

Attending these worship services and observing the diverse portfolio of people who were there provoked me to think about the difference between believing facts about God (which I did) and trusting in God (which they did).[2] As did many other seekers then (and now), I read John Stott and C. S. Lewis.[3] All this led me to fret about how little of my life involved trusting in God. I also worried that I might become too fanatical about God. After all, I was preparing for the professoriate.

But I recognized the contradiction in the status quo. If I believed, as a matter of historical data, that Jesus was the Son of God, it made no sense not to be his follower. If Jesus was who he said he was (and I had believed this for some time), his claim on my life involved far more then regular church attendance.

At a church missions conference one Saturday evening, I asked Jesus Christ to come into my life so that I too might have a personal relationship with him. I reckon I was born again that evening. I became a follower of Jesus of Nazareth. Years later, as I look back on circumstances that would have me attending a missions conference on a Saturday night, I have to reckon as well that the Holy Spirit had me in his net of grace.

Where this newfound old-time religion would take me I did not know. I figured that it would entail teaching at a Christian college. Although the two of them seemed like unlikely co-conspirators, it appeared that God and my graduate mentor had other plans. When I was offered a tenure-track position at the University of Virginia, my mentor insisted that I take it. And I did. A young pastor whom I encountered in graduate school greeted the prospects of my teaching at a secular school with great enthusiasm. He took me aside and began teaching me a biblical view of work. He was persuaded that my "call," as he put it, was to a secular school. I was also influenced at that time by several godly professors who modeled a life of scholarship under the lordship of Jesus Christ.[4]

I feel a mixture of embarrassment and gratitude when I look back on "my decision" to have a personal relationship with Christ. The embarrassment stems from how clinical my decision to follow Christ (in hindsight) seemed to be. There was little understanding on my part of how desperately I needed Jesus Christ; little understanding that I was no "great catch" for God's kingdom; little understanding that I was what the Puritans called a "monster of iniquity"; little understanding that sin was a fatal flaw in my character. Through reading the Bible and consorting with mature Christians, I came to realize what the prophet Jeremiah centuries earlier had articulated—"how deceitful is the human heart," including my own (Jeremiah 17:9). Genuine, heartfelt gratitude to Jesus for what he did when he bore the cross, for his willingness to take the penalty for my sins, came later. And it was later that I came to feel profound gratitude for the people who were not ashamed of the gospel of Christ and were ready to give a defense for the hope that was within them—to me.

Later I experienced what joy there is in knowing God. And it was later still that I learned that worshiping God can be pleasurable. The Bible teaches that faith in God is a gift (Ephesians 2:8-9). Working in a culture that denies God's very existence, I am struck at how rarely I doubt the God of Abraham, Isaac and Jacob—the God of the Bible. I chalk part of this up to my faith's being a gift. Like most of the gifts I have received in my life, it is one that I do not deserve.

For many people the most prominent image of the Christian faith is the crucifix. For me as a teacher, it is the picture of Christ, servantlike, washing the feet of his disciples. The scene illustrates the Bible's paradoxical principle of leadership—the one who leads is the first to serve. Put differently, if you want to be first, you line up last (John 13:3-17).

Becoming a follower of Jesus profoundly affected my view of work. If I want to lead a class of students, I must be willing to serve them; my authority as a teacher is linked to my willingness to serve. For example, a teacher serves by thorough class preparation; a teacher serves by being available; a servant-teacher is not a pal but can be a friend. The servant-teacher is an educator who succeeds when his or her students succeed.

Teaching does not come readily to me. Year after year, before each class, my stomach reminds me that standing before students is not a normal, biological activity. But year after year this visceral feeling of inadequacy has taught me to depend on God throughout the week when I am weak.

I have had the experience of sailing on the *Queen Elizabeth 2*. The anchor on this great ocean liner represents a small fraction of the ship's weight and volume. Yet it is capable of holding the ship against great forces and can stabilize it in unforeseen circumstances. The Bible describes Jesus Christ as an anchor (Hebrews 6:19). Jesus is one who anchors his followers against events and circumstances they cannot anticipate. He offers stability. I take great comfort in the anchor metaphor.

Very few of my life's plans have worked out. I did not plan to remain on the faculty at UVA for over twenty-five years when I accepted its offer of employment; I did not plan to have my wife die of cancer at the age of thirty-three; I did not plan to have my best friends move away from Charlottesville. I never expected to publish, to enjoy the company of students, to overcome my fear of teaching or to be a coauthor of mystery novels. But through it all I have found the Lord Jesus to be a faithful anchor. He gives me strength for today and hope for tomorrow. (What a contrast to most twentieth-century philosophies!)

Jesus has held me secure ever since that peculiar and eventful Saturday evening at the missions conference, and he promises to be my anchor into eternity. I am not ashamed to admit that I need an anchor, a savior, a redeemer. The Bible makes it clear that everyone shares this need.

Why don't more really intelligent people become followers of Jesus Christ? One reason may be that most educated people do not believe, after considering the evidence, that Jesus is the Son of God. They do not believe that Jesus is who he said he was—the Messiah, come to earth as God's provision to save a needy people from their sins, to help them through the disappointments and failures and tragedies of life and to give them joy in knowing God. I do not dismiss the importance of this reason for unbelief. Arguments for the resurrection, for them, have not carried the day.

But another proposition should be considered. Many highly educated people do not follow Jesus because they don't want to. To follow Jesus is, first and foremost, to admit that one needs help—an anchor, a savior, a redeemer. To follow Jesus is to admit that everything —including degrees, credentials, honors, accomplishments, books and monographs—is nothing compared to the riches of knowing Christ. It is to admit that all of the degrees and credentials and honors and accomplishments we accumulate are not going to save us from the central problem we have in God's eyes—our rebellion against him.

"I did this all by myself" is the credo of the self-made individual. "Lord, help me" is the plea of people who recognize their need for a savior. There is a world of difference between the two.

I'm more comfortable with the T-shirt now. I have even worn it at the university. Whenever someone asks me about Jesus, I try to give a "defense" of the "hope that is in me," and I try to do so with "gentleness and reverence." The apostle John presented his "defense" of Jesus in his New Testament Gospel. Toward the end of it he wrote that to tell the whole story about Jesus would more than fill the world with books (John 21:25)—such are the riches and majesty of the One who is "the way and the truth and the life" (John 14:6) eternal.

My favorite Bible verse is the epigraph at the beginning of this chapter: "The saying is sure and worthy of full acceptance, that Christ Jesus came into the world to save sinners, and I am the foremost of sinners." As a teacher of economics, I spend a lot of energy teaching students information I believe is sure and true. I think it is true, for example, that under *ceteris paribus* conditions, there is an inverse relationship between the price and the rate of consumption of crude oil. But I can't, at least with a straight face, claim that this is a truth "worthy of full acceptance." That Jesus came into the world to save sinners, including those living today—that is "good news" worthy of full acceptance.

Notes

[1]Later I had the joy of seeing my father become a committed Christian, a man whose zeal for the things of Christ exceeded his son's.

[2]See J. I. Packer, *Knowing God* (Downers Grove, Ill.: InterVarsity Press, 1973), chap. 2. Packer's book contrasts knowing about God with knowing God personally. Packer's conceptualization of this crystallized my earlier struggle.

[3]John Stott, *Basic Christianity* (Downers Grove, Ill.: InterVarsity Press, 1976); C. S. Lewis, *Mere Christianity* (Riverside, N.Y.: Macmillan, 1975).

[4]One of these professors actually built his kitchen in the basement of his house so that he and his spouse could make their large recreation room open to students for both kinds of bread: bread from the oven and bread from heaven.

12

Hard Question,
Easy Yoke

RONALD D. ANDERSON

Education

University of Colorado

And what does the LORD require of you?
To act justly and to love mercy and to
walk humbly with your God.
—MICAH 6:8

A Hebrew prophet writing at a time of national turmoil in Israel over seven hundred years before the birth of Christ raised the fundamental question expressed in the epigraph: What does the Lord require? In our age, as in that one, this question seems profound and compelling to some, mildly interesting to others and simply meaningless to yet others.

To individuals with a monotheistic worldview, such as Christians, Jews or Muslims, who believe in a personal God, the question is profound and compelling because it addresses the very essence of life.

To individuals with a worldview that is embedded in naturalism—a scientific worldview that limits reality to the material universe and admits no personal God—the question simply has no meaning. There is no God (or no way to relate to this God even if in fact there is a God) and the question should be discarded.

Others are put off by the question because it assumes that God puts requirements on people. A demanding God is not part of their worldview. If God is within us or is simply a vague spirit we can sense in our quieter moments, it is pointless to talk about God's requirements. A New Age adherent rejects both the cold scientism that emerged from the Enlightenment and the idea of a God that has expectations of us.

I find the question profound and compelling, since I have a theistic worldview and I believe in a God who interacts with me personally. The prophet's assertion that God requires people "to walk humbly" with God is a beginning place for reflection and prayer.

Academic culture resists discussing such a question on a personal level. Ordinarily this culture values knowledge and understanding that are acquired in an objective manner. Matters of religious faith are assumed to be matters that are not public or amenable to objective consensus judgments and are usually relegated to the private arena.

The experience of faith is a deeply personal matter that is also embedded in an objective historical context. Thus this essay takes up the concept of culture and the sense of reality of the spiritual dimension of life.

Most cultures take account of a spiritual dimension to life, but an understanding of that dimension may not be firmly embedded in the culture. Fundamentally, spirituality is about a personal relationship with the God of the universe. It is easy for a culture (including a church subculture) to substitute some dimension of its "groupness" for actual spirituality. Unless it is grounded in some sense in the reality of such a personal (not individual) relationship with God, the supposed spirituality is a manifestation of human social interaction. Given the social character of people, there is an obvious relationship between the two, but in my experience they are not the same. It is not uncommon for people's culture to dominate, suppress and warp the spiritual aspects of their personal lives.

The search for meaning, purpose and God is an important part of many cultures and subcultures, and in that sense all of humankind has something in common. As a searcher, I find that I have a lot in common with people of many cultures and stations in life. Thus there are insights to be gained from people of all sorts, including atheists, agnostics and pagans.

The Double Search

An early writer described our search for God as the "double search," denoting our seeking for God and God's seeking for us. I find this image helpful. The search is not just a one-way search, and we are not limited to what can be gained from the human side of the search. As a Christian, I see God as having made the major move in the search; God has enabled me to search for him successfully, resulting in a relationship that is ongoing, personal and influential. Life does not have to be a continuing search for new insights from whatever source about how to find our way to God. It is no longer a search for God; it is a relationship with God in which the two of us jointly search out the path on which we are journeying together. It is a journey—sometimes through great difficulty and intense pain—that has direction and joy because of our relationship and because of the purpose and meaning that only God can give.

God is searching for us. He inserted his Messiah into human history as a part of his reaching out to us and thus dramatically changed the nature of the search. The historical Jesus was not simply another human searcher, even though our secular culture confidently asserts he was. He is a key part of God's search for us. As a result, we can pray with simplicity and confidence, as people have prayed down through the centuries, "Lord Jesus Christ, Son of God, have mercy on me, a sinner." This prayer succinctly captures what God has done, what we can expect from him and the posture we assume before him.

In our society discussions of spirituality tend to include references to organized religious groups such as churches. Linking spirituality with religion raises problems for some people because of their personal history and their disenchantment with institutional churches. Negative experiences with religion need to be replaced by a living relationship with God, a relationship that can be fostered to some extent through healthy Christian community—community that may be found outside the institutional church. (Some people who have had negative experiences with institutional churches try to replace them with different but equally inadequate forms of society and culture. They tend to buy into our secular culture, typically one that has an exclusively human version of spirituality, and become a part of what amounts to a different shallow culture.)

Most church subcultures exert a significant influence over their active participants. They can minimize matters of spirituality and in many cases exert an influence that conflicts with true spirituality. Whether a moralistic code of conduct is substituted for the influence of a living relationship with God, or an academic study of the Scriptures is substituted for letting the Scriptures speak to our lives, or a commitment to the church's subculture is substituted for a commitment to God, the results all lead in the same direction. The result is a good member of the group who may or may not have personal spiritual depth.

The irony of this situation, of course, is that the real church—"the body of Christ" in biblical language—is one of God's great gifts to us. Interaction with the real church allows us to share the results of our search and the ways in which God has reached out to us. Because of the social and institutional nature of organized churches, however, we often have to work through a lot of chaff to get to the wheat. We need the "real" community, not the pseudocommunity encountered in so many of our social and cultural contexts.

The inadequacies of our secular culture—including its many organized religious manifestations—are also of concern. Most people in our culture live in captivity to the culture, be they highly sophisticated academics or simple MTV-generation hedonists. Ironically, they are critical of people they see as captives of a fundamentalist church culture, even as they remain unaware of the extent to which they are captives of a culture—whether expressed in secular or religious terms —that is based on a naturalistic worldview that excludes a transcendent God and has the self as the center of all reality. It is a culture of privatized spirituality: what is real is whatever an individual perceives it to be. It is a relativistic spirituality for a pluralistic society. None of these inadequate cultures—whether characterized as secular or religious—is a substitute for authentic spirituality, a spirituality built on a relationship with the God who actively reaches out to us.

Dimensions of a Christian Commitment

What is authentic spirituality? What kind of relationship with God results from a successful "double search"? The Christian answer to this question may be expressed in three components, which are aspects of the Christian life reflected in the New Testament record of the life and teachings of Jesus Christ. I am assigning them the proactive labels "believe," "do" and "be." We need to give careful consideration to a number of conceptions of reality, including beliefs about the nature and meaning of human existence, the nature of God and the interconnections between the two. The biblical record has much to say about what we should do and about who we should be as a result of this relationship with God, a "being" that some would describe with labels such as "character," "attitudes toward God" and "preferred dispositions to action." Each of these three deserves further elaboration.

Believing—believe. Belief—the holding of certain ideas—is promoted in the life and teaching of Jesus. Certain beliefs are integral to his teaching, beliefs that are central to the Christian life. In earlier translations of the Bible the word *belief* carried more of a flavor of commitment, a proactive response to ideas and less of holding to certain ideas in a simple intellectual sense.

Today's popular and academic use of the word *belief* is more limited to ideas and propositions and does not carry the sense of commitment to certain beliefs found in the New Testament, which asks for more than mental assent. It is more than a commitment to correct doctrine and a discipleship focused on acquiring detailed biblical knowledge. Operationally, correct conceptions are the basis of a right relationship with God.

As a member of the academic community, I have a commitment to truth and knowledge. But my Christian belief is not just a matter of mental constructs—it has a proactive component. A right relationship with God does not necessarily *begin* with correct belief in the sense that this word is found in common usage today. Valid beliefs (in the mental assent sense of the word) may be a partial result of belief (in the sense of commitment, as originally employed). A consistent and well-developed theology is valuable, but it is not the foundation of a right relationship with God. Prayer and an openness to the influence of God have more potential as a starting point.

Doing—do. The New Testament record contains many calls from Jesus for action—actions that reflect love, compassion, caring and sacrifice. But the desired motivation for these actions is not a desire to earn salvation, and the desired actions cannot be summarized in a set of rules. Appropriate actions are of central importance, but they are not the beginning point. The "bottom line" is somewhere else and the desired actions will be the result of this bottom line. Here again, parts of the institutional church may be a bit off the mark. Jesus did not ask us to commit to a particular set of institutional actions or to any particular church program. Being a Christian is not about learning to play the church game according to the rules of any particular church subculture. Spiritual growth could be enhanced by devoting less attention to "doing church" and more attention to what are sometimes called the spiritual disciplines, for example, prayer, withdrawing periodically for silence and solitude, and living simply.

Being—be. A strong case can be made that the most fundamental of the three is "being." To be—matters of prayer, relationship with God and who we are becoming as we live our life—is more foundational than to do. Obviously the three—believing, doing and being—are highly interrelated. Changes may occur in all three simultaneously, but still they must be kept in balance. Possibly the lesser attention to "being" in contemporary church circles is related to having a less than full understanding of belief and action and a failure to ground them in who we are as shaped by a relationship with God.

Commitment: The Bottom Line
Faith is about how we make our life wagers. We all engage in the serious business of deciding where we will put our trust. As psychologist James W. Fowler has explained so well, faith is a significant aspect of human existence. Faith is not the same as religion; one's faith can have a religious or a nonreligious orientation. He also is careful to distinguish faith and belief; they are not the same. Belief is about holding certain ideas; faith is about trusting. Belief, in religious

contexts at least, arises out of the effort to translate experiences of and relation to transcendence into concepts or propositions. Belief may be one of the ways faith expresses itself. But one does not have faith in a proposition or concept. Faith, rather, is the relation of trust in and loyalty to the transcendent about which concepts or propositions—beliefs—are fashioned.[1]

A common cultural image of what constitutes Christian faith, or Christian commitment, is something oppressive, such as bondage to a severe moralistic code of behavior. The reality is quite different; it is a living relationship with God that the Bible likens to marriage. It is a matter of where we put our faith, our trust, our life wagers. This commitment to Jesus Christ ideally is a total commitment, which brings great joy. Paradoxically, the greater the commitment, the greater the freedom and joy. Jesus said, "For my yoke is easy and my burden is light" (Matthew 11:30). We are transformed by this relationship with God, and our behavior certainly changes as a result. But this process is not one in which we are slavishly trying to follow a certain code of behavior. The focus in our relationship with God is on "being." Our forms of "doing" grow naturally from new forms of "being."

Our various church subcultures desperately need to pay more attention to the spiritual disciplines, as described by writers such as Dallas Willard, Eugene Peterson and Richard Foster.[2] Much of contemporary Christian preaching and writing suffers in comparison with the Christian devotional classics of the past twenty centuries.

The many freedoms that come from our relationship with God are truly transforming. This transformation is both a result and a cause of the many freedoms that come from a commitment to Christ: freedom from self-absorption, freedom from status seeking (pride), freedom from the insecurity and freedom from any need to reach my potential or "find myself." It is the paradox of finding freedom in commitment.

We have enormous value in God's eyes. We are not simply blobs of protoplasm, as so many in our science-oriented culture claim. Neither are we strictly human beings who need to reach our potential, as other segments of our culture proclaim. Although the human potential movement has some important insights to offer, it has shallow foundations, is based on an inadequate conception of spirituality, and has substituted human personality for a relationship with the living God. Fundamentally, we have potential because we are "created in the image of God" and can be transformed as a result of a living relationship with God. This distinction is captured in the following quote: "To be healthy and to be whole is no substitute for being penitent, forgiven and holy."[3]

I am in awe of what God has created and what God continues to do in my life. The wonder is about who I am as compared to who I would be without this relationship with God, even though who I am still is less than society's or my ideal. It is about the freedom, contentment and peace that come with Jesus' "easy yoke." This wonder is part of my personal expression of faith.

Notes

[1]James W. Fowler, *Stages of Faith: The Psychology of Human Development and the Quest for Meaning* (San Francisco: HarperSanFrancisco, 1995).

[2]Eugene Peterson, *Working the Angles* (Grand Rapids, Mich.: Eerdmans, 1994); Richard J. Foster, *Celebration of Discipline* (San Francisco: Harper & Row, 1978); Dallas Willard, *The Spirit of the Disciplines* (San Francisco: Harper & Row, 1988).

[3]Michael Ramsey, *The Charismatic Christ* (London: Darton, Longman & Todd), p. 45.

13

Semper Fidelis

MARK T. CLARK

Political Science

California State University, San Bernardino

Besides being complicated, reality, in my experience,
is usually odd. It is not neat, not obvious, not what
you expect. . . . Reality, in fact, is usually something you
could not have guessed. That is one of the reasons I believe
Christianity. It is a religion you could not have guessed.
If it offered us just the kind of universe we had
always expected, I should feel we were making it up.
But, in fact, it is not the sort of thing anyone would
have made up. It has just that queer twist about
it that real things have.
—C. S. LEWIS, *MERE CHRISTIANITY*

Dear Tod:[1]

"Bridge the gap! Bridge the gap!"

Remember that command from training exercises? Our leathery marine sergeants wanted us to jump out over a chasm onto a single line of rope and crawl across it on our bellies to move closer to the enemy position. It has just recently occurred to me, Tod, that "bridging the gap" has been a theme in my spiritual life, from the time you helped me take some beginner's steps till now. I don't think I've ever told you how strategic a role you played in my decision to walk with God. I think it's time to tell you that story and a little about where God has taken me since the last time I saw you.

Before I met you, I had two experiences I'd call "encounters" with God. Neither seemed monumental at the time, though in retrospect I see that they were significant. The first came when I was about thirteen years old. One Friday night my friends left me out of the action. I spent the evening on the back of my Dad's red '57 Chevy pickup looking up at the stars and feeling both lonely and alone. In that aloneness, I remember asking aloud, "Are you really out there, God? If you are, will I ever meet you?" For the rest of that evening I wrestled between believing and disbelieving in God. I never heard any voices. But by the time I went to bed, I do remember feeling certain that I would eventually get a meeting. It was just a sense, but a comforting one at the time.

A few years later, I had another encounter with God. I must have been a high-school freshman or sophomore at the time, for I had begun wearing the same long hair, baggy jeans, jean jackets and cowboy boots my friends wore. The Jesus People came through town (we called them "Jesus Freaks"), and I was invited to an event sponsored by some group or other. I can't remember why I went. In fact, my memory of the evening is vague except for one thing—when the invitation was given to accept Jesus Christ as Savior, I stepped forward, along with lots of other people. The speaker told us we were "born again." I was excited about this new identity for a few weeks, but as the emotions of that night wore off, I wasn't sure what being born again meant. Going to church never occurred to me, and yet something about my life slowly began to change. I could no longer treat life as casually as I had before, and I began to long for a sense of purpose and meaning in what I did.

During the rest of my high-school years, I studied, worked and thought a lot about joining the Marine Corps. I really can't say when I first decided to become a marine. I think it was about the same time as I made this step toward God. I looked forward to joining the marines for several reasons—I wanted the challenge of its rigor and discipline. I also wanted to get away from school, or at least school life and school friends. I slowly came to realize that the path my friends and I were on —partying and pursuing girls—led nowhere, and certainly not to happiness. I could not envision my future. I had no idea what I wanted to do with my life, but I knew I didn't want it to be purposeless. I had to get away, and the marines seemed like the place to go.

Looking back now, I can see how God was leading me. I really loved the Marine Corps. Boot camp was actually fun for me. I've got to say that it was one of the better experiences in my life. I enjoyed the teamwork; it was like football in high school. The drill instructors were a pain at times, and we looked strange with our bald heads. But I drank up the experience. The exercise was less strenuous than I had anticipated, perhaps because I played a lot of sports in high school. I even liked the spit and polish. Becoming an expert marksman with the M-14 was a thrill, but learning combat operations was probably the most exciting. About the only thing I could have done without was all the marching on the parade grounds. Drill, drill, drill. Ugh! I graduated from boot camp with top scores in my recruit training company and was awarded promotion to private first class. Infantry Training School (ITS) was even more fun. Now that I'm forty, I can't imagine how we were able to do all that training—marching, running, infantry maneuvers, and all the rest—on about three hours of sleep a night. As you may remember, I graduated from ITS as company honorman and was promoted to lance corporal. Next came Sea School, which also went well for me, and after that I was assigned duty aboard the USS *Oklahoma City* in Japan, where I met you.

I don't remember exactly what renewed my interest in spiritual matters. Two or three things stand out, though. First, you made a strong impression on me. You were self-disciplined. While self-discipline is supposed to be a hallmark of the marines, most of us applied it to our conduct at work and to our appearance. And we didn't overapply it in either place. I knew many who seemed to do the absolute minimum, just to get by. That bothered me. I saw that the self-discipline taught by the marines did not extend to the moral or spiritual conduct of our lives. You, on the other hand, seemed to exercise self-discipline in every area of your life. I was amazed to watch you spend your free time reading the Bible and writing letters to friends. You even seemed to enjoy these things.

Second, Christianity seemed to support my commitment to serve in the military. When I read some of the literature you had about the

Christian faith, I saw that many of the writers of the New and Old Testament books talked about service, discipline and devotion in words that I understood. In fact, it seemed to me then that the Bible talked about the reality behind the ritual of service. Devotion not just to an ideal, but to a person, namely, Jesus Christ. I began to see that my military service, to that point, represented my commitment to an ideal rather than to something that was tangible, real. I loved serving in the marines, but in many respects, the service was impersonal. The accolades I had received were nice but were in no sense personal.

The third thing that attracted me to Christianity was seeing for the first time in my life how happiness and success might actually go together. This statement will take some explaining. Until I met you, I had enjoyed a good deal of success in the marines. I received honors and promotions—as fast as possible in peacetime—and was promoted at the top of my classes. I was acknowledged by our superior officers as a top-notch marine. But I was not happy. On the outside, I was successful, but on the inside, I was feeling miserable. I started experiencing that sense of aloneness I had felt when I was thirteen. Though surrounded by some forty guys, I did not share close relationships with them. Sure, we would carouse together on liberty. It seemed like the thing to do. But our only bond, if I can call it that, had nothing to do with genuine interest in each other and everything to do with our desire to impress each other with tales of drinking and womanizing. It was high school all over again! My relationship with you was different, of course. But I told myself you were just weird.

My initial attraction to Christianity was diminished by the thought that I would have to give up these so-called good times. I especially remember thinking I would wait until I was older to pursue God-related interests because I wanted to enjoy myself for now. I actually believed that you couldn't be a Christian and have fun. Strange idea!

While alternately toying with and rejecting the inner tug toward Christ during that first year of ship duty, I began to experience some things I had never known before. First, failure. Remember the competition for airborne school? Forty-five of us went after two slots. Although I earned a perfect score on the physical fitness test, you beat me out. We all knew Corporal M. (the captain's favorite) was to get one of the slots, but I was sure I would get the other. Instead, I was sent to Non-Commissioned Officers (NCO) School on Okinawa. Not a bad second choice, but I wanted first.

Nonetheless, at NCO school I worked my tail off, even at extracurricular activities. Do you remember my challenging Sergeant A. to a twelve-mile race through the jungle from our camp—after a full day's training, including a four-and-a-half-mile run—to yours? I beat him, but he wouldn't let me relish my victory. He claimed injury to his ankle, and we had to borrow money from you for a taxi ride back to our camp. Despite all my hard work and setting an NCO school record for fitness, I ended up three-hundredths of a point behind first place! I'd never come in second. To me, second was no better than last. And now I had tasted defeat twice in a row.

That summer I took thirty days of leave and went home. Even with more cash in my pocket than I could spend in a month, that month was the most miserable of my life. I looked up old friends and went to a number of parties. I rode my new motorcycle around town, looking for good times. I even looked up an old girlfriend. But everything I did during that month turned sour. Not one thing gave me pleasure. My parents told me several years later that I had frightened them during that vacation time. They thought I had become wild and reckless. Until then, I could always give at least the appearance of self-control. Apparently even the appearance was gone by then.

When I returned to the ship, things got worse. For the first time in my life, I began to experience a diminished physical capacity for work. Boils on my right leg slowed me down in fitness tests. No more perfect scores. When we went to the Philippines for our annual ten-day athletic competition among all divisions on the ship, strep throat laid me low. Right in the middle of one-hundred-degree weather. Twice!

God had my attention, and I began considering the claims of Christianity more seriously than before. One evening, while lying on my bunk with the light on, I was reading some of the literature you gave me about the Bible. I'll never forget what happened. Corporal R. saw what I was reading and asked, "Are you reading that crap too?" After a year on ship, he no longer was pleasant about his dislike of Christianity. Embarrassed, I said, "No, just looking at some material."

I turned off my light and slid the book back under my pillow. Then a brick hit me! It felt as if God, at that moment, held up a mirror to my soul and showed me my real self. I was a coward. Maybe I was tough physically. And maybe I was pretty successful. But I was miserable. I was letting others control my actions. I shrank from doing what I really wanted because of peer pressure. In other words, I was doing exactly what in high school I had hoped I would escape by going into the Marine Corps.

I realized in a flash that for me to take charge of my life, I would, in a sense, have to give it over to Jesus Christ. I had to obey him in order to be really me. I turned the bunk light back on, grabbed my book, and told R. that I too was reading that "stuff." He just mumbled something derogatory and gave me a funny look. From that point on, you and I became friends. And, by your example, I began to learn how to walk with God.

In retrospect, the struggle I had that evening on my bunk (and through the months before) centered on moral courage. I had to decide, and publicly, to obey the truth. The truth, in my case, was that I believed God to be real and knew he wanted me to "take orders" from him. I had been unwilling to act on what I believed in my heart. I expected to be ridiculed for openly choosing to follow Christ and obey his word. During the first year I knew you I was unconsciously testing you to see whether your walk would hold up under pressure. If it did, then maybe mine would as well.

As timid as I was when I turned my life over to Christ, I began to feel more alive than ever. And to think I used to believe becoming a Christian meant becoming deadly dull. How different has been the reality! For the first time in my life, I began to enjoy studying. Until I became a Christian, I never even dreamed of going to college. No one in my immediate family had gone to college, and I had neither the intention nor the desire to do so myself. But now I could hardly wait to get there.

When I left the marines to enroll at the University of Houston, I left old struggles behind and, of course, I faced new ones. The most difficult one began during my undergrad years and grew worse as I continued on into graduate school—how could I integrate my faith with what I was learning academically? I could do very well with my course material during the day, and then go home and do very well with my faith at night. The trouble, for me, was doing both simultaneously. I had trouble seeing how the two could go together.

As an undergraduate history major, I could at least connect the Roman and Greek history I studied with the biblical account of the world in Christ's lifetime. Learning about the historical context in which Christianity arose could and did enhance my understanding of the New Testament. As a grad student in international relations, though, I couldn't make a connection. Learning about international politics didn't seem to add anything to my faith in God. Nor, for that matter, did my faith in God seem to add anything to my studies in international relations. And it wasn't as if I was doing the wrong thing. Time won't permit me to go into the many circumstances, and desires, that led me to study politics. I was where I wanted to be and, from all the available evidence, where God wanted me to be.

A troubling gap had been created, or at least widened, by an idea I picked up somewhere along the way. I had learned that whereas the church and popular culture disagree on many issues, one belief they seem to share, though perhaps not in so many words, is that faith and practical reality are separate and distinct entities. On the one hand, while the Bible is good for individuals' moral development and spiritual contemplation, it has little bearing on how we are to participate in society (culture's viewpoint). On the other hand, whereas academics may be useful in preparing us for work in the secular world, they have no bearing on how we develop spiritually (church's viewpoint). I found it increasingly difficult, while I was going through college, to live with the tensions this gap produced in my soul.

This conceptual split between faith and practice was sharply focused for me when I encountered the church's (or at least many churches') teaching about origins. I was taught that the only valid interpretation of the biblical creation account demanded a recent creation of the universe and all life, somewhere between six and fifty thousand years ago. Scientists, on the other hand, talked about billions of years. Thus secular science was said to represent a revolt against the God of the Bible. By proposing evidence for an old earth and an even older universe, scientists were promoting atheism—godless evolutionism, to be more precise.

With little science background, I had difficulty verifying this perspective. Not wanting to be heretical, I accepted it. But at the same time, I sensed that something was wrong. Science was pretty intimidating. I mean, of all the disciplines, the natural sciences seem to demand the most brilliance. And these sciences are also the most successful, in terms of explanatory and predictive power. Physics and mathematics are especially powerful. How could we send ships and people into space and return them safely if the sciences were a sham? In the social sciences, lies can (and do) last a long time (remember how many apologized for Stalin in the 1930s, 1940s and 1950s?). But the physical sciences are put to the test publicly day in and day out.

For me, the problem came down to this: If the sciences were wrong, then there was no hope for my discipline. The whole goal of good scholarship is to reduce interpretive bias. Yet according to the recent creation view, the sciences were supposedly based on false interpretations. In fact, the sciences were no better than any ideology. If so, then there seemed no objective reality against which we could measure the relative credibility of our research. And if the physical sciences were subjective, what use could the study of international relations really be? Conjecture and speculation would be as valid as any rigorous study.

This clash between the two worlds of Christian faith and practical facts drove me away from church for a while. Although I never lost faith in God, church became too painfully contradictory. Soon, however, I discovered that I began to act less and less Christlike. I never returned to my former debauched lifestyle, but deceived myself into committing "secret sins." Since other Christians weren't around to see my behavior and be harmed by it, maybe it wasn't really so bad. I saw, once again, a split between what I knew and wanted at the core of me and what I was, in fact, doing. I found myself on the same old horns of the same old dilemma.

The resolution came through a shocking reversal of my understanding and a blow to my pride. My goal throughout graduate school was to work in a policy position in Washington, D.C. Toward the end of my graduate study, I interviewed with a leading Washington agency for an analyst's position. The selection process is lengthy, with all the security clearances and background checks required. A good friend of mine who worked at this agency kept me posted on the progress of my chances. Just as soon as I finished my doctoral dissertation, I was chosen for the position. During two sets of interviews in the next three months I negotiated salary and title. Everything was set. I only had to wait a few days for official "orders." Two weeks passed. Still no word. So I called to find out how soon I might start moving. I was bluntly informed that I was no longer being considered for the position. What a blow! I had pinned a whole year's worth of examinations, interviews and waiting on a job I thought I had in the bag. Now the bag was empty. I didn't know what to do.

A few days later, the echo of that door slam still ringing in my ears, I received a call from a professor I had met several months earlier at a conference. He wanted to know if I was available to take his teaching load while he underwent emergency stomach surgery. Though the assignment extended for one quarter only, I accepted, for his university was one of only three institutions in the United States offering courses in my specialty. That one quarter's teaching led to another and then another. Finally, through an amazing set of "coincidences," the program received approval for a tenure-track faculty position. And then, amazingly, that position became mine. And when my professor friend retired, I was asked by the university president to serve as acting program director. All this in one year!

God surely did grab my attention. First, he prevented me from going to D.C. Then, almost immediately, he gave me a different direction, a career I had never even considered, and yet one that I thoroughly enjoy. Soon enough, he also helped me bridge the schism that tore apart my inner and outer life.

Humbled by his goodness and by my new responsibilities to others at the university, I sensed a growing desire to give church a second try. Even if I didn't learn much, I knew that Christian fellowship would be spiritually strengthening. From my parents I heard that a former Caltech astronomer led Bible classes in a local congregation. Astronomy fascinated me, especially since that night on the back of my dad's truck. But I think I was even more intrigued by this fellow's claim that Christian faith and the facts of nature can be integrated without compromise. I felt sure he must be mistaken, but I had to find out for myself.

My plan was to attend eight or nine weeks of classes, then write him a letter showing him the error of his ways (well documented, of course, with a long list of references). By the end of the second or third week, however, I was humbled yet again. I realized that what I had struggled (and finally resigned myself) to accept was wrong. A reconciliation between the Christian faith and the facts of nature, learned through a variety of disciplines, is not only possible but is mandated by the character of the God we serve. This reconciliation is also necessary to live a healthy spiritual life. Rather than feeling humiliated, I felt liberated, joyful, thankful.

What I discovered was this: Although interpretations of data and theology may differ, the facts of reality—natural and even political reality—and the words of the Bible never do. The reason is simple. Since the one and only God who created the universe (the creation of which science has been confirming since Einstein) also gave us the words of the Bible, and cannot lie, then it follows that both the facts of nature and the words of the Bible must fit together. The difficulty arises with interpretations of one or the other or both. Suddenly I gained a new perspective. Theological disputes over biblical interpretations have a secular counterpart—scientific and scholarly disputes over data interpretation. We should expect that as our research and understanding increase, we will see a greater convergence of that which is scientifically established with that which is theologically certain. We can also realistically expect disagreements over interpretations as our study continues. A little more respect and a little less dogmatism will go a long way in helping us bridge gaps.

This discovery that inner faith and outer life converge rather than diverge has helped me enormously in my teaching, my learning and my relationship with God. It has given me a great deal of inner peace and has helped me become more "peaceful" toward others. When I see others struggle with, or even overtly oppose, Christianity, I see myself when I was with you that first year. I no longer feel the need to respond ideologically to them. I can understand them better because I once felt that way. I also realize that some may even have legitimate concerns that need addressing—concerns about complex questions found in the Bible or concerns that arise from the ill-treatment people have suffered at the hands of other Christians. It's okay not to have all the answers. This side of heaven, we probably don't even have half of the questions.

On the other hand, having greater confidence in the compatibility of the facts of nature and the words of the Bible gives me greater confidence in sharing the truths of the Christian faith. I really wish my non-Christian friends could see how much it helps us live well. The great search for meaning that goes on at the university has a deeper significance and an eternal value when imbued with the "wholesomeness" of Christianity—to be a Christian at the university means that you can experience learning with your whole body, mind, soul and emotions in the quest for truth. Once found, the truths are not passing fads. The human spirit can only take so many crashes of falsely hyped expectations before producing the inner rot of indifference, skepticism, cynicism or despair. At the very least, for the Christian, learning is great fun.

This resolution helped me in my profession as well. There is an objective reality against which the soundness of my research and teaching can be measured. I strive to find the truth, in every area, and integrate it with ever-increasing consistency. For example, in my field of strategic studies, I have always been concerned about the ethical or moral dimension of war. As you will remember, this concern dates back to our days in the marines. Well, I spent an entire summer and a good deal of an academic year researching this subject further. I studied a variety of fields including the Bible, history, politics, ethics and international law. I developed a resolution that I'm comfortable with.[2] In fact, one commentator told me that it was probably the most original critique of the "just war" doctrine he had ever seen. I've got a few more projects in mind.

For the last couple of years I've been leading a Bible study for graduate students on integrating faith with decisions, attitudes and actions. God is using my experiences and training to help future leaders and teachers avoid some of the pitfalls that have tripped me up. In this way, Tod, God is still using your faithfulness to him in those early days of our acquaintance to impact many others today. Thank you for showing me the strength of the Bridge between God and humanity. Thank you for nudging me across the gap.

Semper Fidelis![3]
Mark

Notes

[1]Tod is now an orthopedic surgeon in private practice in Arkansas. He is a medical officer in the reserves, and he served in the 1991 Gulf War.

[2]Mark T. Clark, "The Paradox of War and Pacifism," *Perspectives on Science and Christian Faith* 47, no. 4 (1995): 220-32.

[3]Latin for "Always faithful."

14

A Prodigal Child
Finds Faith

LOUISA (SUE) HULETT

Political Science

Knox College

I do not seek to understand that I may believe,
but I believe in order to understand.
—SAINT ANSELM, *PROSLOGION*

Now faith is the assurance of things hoped for,
the conviction of things not seen. . . . By faith we
understand that the world was created by the word of God,
so that what is seen was made out of things
which do not appear.
—HEBREWS 11:2-3 RSV

I was a prodigal child who wandered to a distant land far from
God. I had no time for God. I was busy with my life and preoccupied with career advancement. Hanging on to a passing acquaintance with a blurry, generic God, I attended church until college. But
my weak and passive faith was no match for the skepticism, intellectual arrogance and blissfully self-gratifying lifestyle learned and
embraced in college. After college I studied hard, earned my Ph.D. (my
first idol) and started teaching international relations at Knox College,
a secular liberal arts college in the Midwest. I wrote several articles

and books (publications, my second idol) and was well received in the classroom even though I sometimes sacrificed time with students in order to do research. I earned tenure (my third idol) and received several prestigious research grants. I relished my success (my fourth idol) and the acclaim of being a big fish in a small pond. I controlled my fate, or so I thought.

My other passion is sports. I played team sports in high school and college, and as a young adult I played competitive (possibly overly aggressive and frenetic) tennis, racquetball, softball and so forth. I loved to win and I hated to lose. I succeeded at sports in a small town, my health was good and the future looked bright.

I believed that success in career and sports came from my own effort, not God. As a successful person, I would live the way I wanted to. I had no time for people or things that interfered with what I wanted to do. Despite this great life, however, I began to feel that something was missing. Career and sports were not enough. I still hated to lose, but winning and succeeding offered no joy. I wasn't seeking God, but I was questioning the value of life. What was my purpose in life? Why is there a universe?

I raised these questions with a Christian colleague, who recommended a Christian retreat. I agreed to attend, although I didn't know why. As the date of the retreat approached, however, I dreaded the thought of giving up three and a half days of research time. Satan was working overtime sowing doubts. I actually did think of prayer at this time—I prayed I would get sick so that I could avoid the retreat. But this prayer was not answered. God had a different plan for me. Since I did not get sick and I did not want to disappoint my friend, I went to the retreat. I hated it, resenting the wasted time and the wasted tennis weather. People talked about God all day long as they plied me with cookies and conversation.

By the third day, my attitude began to change. At first I attributed this to a sugar high from the cookies. But as I listened to the Christians around me and grappled with questions about values, faith, worship and spirituality, I began to do some serious soul-searching. I realized that I was very far from God and was missing out on something. Then, during one of the quiet times, I felt the loving presence of Jesus Christ.

God, the merciful and forgiving God, opened his arms to me, despite my twenty-five years of accepting the deceptive and conceited notion that we make our own destiny and rules of conduct. I had selfishly concentrated on material and intellectual things to the exclusion of other people and God. Overcome, I asked God to forgive me and to take me back. I was, as C. S. Lewis wrote, "surprised by joy" when Jesus welcomed me home after so many years of being lost.

I had gone to the retreat still wrapped up in my egotistical and obsessive world of work, pleasure, desire and grim determination to succeed. In this world without God, only one thing had mattered: what I wanted and when I wanted it. I had squandered the gift of life until I, like the repentant prodigal son (Luke 15), came to my senses and saw the selfishness, narrowness and emptiness of my past. After experiencing Jesus' embrace at the retreat, I knew what I could become. I knew God was there to help show me how I could change. God's love overwhelmed me and set me on fire with a new perspective on life and the depth of the Father's love for this prodigal child. He let me make choices about how to live; he gave me everything—life, intelligence, laughter, family, friends and joy. He allowed me to gamble and nearly lose all of these. When I abandoned him, he mourned and yearned for my return. When I asked to return, he assented and rejoiced over the one who was lost. As my nephews say, "Way cool."

My life changed dramatically after I was born again. (It took me nearly a year to use this decidedly nonacademic phrase to describe my transformation from agnosticism to a personal relationship with Jesus, whose sacrifice on the cross bought my salvation.) My career remains important, but it no longer dominates my life to the exclusion of everything else. Much to the shock of my students, I shared my experience with them the day after the retreat. As a new disciple, I shared my story with students, colleagues, friends, family and tennis partners. In my newfound Christian enthusiasm, everyone was a target for a conversation about God. In my first swing at evangelism, I invited students to talk to me anytime about anything. On the same day I made this offer, a student came to my office and said that hearing my testimony made him brave enough to see me. I was elated. Then he proceeded to complain that I graded too hard. I deflated quickly. But we discussed grading, striving and overcoming challenges, and I learned to listen more attentively to my students. I now spend more time with students, helping them in the classroom and being more available to answer their questions about life and God.

I took on the role of advising the three embryonic Christian groups on campus. This rewarding experience taught me more about God as my students taught me about their faith and as God revealed his plan for Christian growth at Knox. Nothing has given me more joy than being a part of these groups for the past ten years. It even reinvigorated my teaching, as I searched for ways to adjust the substance and style of my teaching to the universal truth that God exists and desires comfort, peace, justice and virtue for all people. I do not proselytize in the classroom, but I ask students to seek the truth, to be open to the idea that truth that can be found and to question their purpose in life. In my search for a fuller revelation of truth, I created a new course, Christianity and Politics, so that students and I could chew on issues like the existence of God, the religious origins of the founding of our country, the impact of Christian principles on American political ideas and history, the role of religious political movements and the moral ethic behind ideas like pacifism, Christian realism, liberation theology and social justice. The experience of preparing for this course led me to write a book on these topics, which are far removed from my primary research area of Soviet-American relations. I now realize that God took good care of me. When the Soviet Union collapsed, I lost my main field. Now I have a new purpose in life, a new field and new life in Christ, who makes all things possible.

I wish I could say that I am perfect now. But being a new creation is hard. Having a change of habit as well as a change of heart is hard. On bad days I catch myself exhibiting the same impatience and short temper that I exhibited before becoming a Christian. I still get caught up in the race to succeed and become too busy to help students in need. I know in my head that God changed me and that joy does not reside in circumstances, sports, friends or family. As Lloyd Ogilvie wrote in a commentary on Colossians, "When we know that we are loved and cherished by God, joy floods our emotions. It is far superior to happiness, which is dependent . . . on circumstances and people. Joy is love growing in the soil of difficulties and suffering. . . . Only fellow-ship with God can fill the emptiness of our emotional natures."[1] I believe these in the abstract, but what kind of new creation am I when setbacks crush me? The apostle Paul bemoaned the same thing when he wrote, "For that which I am doing, I do not understand; for I am not practicing what I would like to do, but I am doing the very thing I hate" (Romans 7:15 NASB). I still get depressed, angry, impatient, selfish and moody. That I am contrite and often surprised by my lapses does not answer the question of why I revert so easily.

I find comfort in Paul's assertion that when we accept Jesus we become a new creation. Jesus tells us that when we believe, we are his and belong to him. ("Therefore, if any one is in Christ, he is a new creation; the old has passed away, behold, the new has come," 2 Corinthians 5:17 RSV.) I am a new creation, not because I want to be one or work hard to be one but because of Jesus' promise to make me one. When I fail/sin, Jesus forgives me and provides the strength for me to continue to grow and change. And how wonderful of God to give us his word in Scripture—to tell us how much he loves us despite our inevitable failures, to encourage us, to forgive and redeem us and to draw us to him. Sometimes I think he is shouting at a deaf person, or maybe I'm not always listening. On the other hand, I know that the soul-searching and prayer that accompany each crisis help me in my walk with Jesus. He called me and spoke to my heart, and he is faith-ful. I may not always feel his presence, but I remember vividly the miracle of his touch ten years ago. The reality of that memory sustains me in dry times.

In the meantime, as a born-again Christian, I have a mission-not-impossible: sharing my faith with faculty and students in the surround-ing secular academic world. It is not easy to speak about Jesus in a world dancing between a modernism that worships humanity and reason and a postmodernism that denies the existence of universal truth. How do I persuade students that the quality that makes us human is our soul or spirit, which does not emerge simply from the brain or result from psychological needs to please or reject our parents and others? I remind students that most of them are in college today because they acted on faith. They believed that a college education was important. They took on faith the beliefs of their parents, friends and counselors. We are creatures of faith. We go to sleep each night believing we will wake in the morning. We believe there are solutions to problems. We may not know what they are, but we believe in solutions and correct answers. This describes part of the scientific method. We assume rationality, explanations and axioms—rules we assume to be true without a priori proof in order to study the actions or consequences that follow from them. We believed in manned flight before there were airplanes, in atoms before we could see them, and in the promise of science before there was proof. We act on faith and could not function without it.

With students I talk about the most fundamental forms of faith: belief in God and in God-designed universal truths. To understand and believe, we need to find answers to certain questions. Do our lives have purpose beyond ourselves? Was the universe created by mere chance and circumstance? Is what distinguishes us from the animals our awareness of self and the sense of God the Creator? Who are some models of faith and what can they tell us? Let us briefly look at four answers to these questions. The "father of faith," Abraham, believed in God, obeyed God (most of the time and at the most crucial times) and worshiped God. Socrates believed in a higher power, universal (not self-determined) truths and divine purposes. He lost his life for teaching and defending these beliefs. Martin Luther King Jr. believed that God had a plan for his life, and he dedicated his life to the Christian ministry and to seeking justice and mercy for all God's people—black and white. King served God by being a minister, a civil rights leader and a voice of conscience to the nation. Mother Teresa sacrificed every creature comfort to live in abject poverty to serve God by caring for the wretched of the earth.

We can teach about faith by our own testimony, by examining models of faith and by comparing points of view on the value of faith. Looking at Holy Scripture, ancient and modern philosophy, great literature and people of action can reveal much about the linkages between faith and human nature. Let us review some of those who promoted or dismissed faith as a foundation for human behavior.

We see in Tolstoy's *Death of Ivan Illych* the tragedy of living an unexamined life and the miracle of a spiritual awakening as Ivan reassesses his past. Socrates saw individuals as hopeless and lost unless they used reason to ask questions. What is the purpose of life and what does it mean to believe in piety, justice, honor and virtue? Dostoevsky, in *Crime and Punishment*, portrayed the danger of our depending only on intellect and will without recognizing our dependence on God. He once wrote that if he had to choose between Christ and truth, he would choose Christ because "without Christ there is no truth." On the other hand, Jean-Paul Sartre argued that each person designs his or her own truth, makes his or her own purpose and rules in a world without God, hope or meaning. According to Sartre, we live in despair and aloneness because we have lost faith in a nonexistent God and, presumably, this loss also produces freedom and self-reliance. Karl Marx saw people as creatures imprisoned by their economic environment and the exploitation of one human being by another. The state run by the proletariat will produce heaven on earth, and since there is nothing beyond this earth, we should strive for this goal alone. Sociobiologists explain that our genetic makeup determines our thinking, choices and goals. Freud speculated that deep-seated, repressed and often denied primal psychological injuries and urges form our self-image, motivations and emotional responses to outside stimuli. Feminists insist that gender bias damages our ability to relate to one another. Malcolm X and Louis Farrakhan blame racism for distorting human behavior. Sociologists and anthropologists insist that society and culture influence our responses to and attitudes toward life, death and the hereafter.

Are we merely a chaotic composite of creatures who reason, struggle to survive and procreate, and selfishly seek economic or political power and/or personal well-being in a world without meaning or God? For Christians and Jews, people are indeed reasoning beings plagued by doubts, psychological urges and temptations, and by environmental, mental, biological and cultural limitations. But, above all else, human beings search for meaning. Viktor Frankl, a psychotherapist who spent years in a Nazi concentration camp, agrees.[2] Based on what he saw in the camps, he concluded that the main concern of human beings is not to gain pleasure or to avoid pain but to seek meaning in life. Frankl rejects Freud, Marx and sociobiologists who argue that values are nothing but defense mechanisms, reaction formations, herd instincts, or social or class conventions. We live and die not because of defense mechanisms or action-reaction dynamics but for the sake of ideals and values. The author of the book of Genesis in the Bible would agree and would highlight the need for faith in God, who alone gives meaning to life.

The book of Genesis reveals the origin and history of humankind, the evolution of God's chosen people, the emergence of key prophets and servants of God like Abraham, and the declarations of God's character, plans, teachings and promises such as transcendence, omnipotence, the nature and consequences of sin, judgment, reconciliation, messiah and salvation. Abraham believed in and experienced God. He endured the greatest test of faith when he obeyed God's astonishing command to sacrifice his beloved son.

Earlier God had called Abraham to leave his nation. Abraham "went as the LORD directed him" and built an altar to the Lord who promised to give Abraham many descendants and to "make of you a great nation" (Genesis 11—12). Abraham responded to God's call, yet he also questioned God about the destruction of Sodom and Gomorrah, and when in fear for his life in Egypt, he lied about being married to his wife, Sarah. In other words, Abraham was a sinner, as were David (adulterer) and Moses (murderer). But God loved Abraham, spoke to him and taught him about hope, covenant, forgiveness and trust. When he obeyed God's command to sacrifice his son Isaac, Abraham learned the depth of his faith, his willingness to subordinate his will to God's will, and his joy in being a part of God's perfect plan to instruct all of us about the meaning of faith and the bankruptcy and despair of life without God's grace and direction.

Abraham's act of obedience stands as a beacon and a living embodiment of faith for Abraham himself and for all his descendants— including all who accept Abraham as the father of faith. God rewarded Abraham by sparing Isaac, multiplying his descendants and making his people into a great nation and the earthly home of Jesus Christ. Abraham is a wonderful model of faith and action (obedience). Christians may contend over which is more important, but as C. S.

Lewis wrote in *Mere Christianity*, disputing over this is "like asking which blade in a pair of scissors is most necessary." As the apostle Paul writes in the book of Philippians, "Work out your own salvation with fear and trembling. For it is God which worketh in you" (Philippians 2:12-13 KJV).

I don't claim to know God as Abraham did, but I know that God exists because I have experienced his presence in my life. This experiential proof is impossible to dissect, verify or test. I could approach you and touch your arm. You would feel my touch, but no one except you and witnesses would see the mark of my touch. But you feel it and know it to be real. That is how I feel, and it is how Abraham felt. We are people of faith, called to put this belief into action by living in obedience to God. As John Calvin, echoing the words in chapter 6 of the book of Romans in the Bible, wrote in the *Golden Booklet of the True Christian Life*, "The gospel is not a doctrine of the tongue, but of life. It cannot be grasped by reason and memory only, but it is fully understood when it possesses the whole soul, and penetrates to the inner recesses of the heart. . . . But our religion will be unprofitable, if it does not change our heart, pervade our manners, and transform us into new creatures."[3]

Notes

[1]Lloyd J. Ogilvie, *You Are Loved and Forgiven: Paul's Letter of Hope to the Colossians* (Ventura, Calif.: Regal Books, 1977), p. 34.

[2]Viktor Frankl, *Man's Search for Meaning: An Introduction to Logotherapy*, 3rd ed. (New York: Simon & Schuster, 1984).

[3]John Calvin, *Golden Booklet of the True Christian Life*, trans. Henry J. V. Andel (Grand Rapids, Mich.: Baker, 1952), p. 17.

15

From the Ends
of the Earth

GLENN TINDER

Political Science
(Emeritus)

University of Massachusetts, Boston

All things work together for good to them that love God.
—ROMANS 8:28 KJV

*A*n account of one's faith, at least for a Christian, is an account of one's life. It cannot be simply a statement of propositions and the reasons underlying them. A Christian's faith may, to be sure, involve certain propositions, along with supporting reasons. But it is necessarily more than a rational structure. It is a way of living and is affirmed through the daily and hourly activities that make up a life, not merely through an explicit act of assent. It might be said that a Christian's faith is a destiny—a life and a purpose bestowed by an unsurpassable authority, and the commitment by which that life and purpose are pursued.

Moreover, any Christian statement of faith, as an account of a life, must be confessional. It must deal, in the words of the Anglican Book of Common Prayer, with "things left undone which ought to have been done, and with things done which ought not to have been done." You do not become a Christian because you view your life with pride and satisfaction. If that were the case, you would have no need of a Savior—of Christ. So a Christian profession of faith must be an acknowledgment of insufficiency and guilt. To tell about a journey toward Christian faith as though it reflected creditably on your intellectual discernment and personal goodness would be to betray, in the very telling, the faith described.

Finally, note must be taken of the paradoxical fact that, even though an account of one's faith must be an account of one's life—which might seem to be a complete explanation—the faith accounted for must be in some sense inexplicable. This is simply because faith is given by grace. This is why it is more than a set of concepts accepted for good and sufficient reasons. As a gift of grace, however, it is more even than the logical outcome of interconnected events of the kind that make up a life. Faith is an incursion of the encompassing mystery into our prosaic, explicable lives. Of course some gifts are deserved, and are in that sense explicable. But according to Christian principles, the gift of faith is an act of divine forgiveness and is thus, in its very nature, undeserved. It is gratuitous, which is defined in the dictionary as being "without apparent reason, cause, or justification." Thus somewhere in the story of a Christian life there must be a gap.

I must begin the account of my faith with a description of this gap. Karl Barth speaks of the Incarnation in terms of a journey by Christ into "a far country." My own encounter with Christ began in a far country.

I was raised, very intensively, in Christian Science. I say "very intensively" because I was an only child, and my mother was not only a Christian Scientist but also a highly intelligent and conscientious woman. Understandably, she saw one of her main responsibilities as a mother to be that of instilling Christian Science as deeply as possible in her one and only child. She was in a good position to do this, since not only was her attention, as well as mine, undiverted by brothers or sisters; my father, although a gentle and sensitive man, was rather detached as a parent (for reasons not entirely clear to me and in any case, so far as I know, without appreciable bearing on my present subject). From my early years every day began with readings from Mary Baker Eddy's *Science and Health* as well as from the Bible. In addition, throughout my childhood and adolescence, the world and daily life were construed for me according to the standards of Christian Science. I do not mean to make this sound like indoctrination in the pejorative sense of that term. It was a conscientious mother's effort to raise up her son in the truth.

I must make it clear at the outset that Christian Science is not a form of Christianity. It is not even near enough to Christianity in the traditional sense of the term to be called a heresy. It is often thought of as centered on faith healing, and it is true, as the very title of Mary Baker Eddy's book suggests, that it is centered on the achievement of health. This is not strictly speaking a matter of healing, however, for the very reality of sickness is denied. Sickness is an illusion. Faith therefore does not bring healing but rather a realization that one was never sick to begin with. No phrase is more common among Christian Scientists than "knowing the truth," and this means telling yourself continually, when the illusion that you are sick arises, that in actuality you are perfectly healthy. This of course is apt to bring peace of mind, and this in turn may be physically beneficial. Hence in many instances "knowing the truth" unquestionably plays a part in the restoration of health. When that happens, however, it is not a healing that has occurred, in the view of Christian Scientists, but rather a realization of what has been true all along. The signal point in all of this is that Christian Scientists deny the reality not only of sickness but of all evil. This means that they deny the reality of sin, and in doing this they deny the very fallenness of the human race. The crucifixion becomes pointless (although the symbol of the cross is retained, a crucifix is never seen, as far as I know, in Christian Science churches or publications). The core truth is not that we are saved. It is rather that we have never been lost.

To common sense, much of this may seem absurd. It is, however, a daring and quite logical response to what is often called "the problem of theodicy": how can there be evil in a world created by a good and omnipotent God? Mary Baker Eddy answered, simply, that there can't and therefore isn't. Christian Scientists are people with the nerve required for living according to this answer—the nerve, for example, to spurn all medical help in time of illness. My mother had this kind of nerve, and for the first seventeen years of my life (until I left for college) my mother did her best to instill it in me.

There have probably been worse doctrines in the twentieth century than Christian Science—communism, for example, and fascism. Nonetheless, it is radically in error and, in spite of its benign appearance, can be profoundly harmful. For one thing, in teaching you to avert your eyes from evil, it teaches you to ignore your own sinful impulses—your pride, callousness and sensuality. The Christian Scientists I have known have been quite decent people. This is owing not to their principles, however, but in most cases to the kind of training they received before becoming Christian Scientists. I consider my mother to have been quite a good person, but in my view this was because she had been raised as a Quaker and never succeeded in becoming an altogether logical Christian Scientist. A logical Christian Scientist does not deplore and try to eradicate sinful desires but tries simply not to notice them. Nor does a logical Christian Scientist who has committed a grave wrong suffer pangs of guilt and seek redemption; rather, the whole matter is as far as possible erased from one's mind. Christian penitence becomes impossible.

Equally dangerous is that Christian Scientists who learn to avert their eyes from evil learn to ignore the illnesses and other troubles being undergone by friends and relatives. As strange as it may seem, Christian Scientists who are rigorously practicing their creed do not ask someone who has been ill, "How are you feeling this morning?" or "Are you feeling any better?" Rather, they "know the truth." They are often nice to other people, in many ways, but they do not commiserate with those who are suffering. Instead, they resolutely deny the reality of the suffering. Such a habit is compatible with graciousness and cheerfulness, but not with deeply felt expressions of sympathy or concern. To put it bluntly, Christian Science undermines compassion. This does not mean that no attention is paid to others. It means rather that those who are ill, bereaved, depressed or in any other way afflicted are subjected to a process of silent reconstruction. They are seen as not ill, not bereaved, not depressed and not in any other way afflicted. This of course means simply that they are not seen.

As I have already suggested, whereas my mother was a very serious Christian Scientist she did not rigorously work out or adhere to the implications of her creed. When I had the measles, she illogically saw to it that I was shielded from the light that would have damaged my eyes, and she illogically allowed me to be vaccinated against various other illnesses. Above all, I want to say that she had little resemblance to the monument of self-righteousness and self-absorption that her creed implicitly encouraged her to be. I doubt that she ever more than half believed in the principles of Christian Science, even though she thought she believed in them wholeheartedly. After all, she had not been raised in those principles. I of course had, and unfortunately I embraced them, at least for many years, quite unreservedly.

My purpose here is simply to show that I came to Christianity (well along in my life) from a place very distant from Christianity. Although painfully conscientious, I was insensitive to my own sinful potentialities and not much attuned to the feelings and sufferings of others—conditions fateful for my life, as I will show. The principles of penitence and forgiveness were meaningless to me. In the book of Isaiah, God addresses "Israel, my servant, Jacob, whom I have chosen," as "you whom I took from the ends of the earth, and called from its farthest corners" (Isaiah 41:8-9 RSV). I am conscious, in my Christian faith, of having been taken from the ends of the earth. I am of course speaking spiritually. But the spiritual fact is symbolized physically. I was born on a cattle ranch near a very small town in the far West. The scenery, with towering mountains a few miles away on both sides, standing forth in the crystalline desert air, was dramatic and testified daily to the Creator of the physical universe. But the nearest city was almost three hundred miles away and could be reached only by crossing a great, arid desert. In that sense, I was at the ends of the earth physically as well as spiritually.

It was not only Christian Science, however, which placed me at the ends of the earth. After graduating from college and spending three years in the navy during World War II, I entered a spiritual environment very different from that of Christian Science yet no less distant from real Christianity. This was the world of American social science.

On my release from the navy I undertook graduate work in political science, first at Claremont, then at Berkeley, where I finally received a Ph.D. No longer was I a Christian Scientist. But I was not a Christian either; indeed, I scarcely knew what Christianity was and did not really care. I was interested mainly in political philosophy, and I was, to be sure, attracted to certain thinkers who were in a broad sense religious (although not Christian), such as Plato and the English Hegelians. But I had little interest in the great Christian political philosophers such as Augustine and Aquinas. And my intellectual mentor among the major political philosophers was an outspoken atheist, John Stuart Mill. What needs emphasis, however, is not the canon of political philosophy, which includes figures of unquestionable spiritual stature, but rather the atmosphere of social science in most American universities.

There were Christians in the political science departments of secular colleges and universities. But they were very quiet about their faith, and for the sake of professional survival and advancement they had to be. The reigning assumption was that a respectable intellectual not only had no belief in God but had no interest even in the possibility of such a belief. Religion was not a live issue for anyone in pursuit of the kind of truth sought by political scientists. No one said this; the assumption was so dominant and unquestioned that no one had to. (The situation today is somewhat, although not entirely, different.) In the time I spent as a graduate student and professor before becoming a Christian—a period of about twenty years—I never had a single professor, or a single friend or colleague, who expressed any definite interest in Christianity. Two or three friends were Christians, but, obedient to the reigning code, they were very quiet Christians, and I knew of their faith only from chance remarks and not from anything we seriously discussed.

It was in this setting, and contrary to every reasonable expectation, that I became a Christian. It happened so gradually that I am embarrassed by my slowness of heart; yet in looking back it seems to have happened inexorably, as though some irresistible force (like grace!) was behind it. I dislike the casual way in which some Christians speak of miracles, as though we see them all around us, every day; the mystery and wonder of divine action tend thus to be obscured. But I am willing, soberly and tentatively, to think of my conversion as a miracle. There was nothing in my childhood and youth, and nothing in the spiritual setting I inhabited as an adult, to explain it. When I was finally baptized, in my early forties, I had spent all of my life at the ends of the earth. I do not want this statement to carry any overtones of disdain for particular persons. My parents were fine people, and I loved them deeply, and still do; and I have had numerous colleagues for whom I have great respect, and several of them have been, and still are, cherished friends. But nowhere in my background or environment were there Christians (the quiet sort aside). In spite of this, I became a Christian—one for whom, as for any Christian, Christianity is not one among several activities and interests but is rather the center of the universe, the axis of history, in a word, life itself.

There was another circumstance, however, that placed me at an even greater distance from God than did Christian Science or academic life. This consisted not in conditions to which I was subject but in acts for which I was responsible. It belongs to the time that separated my life as a Christian Scientist from my life as an academician—the three years I spent in the navy.

Aside from some months of general education and nautical training, which I received on entering the navy in July 1943, the bulk of my time in the service was spent aboard a large landing ship in the Pacific, mainly in the Philippine Islands. I was an officer, for some time in charge of the deck force and responsible for the general maintenance of the ship, and later navigator and general manager of the ship under the captain. The crew was made up of something like ten officers and a hundred men. We carried trucks and tanks, along with soldiers, and took part in most of the major landings in the Philippines—usually, however, coming in sometime after D-Day, and usually in rather undramatic circumstances. We would beach the ship, open our bow doors, let down the bow ramp, spend a few hours discharging trucks and soldiers onto a beach that Japanese forces had evacuated hours or days earlier, and then leave for another island and another operation. There were occasional air raids, once a period of shelling from a large Japanese gun inland, and now and then sounds of combat in the distance. If I was "seeing action," however, I was doing so in almost the literal sense of the phrase—*seeing* it without being very much involved in it.

In March 1945 our ship put into Manila Harbor. A month earlier we had taken part in the landings in Lingayen Gulf, perhaps a hundred miles north of Manila. American forces had been fighting their way down to Manila and, after some of the bloodiest combat of World War II, had finally taken the city of Manila. In approaching Manila, we were made acutely conscious of all that had been going on. The ship more than once passed through clusters of dead Japanese soldiers, bobbing about on the waves of the sea, and as we passed Corregidor we watched an American plane dive-bombing Japanese positions. Most of the fighting in Manila was over. But there were isolated centers of Japanese resistance on the outskirts of the city, and Japanese bodies, often grotesquely bloated, were a common sight in the water and on the beaches. A particularly fateful circumstance in my own destiny was this, that scattered throughout the bay were dozens of Japanese cargo ships, sunk by American planes and resting on the bottom of the harbor, but with superstructures and upper decks still protruding above the surface of the water.

These looked like fascinating objects of exploration. They were oceangoing vessels, and most of them were largely intact. We were drawn by the prospect of seeing staterooms, bridges and other operational areas so recently occupied by the Japanese, now for over three years a mysterious and fearsome antagonist. So a day or so after coming to anchor, a group of us, with me as the officer in charge, got together and set off in a small boat to look at some of the ships. Only one thing kept the expedition from being an altogether carefree outing. There were rumors that Japanese soldiers, resisting capture to the last, perhaps with guns or hand grenades, had found their way out to some of the ships. We did not really expect to encounter any such soldiers, but as a precaution we armed ourselves, many with automatic weapons, before embarking on our explorations.

We had gone through two or three ships and were tying up our boat at the side of another. Suddenly there was shattering gunfire right at my side. One of our sailors had seen a Japanese soldier on the ship, only twenty or thirty feet away. We were all so absurdly frightened that we were afraid to expose ourselves even to the extent of standing up to cast off the line secured to the ship. We severed it with gunfire and immediately went to the beach and found an American army officer, exhausted and unshaven, stretched out languidly in a folding chair outside a large building in which we could hear occasional gunfire; inside were Japanese holdouts. We told him what had happened. He was courteous but completely uninterested. He gave us a hand grenade and left it to us to decide what to do next. We returned to the ship and, trembling with fear, went aboard. We thought the Japanese soldier had been hit and probably killed. But we weren't sure; he might still be alive and he might have companions. I crept up to a porthole and looked into a cabin where we thought the soldier might be. Inside, in the semidarkness, I seemed to see a figure on the deck, perhaps reclining against a bulkhead; shielding myself as fully as possible, I reached through the porthole and fired several times. We found the soldier, indeed dead, in the cabin into which I had fired. In a fever of tension and fear we explored the ship, finding no other soldiers.

The soldier we had killed was unarmed. At the time, I thought little about this signal fact. He had made no effort to surrender, as far as I knew, and I assumed we could not have safely tried to capture him. I assumed also that a Japanese soldier would rather die than be captured. These were sound assumptions, but they rendered me insensitive to what had happened. When we returned to our ship, I was in an untroubled frame of mind.

During the next few days, as I recall, no one said much about the killing of the Japanese soldier. And probably no one thought much more about it than I did. But one afternoon some sailors asked if I would serve as officer in charge of another exploratory expedition; we had looked into only a few of the many hulks out in the bay. Unthinkingly, I agreed. Again we armed ourselves and set out. Again we crept, tense and frightened, yet feeling a sense of adventure, down passageways, around corners, into staterooms, able often to see only a few feet ahead, fearing that at any moment we would be faced with one or more armed and suicidal enemy soldiers. The fascination we felt probably resulted from the risks we were running, but mainly, I think, from these great abandoned ships.

Nothing eventful occurred, however, until I had gone out on the main deck of one of the ships while a group of sailors were prowling around inside. Then, from somewhere within the ship, came the sound of gunfire. I was told that another Japanese soldier had been killed. When I arrived at the scene the soldier, presumably dead, lay on the deck with his back to me. Assuming it would be unsafe to approach him, since conceivably he was armed and only feigning death, I fired into his body. As strange as it may sound, this all happened rather casually. I saw no blood; I had seen no one fall under a hail of bullets. Movie violence today is far more horrifying and "realistic" than this was. I scarcely even looked at the body. Only later did someone tell me that this soldier too had been unarmed.

I was still untroubled, cushioned as before by the assumptions that the shootings were unavoidable and that the dead soldiers preferred death to the disgrace of being captured. There was nothing in my motives (or, so far as I knew, in the motives of the sailors) to trouble me. We had not set out to kill Japanese soldiers and found no satisfaction or thrills in the fact that we had. If we had somehow found ourselves with a captured and unarmed Japanese soldier in our custody, I am quite sure that we would have done him no harm. Our aim had been to find relief from the boredom of shipboard life by exploring some great deserted oceangoing vessels. The killings seemed incidental, unavoidable, devoid of hatred or pleasure. It is no doubt significant in relation to my own state of mind that I, personally, had not faced and shot a living man. So again, some days passed during which I carried on my normal shipboard duties and thought little of what had happened.

I still don't know why this period of complacency ended as suddenly as it did. But I vividly remember, and will always remember, the moment it happened. It was a few days after the second exploratory expedition. I was stepping into my stateroom. Suddenly I was nearly felled with the realization that I was responsible for the needless loss of two human lives. I had been officer in charge of the two exploratory expeditions, and I had fired my gun into the bodies, probably dead but possibly living, of both of the soldiers we had killed. I was not simply conscience-stricken. I was incredulous that I, a rather conscientious and even strait-laced young man (in college, for example, I neither smoked nor drank; I cried in pity over the first fish I caught as a child; I could never bear the idea of hunting; on the ship I meticulously enforced all safety regulations, thinking how awful it would be were there a fatal shipboard accident), had fallen into such a moral abyss. The terrible word *murder* invaded my mind. It was as though I had been dreaming all during the preceding week, during the ship explorations and the killings, and suddenly the dream had turned into a terrible, and entirely unacceptable, reality. There is no exaggeration in saying that at the moment this happened my life changed forever.

The ensuing weeks are unclear in my memory. I do know that they were spent in a state of what might be called metaphysical panic. I realized that I had committed an offense against something holy and, as far as I knew, remorseless and unforgiving. I had never had anything like "a religious experience." God, for me, was merely the One who had created a good universe and then conveniently disappeared, leaving the human race to know the truth about it and enjoy it; this was the general understanding of things I had gained from Mary Baker Eddy. Now, unexpectedly, an angry God, or at least a divine and implacable law, menacing and offended, towered over me. Christian Science gave me no help at all; denying evil, it had nothing to say about forgiveness. Yet it had made me a stranger to Christianity. It is a mark of this estrangement that there was a Christian chaplain on our ship and, although I was nearly drowning in anguish, it never occurred to me to talk with him. I talked with no one. I went through the motions required of me by my shipboard duties while despairingly casting about in my mind to discover how I could go on living.

This period abruptly ended, after perhaps two or three weeks of moral agony. I had with me on the ship not only *Science and Health* but also a Bible, given to me by my mother on my ninth birthday. One afternoon I was leafing through the Bible in a mood of desperation. My eyes fell on the words of Psalm 118:24: "This is the day which the LORD hath made," I read, "we will rejoice and be glad in it." I knew in an instant that in spite of what I had done God's universe remained intact, that I inhabited a day that God had made, and that I could live. The inward experience immediately found an outward symbol. The sunlight on the waves of the blue Pacific Ocean took on a splendor and significance they had never before had but never lost during my time at sea. In the sunlit waves that were all about me every day I saw a sign of the divine power that could, in a way still utterly beyond my understanding, deliver me from guilt and give me life. Not that I was thereafter happy. For years I would recurrently go through hours and days when my heart was burdened with the memory of what I had done. Nor did I quickly gain understanding. It took not merely years but decades for me to comprehend, and to live under the authority of, the act of divine forgiveness that took place on the cross. I was still a Christian Scientist, not a Christian. But from the moment I came upon the psalmist's words about the Lord's day, I knew that my life had not ended on those ships out in Manila Bay.

These events reached a climax only when I became a Christian. Only then did I begin to understand that the light of God's day came not only from the act of creation but also from the act of redemption that was accomplished on the cross. For a year or two I resorted to the most absurd theological expedients to explain to myself how God was able to shield the day he had made from the destructive impact of deeds like mine. Humbled and lost though I was, I'm afraid God found me a slow and halting follower. Nevertheless, his mercy endured, and I began my long journey toward Christianity on that terrible and wondrous afternoon when my eyes lit on verse 24 of chapter 118 in the book of Psalms in the Bible.

This was a highly intellectual journey, even though it began with traumatic physical events. I don't mean to suggest that I set out in a mood of moral serenity and devoted myself single-mindedly to the search for truth. I recurrently experienced great anguish over the events in Manila Bay. Although I told myself that I would put those events behind me by becoming a good person, I certainly did not succeed in becoming any better than the average person, who is shackled by pride, sensuality and callousness. But I did get myself seriously involved in the quest for truth. I became a professional intellectual.

Soon after being discharged from the navy, I entered into graduate work, which lasted for six years, and then into university teaching.

It would be roughly accurate to say that for about twenty years I stumbled along in the dark but caught occasional glimpses of light far ahead; gradually the light grew brighter. Many of these glimpses came through a pagan of great spiritual stature—Plato. I read his main dialogues again and again. I think that the natural setting in which Plato lived and wrote, with the dry air, the lucid sunlight, and the sharply etched mountains one can still experience in present-day Greece, was enough like the desert setting in which I grew up to render his thought particularly evocative for me. In teaching the history of political philosophy, I always devoted many weeks to Plato. Subsequent history, as I taught it, tended to become a record of decline from Plato on (although, in opposition to Plato, I emphatically endorsed the separation of temporal and spiritual authorities that arose from Christianity as well as the ideal of liberty to which this separation eventually led). Glimpses of light were also provided by more recent thinkers. I became intensely interested in existentialism, which was very fashionable in the postwar years. I was attracted mainly to existentialists who were religious and Christian, not atheists such as Sartre. I read extensively in Kierkegaard, Karl Jaspers and Gabriel Marcel.

To speak as casually as this about writers who interested me, however, conveys an inadequate impression of the crucial role that books played in my spiritual progress. Although I had many good friends as a graduate student and then as a young instructor, I always had religious concerns that set me apart from practically all of the young political scientists and historians with whom I associated. That these concerns were inchoate and exceedingly vague, although deeply rooted, increased my isolation, for I was unable to articulate them. The consequence was that books assumed a peculiar importance in my life. I was nourished and kept alive by certain writers, and it was these writers who gradually led me to Christianity. So dependent was I on them that an account of my spiritual journey would be false without a few words on the most important of them.

Standing slightly taller than any of the others in my memory is the great, but now largely forgotten, Christian philosopher *Nicolas Berdyaev*. I'm not sure why a naive young man from a small town in the American West should have been so powerfully drawn toward an exiled Russian aristocrat. Some of his key ideas were never acceptable to me, his emphasis on creativity, for example, and his concept of a primal, cosmic freedom that placed limits even on God and introduced into God's life a tragic note. Moreover, Berdyaev paid little attention to the Christian theme that concerned me above all others, as a consequence of my war experiences: sin and forgiveness. I can only say that his writings enchanted me. And he influenced me decisively in spite of my reservations respecting his philosophy. First of all, he set an example of bold, wide-ranging thought—on a Christian basis. Beyond this, he taught me to take the mystery of human freedom very seriously, although I incorporated it into a Western liberalism, which was not at all what Berdyaev had in mind; he swayed me in the direction of a sharply dualistic metaphysic (most authoritatively expressed, perhaps, in Paul, although approaching the extreme of gnosticism in Berdyaev himself); he made eschatology—the idea of the reappearance of Christ and the end of history—a dramatic possibility among the ideas that occupied my mind; and he enabled me to understand the spiritual significance of Kant, and especially of the first Critique. I will always think of Berdyaev as an old, revered teacher (although I think Berdyaev, seemingly without pride or pretense, and wishing to impel his readers to be free rather than to follow him, would have been made uneasy by my reverence). But Berdyaev did not make me a Christian, at least not he alone.

It is harder to define the impact on my intellect and feelings of *Fyodor Dostoevsky*; the influences emanating from novels are probably more subtle and various than those emanating from philosophical writings. However, I read all of Dostoevsky's major novels five or six times over a period of several years, and I'm sure those works did much to confirm and shape my Christian faith. Thus Dostoevsky reinforced my awareness, gained first from Berdyaev, of freedom as the incomprehensible and uncontrollable core of a human being; he helped me (as Berdyaev had not) to see freedom as a bottomless reservoir of evil but, at the same time, to see God's mercy as more power-

ful than human sin; he enabled me to realize that sin cannot be
overcome by human devices of the kind that governments wield but
only by suffering and by grace; and he implanted deeply in my mind
the sense that when Christianity fades, as it has in our time, and as
Dostoevsky prophetically foresaw that it would, strange and terrible
consequences are apt to follow, consequences like those dramatized in
Raskolnikov (*Crime and Punishment*), Stavrogin (*The Possessed*) and
Ivan Karamazov (*The Brothers Karamazov*).

A third great thinker who always comes to mind when I try to
remember those who drew me into a Christian universe was, paradoxically, not a Christian. This is the Jewish philosopher *Martin Buber*.
Buber's thought is perhaps too simple to be quite adequate; the
concept of I-Thou relations leaves numerous metaphysical issues
untouched. And his political thought is not only too simple but too
optimistic as well; it seems that only a wondrous naiveté could have
allowed Buber to ignore the questions about his socialism that were
tacitly posed by thinkers such as Augustine, Machiavelli and Hobbes,
as well as by various modern writers influenced by the Christian
doctrine of original sin. Nonetheless, Buber was a very great intellect,
if we mean by that someone possessed of profound and exceptional
insights. Buber's concept of dialogue, an activity embracing not only
human beings but also God ("the eternal Thou"), is among the permanent furnishings of my mind. And it has decisively shaped my understanding of Christianity. If Christ is the Word, then he is a dialogic
figure, an interlocutor, so to speak, in conversations between God and
human beings.

Berdyaev, Dostoevsky and Buber did not merely affect the way I
looked at things. Partly from a natural affinity that seemed to bind me
to them and partly because I read them so fully and frequently, they
became, as it were, permanent residents in my intellectual universe.
My thinking tended to be a kind of continuing consultation with them.
This is true of two other thinkers as well, one of whom was *Karl Barth*.
I still remember the moment I came across one of the huge, black
volumes making up the *Church Dogmatics*. The book looked most
forbidding. For one thing, it was long (just short of seven hundred
pages) and the print was small. Also, Barth discussed matters like sin

and damnation, and I dreaded reading something which would make me feel that, due to my deeds in the Pacific, I was lost.

But I purchased the volume and read it. I found not only that my fears were unfulfilled (far from it, in view of Barth's eloquent emphasis on God's mercy) but also that I received doctrinal instruction of a kind not gained from anything else I had read. In subsequent years I purchased and read the rest of the twelve giant volumes making up Barth's masterwork (and some of them twice). Barth was a rigorous and highly orthodox theologian; he was also a dramatic writer. The *Church Dogmatics*, along with the electrifying *Epistle to the Romans*, provided me with a kind of theological education. Barth was an extremist, a theological Bolshevik, one might say, and I have never in any strict sense been a follower of his. But for years he has been indispensable to my spiritual morale, and he has probably taught me more about Christian doctrine than any other author.

Finally, I must mention the one American among my regular intellectual instructors and companions—*Reinhold Niebuhr*. By the time I started reading Niebuhr, shortly after finishing graduate work, I had given up Christian Science entirely (which did not happen in a single dramatic moment but through a slow process of erosion). Niebuhr greatly helped me to consolidate this development. He presented a pessimistic (or, more accurately, realistic) view of human nature and history; he did this in an eminently clear and logical fashion; and he brilliantly related his insights to the contemporary political world. His assistance was indispensable in enabling me to get on my feet, not only as a Christian but also as an inhabitant of the harsh political world of the twentieth century. If Niebuhr had a single guiding idea, it was that of original sin—sin as not merely one human trait among others but as an orientation of the soul, distorting and misdirecting all human traits. He wielded this idea with powerful effect in examining the political illusions of our time, and I still see it as one of the few indispensable components of political wisdom. Much of the tragic folly of our times, not only on the part of extremists such as Lenin but also on the part of middle-of-the-road liberals and conservatives, would never have arisen had we not, in our technological and ideological pride, forgotten original sin.

The twenty years during which I was inching my way toward Christianity was a time of intense study and reflection. I was absorbed daily and hourly by the enigmas and demands of the intellectual universe in which I dwelled, a universe populated not only by the five names I have mentioned but by numerous others—philosophers, theologians, political writers and novelists. I lived with books, as well as with notepads for jotting down the thoughts that came to me. I was absorbed in trying to understand my life, and life generally, and the short steps forward that I made were recorded in the lectures I inflicted on my students and in the articles and books I began to write.

It may sound as though my days, and my journey toward Christianity, were very cerebral, and indeed they were. Too much so, probably. I had a wife, someone of worth so inestimable that I count her along with my faith as one of the signs that God has not given me up. I also had two sons, little boys whom I delighted in and loved. I fear, however, that I was too deeply involved in intellectual trials and undertakings—and too wearied and exasperated by my failures—to be very satisfactory as a husband and father. But God does not forgive us just for grave misdeeds, long repented of, such as those I committed in Manila Bay. He forgives us, I believe, minute by minute, in response to the continuing stream of minor and not-so-minor misdeeds that, for most of us, mark the course of our fallen lives. Hence in spite of my inadequate performance of family duties I continued to be carried ahead on the raft of divine grace. I finally completed the long voyage that had begun in Christian Science and ended in Christian faith, the journey that led me from Plato to Christ, and from John Stuart Mill (of whom I wrote a systematic, if inept, defense in my doctoral dissertation) to such mentors as Berdyaev and Barth.

I still have not described the actual event of my becoming a Christian. There is good reason for this: no such event occurred. I can say only that I was not a Christian during my time as a graduate student and a young instructor whereas well before reaching the age of fifty I was. I can see two main reasons behind this development, one "existential," or personal, the other intellectual. The existential reason is that with my scarcely insignificant moral failures, I could only live as one forgiven by God. After Manila Bay I felt I had forfeited the right to live; only grace could restore that right. The intellectual reason is that among all the numerous creeds I studied, Christianity was by far the most interesting and convincing. Whether it would have been so interesting and convincing apart from my war experiences, I cannot say. It is rather unchristian, however, to give reasons for being a Christian. I have learned this, I suppose, from studying Barth's doctrine of election. If you are a Christian, this is not because *you* have made a choice but because *God* has made a choice. Christianity was written into your destiny on the day of your creation. This is not so arrogant a statement as a non-Christian might suppose. As my own case makes so starkly manifest, to be chosen by God presupposes no merit whatever of your own; nor is it in any other sense an achievement that redounds to your credit. It is only a matter of unending gratitude.

Just as Christianity is not something you choose, nor something you hold on to for certain specific reasons, neither is it something to which you can assign a value. Living as a Christian does, to be sure, bring hints of ultimate peace and joy that impel us to think of Christianity as possessing great value. Thinking that way is risky, however. It may subtly insinuate into our minds the idea that there is a higher standard in terms of which the value of Christianity can be judged. But that demeans Christianity, which is itself the highest standard. We judge all else by the Christian standard and cannot judge Christianity itself. In other words, attributing value to Christianity may cause us to forget that Christianity is not a part of life, not even a part that is immeasurably more valuable than any other part. It is simply life itself.

Judging the value of Christian faith is risky too because it may tempt us to exaggerate the degree of our happiness. Christians often do this. They seemingly feel obliged to paint their daily pleasures and satisfactions in glowing spiritual colors. But Christianity does not promise earthly happiness, not even the happiness of feeling the immediate presence of God. Can you, for example, read the letters of Paul and then embrace Christianity in the expectation that it will, in any ordinary sense, make your life better? Christian existence, one must remember, is a drama of estrangement (for me, Christian Science) and reconciliation, of sin (Manila Bay) and redemption. Living through such a drama is likely sometimes, surely, to be trying and difficult. Even grace may be harsh. Suffering may be the fire in which a new soul is forged. In my own experience, only once, far out in the Pacific Ocean—at the ends of the earth—have I been consciously lifted up by grace. This was on reading Psalm 118:24. But of course I am not saying that grace has had no part in my life. Let me illustrate the part I think it has had by something told me by a friend.

The friend lived in my hometown in the West. He would often hike, alone, into the Sierra foothills prospecting for gold, also, I think, glorying in the dramatic mountain and desert scene that lay all about him. There were known to be mountain lions where he hiked. Mountain lions are mysterious, even mystical, creatures. They are almost never seen, even in areas they inhabit; they are benign, for rarely do they attack human beings, although they are among the large predatory cats and can kill sizable animals in an instant; and they possess great beauty and grace. I once asked my friend whether he had ever seen a mountain lion on any of his prospecting ventures. He said that he hadn't. He said also, however, that often when he hiked into a mountain canyon, then late in the afternoon turned back, retracing his steps, he would find the tracks of a mountain lion near his own tracks, made earlier in the day. He would know that a mountain lion had been paying him close attention, even though he never saw the lion. My friend's experience might serve as a parable of my own life with God. I can't claim ever to have had even a glimpse of God. When I look back on my life, however, I see his tracks all around the places where I have been.

16

Down by the Cross

PATRICIA RAYBON

Journalism &
Mass Communication

University of Colorado

When you've got too much religion that you can't mingle
with people, that you're afraid of certain people,
you've got too much religion.
—BAPTIST PREACHER C. L. FRANKLIN

---

*H*e came at daybreak. That's when I first met Jesus. I was just twenty-three but I was divorcing a husband. I was a young mother with a year-old child. I was jobless, despite a new college degree. And I was broke, a prodigal daughter come home for atonement and renewal in my good parents' home.

Come on back, they said. So I went.

Then they did the remarkable. They never once said "we told you so." They just put up a crib in my old bedroom, a girl's room still dressed in pale blue and soft ruffles. They bought baby food and diapers. They ordered nursery books and toys.

Then my daddy, a tall brown man with strong arms and quiet ways, spoke in his soft voice the words that would change forever my mortal life: "You need to open your Bible."

He didn't elaborate. There was no fussing or lectures. On that morning, Daddy just quietly left me in his living room, leaving me a choice. So I lifted the big Bible from its place on my parents' coffee table and I opened it, surprised that the words of my recovery had been underlined years before with my father's black-ink pen.

There is therefore now no condemnation to them which are in Christ Jesus (Romans 8:1 KJV).

I saw my daddy's past, linked up with my mother's dreams, all these things tied together with my future and underscored in ink years ago by my father's hopeful hand.

And we know that all things work together for good to them that love God (Romans 8:28 KJV).

I saw the themes of colored Easter plays and children's choirs and sunny Sunday-school rooms where sweet brown women in white missionary dresses once taught children like me the words of their Savior.

Father, forgive them; for they know not what they do (Luke 23:34 KJV).

Through fresh tears, I dared now to ask that Savior for forgiveness for myself, calling on a God I'd sung about as a child and now was crying before as a woman.

Help me, Jesus.

I cried at daybreak. *Help me, Jesus.*

It is a believer's first prayer.

But I'm not just any believer.

My skin is dark.

And Jesus was a white man when I was growing up. He was blond and meek, a beautiful white shepherd smiling in a portrait hanging in the Sunday-school room. A Savior with long hair and blue eyes. A man meant to be loved. So we worshiped him.

We sang in our little black church, lifting our voices with complete conviction to the lovely Messiah:

"Oh, how I love Jesus!"

From a toddler, I knew all the melodies, all the words.

Jesus loves me, this I know,
For the Bible tells me so.
Red and yellow, black and white,

They are precious in his sight.

The Christian message, with all of its fantastic paradoxes, provided our framework for coping in a hostile world: Love your enemies. Do good to those who hate you. Pray for those who persecute you. Do not repay evil with evil. Trust in Jesus.

Trust in Jesus.

I heard it every Sunday, every week, every year of my life as a black child in that small church in northeast Denver, and over time I just believed the message and every angle that went with it. Kneeling at an altar to "eat his body" and "drink the blood of the new testament" seemed not only perfectly reasonable but absolutely desirable. And sweet-smelling dark women who fried chicken for church dinners and served up lemon cake and iced tea and soft hugs affirmed this.

Trust Jesus, they told me. Ask him for anything, honey. "Just call him up and tell him what you want." The gospel song directed me, but so did the unshakable belief of the colored preachers and teachers and family and friends who filled every corner of my life. They talked about Jesus as if he were sitting right there in their kitchens, as if he were walking around the sanctuary of the Cleaves Memorial Christian Methodist Episcopal Church, a living and breathing real-time God, right there in our northeast Denver ghetto, in our very midst. So, almost casually, the preacher and the missionary sisters and my daddy would every Sunday tell each other so matter-of-factly: Just tell Jesus. Just tell the Lord. He will save you *now*.

Jesus was white, but he would save me. He was depicted as white, anyway, but that didn't deter us. In fact, it didn't occur to me to challenge this racialized depiction. Years later, when I was in college, the black power movement questioned the irony of black Christians in America loving a "white" God. In response, black churches started displaying paintings of God and Jesus as black men. But I experienced as much tension with this latter racialized "makeover" as I did with the earlier blond representations of our Messiah.

But during my childhood, I wasn't perplexed. Maybe that's because Jesus seemed more than a man. He symbolized a way of life, a moral code, that directed our thinking. He set our strategy, so critical to colored people in the unfriendly fifties—with their Jim Crow laws and hostile looks. His two-thousand-year-old lessons fit our personal crises —not just for important matters, such as illness or job discrimination, but for the smallest affairs of everyday colored life. I share the following personal story as an illustration.

As a child I dreaded getting my rough hair pressed straight by a hairdresser whose hot-comb technique left my scalp feeling scorched— too sore to touch for days. Every two weeks, on Saturday morning, the dreaded pressing comb—heated under a high flame on the hairdresser's kitchen stove—was dragged across the hairs on my scalp, flattening my woolly kinks into something close to smooth, a high hiss from the sizzling comb accompanying each curl. It took two hours to finish "one head," and I was in agony every searing minute. Any phone call to the hairdresser, on the fortnight, left me reeling with dread.

But this Saturday I was praying—eyes squeezed tight, clinging to the bedpost in my bedroom, whispering hard to Jesus, asking him to *please, God, save me today. Jesus, please help me.* My mother found me on my knees, but she didn't ask what I was doing. Instead, she seemed bothered about something and launched into a complaint about the hairdresser. It seems the woman had a conflict that day and couldn't fit me into her regular hairdressing schedule. Without notice, she'd canceled my appointment!

Hallelujah!! Trust Jesus! Trust him all the time. Call him up. Any time. All the time. He will save you from sickness and Jim Crow and hot pressing combs. I believed this.

This primal faith called "religion" was the deepest part of my black life as a child—the part that I hid, as much as I could, from the few white people I knew then.

White people, indeed, seemed so rational. So controlled. They defined religious civility with their own quiet hymns that they sang so carefully and so neatly. I watched them on television, wearing choir robes that fit and singing every word so perfectly, worshiping their Christian God who looked so much like them. At the same time, our black expression of that same faith was raw and wild, and utterly transparent. *Help me, Jesus! Help me, Lord!* Every Sunday our church sanctuary was filled with this open, unbridled worship, unhampered by form or pretense. These brown saints loved the Lord, and when it came to praise, they didn't hold back.

So, quite naturally, when our church invited a white Lutheran pastor and his youth group to our service one Sunday, I was horrified. It was the right thing to do. A good thing. A very decent thing to do in those times—the late fifties. But I was terrified, fearing that the Holy Ghost would sweep up the saintly sisters and lay them in the aisles, leaving them shouting and jumping and wailing, "Thank you, Jesus! THANK YOU, JESUS!"

All my senses were on alert, knowing the inevitable would soon envelop the little sanctuary. The service started without incident, marked only by the usual murmured "amens" during the opening prayers and songs. But with white people in attendance, even quiet amens sounded uncomfortably loud that morning. I flinched a bit every time I heard the word, worried it would offend the ears of the white people there, praying at the same time that nothing uncomely and "wild" would mar this Sunday gathering—hoping against hope, really, because the air already was tense, with racial strain certainly but also with pent-up praise.

Then, as if on cue, a favorite singer stood up in the choir loft and walked solemnly to a microphone near the pulpit. It was time for her solo. Some of the saints were on their feet already, clapping their hands wildly and shouting amen at the woman, and she hadn't even started singing. The soloist, a thin, short woman nearly lost in a billowy blue choir robe far too long for her petite frame, waved a tiny brown hand in acknowledgment and looked soulfully heavenward. Then the pianist launched into the opening strains of "Precious Lord," and one long wail rose from the audience.

A missionary sister was already crying, moved by the opening notes of the gospel song. She waved her old brown hands in the air, and I slumped deeper in my chair, knowing that on this song the Holy Ghost would take over, surely terrifying the white people.

Then it happened, of course. A whole row of missionary sisters leaped to their feet almost in unison, shrieking and shouting and swaying with emotion and praise. I couldn't breathe for a moment. And I felt betrayed. We were seen raw, emotionally naked before white people, and my embarrassment nearly suffocated me. I closed my eyes, shutting out the spiritual display—the moaning and jumping and falling and shouting. The church atmosphere was flush with the sounds and sights of Holy Ghost emotion. This was how black people worshiped our Jesus, and white people, surely, couldn't understand it. When I got enough nerve to look over at the white teenagers, to gauge their reaction, it was worse than I had imagined. Their eyes were wide as plates, their faces red with discomfort, maybe even fear, as they watched the missionary sisters whirling like tops in the aisles and shrieking, "Thank you, Jesus! THANK YOU, JESUS!"

Then the ushers rushed down with their fans and handkerchiefs, ready to calm the overwhelmed saints. But the soloist wouldn't stop singing, her choir backing her up on every note. The pianist kept the pace, pounding out chords, her head thrown back, her own mouth opened wide like a tunnel—shouting the song herself toward the lights on the ceiling. "Precious Lord! Take my hand!" The atmosphere in the church had grown taut as a swollen balloon, and the sound pressed against the walls, the ceiling, the stained-glass windows, the frayed red carpet and the funeral-home fans, threatening when it exploded to splinter every eardrum and every window and every inch of plaster and wood holding up that little black church, as the sisters moaned, "THANK YOU, JESUS! JESUS, THANK YOU, MASTER!"—not caring that the wide eyes of the white people were glued on the scene, unbelieving.

Just as it seemed that we would all just vaporize right there from the heated tension in the room, the singing slowed and finally stopped. I was thankful.

A queer quiet descended on the sanctuary. The only sounds coming from the missionary ladies were soft moans. The ushers wiped one last drop of sweat from one last overheated brow. Their God had reigned.

And now, years later, my daddy was directing me to this same God, a Savior who might take me out of myself and leave me unbridled and raw with gratitude, a God who could save me from a sad divorce and bad mistakes. And, my daddy's Bible said, that Savior's name was Jesus.

Where does Jesus fit when you're twenty-three and brown and confused? You can't say his name out loud. That means you're crazy. You can't confess him as Savior because in his picture he's white and, if you love him, you're a traitor. A honky lover. A kook. An oreo Negro stunned by religion, numbed by too much pork fat and fried chicken and gospel singing.

It takes a deep, deep breath to call on Jesus.

I was colored in America in the seventies. It took all the faith I could muster to call on him then—knowing that my troubles were more complicated than divorce.

That's what I love about Jesus, in fact. I pray to him and he answers, not with the conclusion I expect but with a new insight and a fresh hope.

So I prayed to Jesus and, in a miracle, I experienced first that "peace that passeth all understanding," an odd calmness, actually, that granted me an undeserving assurance that everything would work out okay.

As the miracle evolved, I was directed not just to work out of a sad marriage but to remake my heart and my eyes and my soul. Eventually I remarried, and my new husband said years later that Jesus completes everything and that, in particular, Jesus was rounding us out. Forging us. Finishing us according to *his* will.

For me, the completion came first in my soul, stung for so many years by the complication and convolution of race in my nation. Here, indeed, is the awful truth of it:

I hated white people.

I was angry at a former husband. But I hated white people.

I hated that they had seemingly ignored my crisis, all of it for me involving our American configuration of race. And I hated that some had done this in church, using the Bible to justify unthinkable laws and bad thinking, barring us from their sanctuaries and their schools and their neighborhoods and their lives, and saying that God ordained it, when God didn't ordain that brokenness. And I hated that they got to say who counted—and I didn't count. And I didn't know how to fix any of this. And *that* problem, said Jesus—this racial turbulence in my soul—was the problem I needed to tackle now.

Confusion about race, which had overwhelmed me from my very first breath, was the matter I needed to scrutinize. So I wrote a book about making peace with white people, *My First White Friend*.[1] It carried me into crevices in my soul that only a merciful God could heal. But I found those fissures burning not just with rage at white people but with festering resentment against old family hurts.

I was stunned by this. The book I was writing became a book about making peace first with my family and with myself and even with my God. And I cried as I wrote the book because the damage was big.

It was an old hurt with bad scars, and the surgery was messy. But, thanks be to God, Jesus cuts clean, healing those wounds and covering them with a fresh outlook. And the pain ended.

That is why I am a Christian. When I called on Jesus, he delivered a remedy. Prayer begat peace. Scripture begat insight. Worship begat wonderment with the triune God—the Father, the Son and the Holy Ghost. And Jesus was the door. I crossed that threshold in faith, believing that in the spiritual life, as prescribed by Christ, I would find a resolution for hate. I did.

However, please consider this: I could have hated Jesus as the symbol of everything that had stopped my early progress in America —the symbol of the "white" church and everything it seemingly had failed to do and the moral conscience it seemingly had failed to be, for having more religion than love.

But I called Jesus' name. *Help me, Jesus.*

And that prayer of belief changed my essential life, not because I held onto that life but because I was willing to let it go. I conceded that hate was bad. It was killing me, in fact, even though some days I confess that the hate felt so good. But hate sours. I had to open my heart and release it. All of it, one day at a time, as much as I was able, with Jesus' help, to just let that hate fly away.

But this is the first unspeakable thing about the Christian faith, this thing that, indeed, is inexplicable because trusting Jesus is first about surrender. It is a giving up of old ways and worn-out ideas and festering fears, not just about white people but about all people, even myself.

I had to admit that Christianity was not a "white" thing or a "black" thing but a "Jesus" thing. That's the slogan of a local megachurch in my suburb that attracts thousands of worshipers every Sunday with its white gospel preacher, its black gospel music, its Hispanic associate pastors, its Asian immigrant services, its women's ministry, its televised prison ministry, its deaf translation for the hearing-impaired ministry and, its latest addition, a translator for Russian-speaking immigrants who have been moving in significant numbers to my area. It is a church for all people that worships a Christ for all nations. Not a white Christ. Not a black Christ.

And the place is overflowing, liberated from old ideas about "white churches" and "black churches," striving instead to be Christ's church. Period.

I, likewise, had to uncouple Christ and whiteness to make peace with blackness, to transcend all of that and finally learn to hear my essential God.

And God's music was even sweeter than gospel singing. It was liberation music, affirming the New Testament promise that to be set free by Christ is to be set free indeed. Maybe that's because Jesus understood that hunger to be free.

He himself was an outsider, a marginalized Jew, mocked by the slanderous question, recorded in the Fourth Gospel, about Jesus' humble hometown: "Can there any good thing come out of Nazareth?" (John 1:46 KJV).

Nazareth was "no place," in other words, a small village partly secluded in the hills at the northern edge of the Plain of Esdraelon, halfway between the Mediterranean Sea and the Sea of Galilee. Its mud-brick houses were huddled together on the side of a small hill, "some distance from the main road," according to one account. About a hundred people lived in Nazareth in Jesus' time, mostly farmers and a few craftsmen like Jesus' father, Joseph the carpenter. The setting was humble, but the view from the tops of nearby hills around the tiny hamlet was spectacular, a vista that stretched for miles across the immense Plain of Esdraelon where heroes like Gideon, Barak, Saul and the Maccabees had fought Israel's enemies. Conquering armies of Assyria, Babylonia, Persia and Greece had all marched through it.

Jesus' family was poor and unlearned, just common folk in the eyes of the temple elite who were outraged when Jesus, as a young man, began his ministry by teaching and healing without sanction in the local synagogue, even on the sabbath.

The locals were appalled, asking, "Where did this man get these things? . . . What's this wisdom that has been given him, that he even does miracles? Isn't this the carpenter? Isn't this Mary's son?" (Mark 6:2-3).

He was just a neighbor boy, now grown up. And here he was teaching and exhorting and healing. And the locals were outraged, scandalized by Jesus' boldness, his assurance as he preached in "their" temple —the only temple in tiny Nazareth.

In their eyes he was out of line, a line that I walked every day as I vainly tried to be more than "colored" by declaring my dignity. I was very much an outsider in the temple of America and felt like one. At my university I am sometimes forced to answer questions from people who think that I, as an African-American, must have obtained my faculty position without honor. It has been an exhausting existence, often on the defense, rarely good enough or smart enough or orderly enough to satisfy every standard of this exacting and skeptical world.

But now I turn to the words of Jesus, my Savior, for comfort. He cuts through every moment of stress and doubt: "Come to me, all you who are weary and burdened, and I will give you rest. Take my yoke upon you and learn from me, for I am gentle and humble in heart, and you will find rest for your souls. For my yoke is easy and my burden is light" (Matthew 11:28-30).

It is an invitation I can accept only by faith.

Believing in Jesus feels good because it is not, at least initially, an intellectual activity: it is an expression of pure faith. And I need faith to live in America. More than learning or money or credentials. I need faith, and Jesus supplies it to me just as I am. I can't be smart enough for Jesus, or clean enough or good enough or nice enough. My hair will never be straight enough. But I am enough for Jesus. Just as I am. Thus I sit quietly with a Bible in my arms, and before even opening it, I experience that unlikely "intercourse between dust and divinity," as my church pastor describes the spiritual path.

It is a spiraling road that leads ever upward and is barricaded with obstacles I can't fully negotiate. I can't offer proof of Jesus' virgin birth or his resurrection from the dead or his promise of eternal life. I just read my Bible and ponder the stories and the words and the insight. This experience of understanding and hope adds up to a walk with the now and living Christ.

And race isn't even in the picture.

And that makes me laugh out loud and jump around and wave my arms and lift my hands with joy and praise. I have become a mission-ary sister, looking on Sunday mornings and Wednesday-night worship services for all the world like the brown holy women who filled my childhood church with their heated hallelujahs and joyous praise.

I am elevated by Jesus. With him I rise above the fickleness of race consciousness. And that feels good—an emotional response, not an intellectual one, but an undeniable response nevertheless. Believing in Jesus and worshiping him and feeding on bread from heaven—his word—takes me above and beyond the secular experience of trying to figure out myself to myself. It takes me beyond our artificial human orders, our segregated Sundays and our pious proclamations that are heard in both black and white churches.

It propels me into a realm that animates my spiritual core. This goes beyond mere meditation, however. Believing in Jesus introduces me to a knowledge that I can't fully know, but I do know that I can't stop searching for it. However, just the partial knowledge of the Energy that I call God excites an element of my being that I can't dismiss or ignore. In that manner, Jesus absolutely activates all of my intellectual connections.

Thus the effect of Christianity is that I can now understand and accept things I'm supposed to decry. I can now love people I'm supposed to hate. I can go places I'm supposed to fear. I can do things I'm supposed to avoid because according to the world I'm not supposed to be smart enough or good enough to try them.

But Jesus tells me that I am enough.

I can't explain why it works. But I know that trusting the triune arrangement of Christianity nurtures, affirms, assures and thoroughly vitalizes me, mostly because I can activate it only by faith.

Billy Graham, the renowned evangelist, wrote in his 1997 autobiog-raphy, *Just As I Am*, of this "impenetrable mystery," describing his early struggle to accept the Bible as completely true. One night as he was walking alone in the moonlight at a retreat center in the San Bernardino Mountains, he dropped to his knees and placed his Bible on a tree stump, able only to "stutter" into a prayer: "Oh God! There are many things in this book I do not understand. There are many problems with it for which I have no solution. There are many seeming contradictions. There are some areas in it that do not seem to correlate with modern science. I can't answer some of the philosophical and psychological questions [that a friend, Chuck] and others are raising."

Graham wrote that he was trying to come clean with God "but something remained unspoken." At last "the Holy Spirit freed me to say it. 'Father, I am going to accept this as Thy Word—by faith! I'm going to allow faith to go beyond my intellectual questions and doubts, and I will believe this to be Your inspired Word.'"

When he stood up, he said he understood that not all his questions were answered. But "I knew a spiritual battle in my soul had been fought and won"—with the pivotal factor in this war being a declaration of faith.[2]

Likewise, I trusted that morning twenty-five years ago, sitting in the sunlight in my parents' living room—trusted that a holy and loving God was hearing my cries and would deliver me. I needed immediate comfort and the assurance that I could recover myself and move on from that sour divorce. I found that promise in the words of Scripture: "There is therefore now no condemnation to them which are in Christ Jesus." This quote is found in the eighth chapter of the apostle Paul's letter to the early Christian church at Rome, written in about A.D. 56 or 57. But when my daddy, in the A.D. 1940s, underlined the words with his black-ink pen, and when I read the words in the A.D. 1950s, we both were encountering an answer to all of our many dilemmas—starting with race, certainly, but transcending even that large pain.

In Jesus, colored Americans find that balm.

But white people, it turns out, were looking for it too.

So Jesus comes at daybreak. He is the daybreak—bursting through our human frailties with the light that fills up our shadows. Thus he completes us with himself—saving us from having too much religion, gifting us instead with enough faith to become the sons and daughters of the great, eternal and essential God. At the same time giving us the courage to meld as sisters and brothers and, in that bond, to become one with our God.

He helps us do the impossible.

The psalmist, praising God, put it this way: "With your help I can advance against a troop; with my God I can scale a wall" (Psalm 18:29).

The wall of racial malevolence gripping my heart crumbled like the wall around Jericho (Joshua 5:13—6:20), not because I convinced white people to change themselves but because I allowed God to change me.

The gospel language of colored church songs puts it more plainly: "It's me, it's me, it's me, O Lord, standing in the need of prayer. Not my brother, not my sister, but it's me, O Lord. Standing in the need of prayer."

Or consider this: From deep space, the weary Earth looks like a tiny blue dot—our human affairs reduced to a pinprick; our wars and conflicts a mere jot in the vastness of heaven.

Surely, on this isolated ball, we can make some peace.

The holy people say it best. Here is Nelson Mandela: "We have forgotten our differences."

Yebo! Yebo! Abba Mandela. Nelson Rolihlahla Mandela: "We have forgotten our differences."

And Jesus: "My command is this: Love each other as I have loved you" (John 15:12).

We can forget our differences, the Messiah promises—even that odd and odious complication of "race"—and along the way, as we press our way home, we will find uncommon rest for our weary souls.

And the sun will rise on our efforts.

And the people of God all said amen.

Help me, Jesus.

Thank you, Jesus!

Amen.

Notes

[1]Patricia Raybon, *My First White Friend: Confessions on Race, Love and Forgiveness* (New York: Viking/Penguin, 1996).

[2]Billy Graham, *Just As I Am* (San Francisco: HarperSanFrancisco/Zondervan, 1997).

17

Marxism and Me

MARVIN OLASKY

Journalism

University of Texas

Man without God is a beast, and never more beastly
than when he is most intelligent about his beastliness.
—WHITTAKER CHAMBERS

The debate at Big University in 1995 was ostensibly about welfare reform, but the real subject for the professor of social work and his coterie of students was capitalist exploitation. "Some of us fight against exploitation [hooray] and some of us join in [hiss]." The rhetoric and response did not irritate me because twenty-five years earlier I had been a student member of the hurrah-and-hiss drill team. But the professor had more to say: "And the immigrants at the beginning of this century, whom Olasky claims were helped by the provision of effective compassion, were even more ruthlessly exploited."

That was too much for me. Insult me, insult my intellectual and political teammates who are working to replace welfare, but don't insult my grandparents by saying they were exploited and too dumb to notice. They all came from the Russian empire shortly before World War I and found the streets of America paved not with gold but with liberty, which, in the hands of people who wanted to work hard, amounted to virtually the same thing.

My father's father had the wisdom to desert from the Russian army and make his way through Europe to New York and then to Boston, where he became a boilermaker. Louis Olasky worked for a capitalist so exploitive that he was able to save money, buy a home, go to the synagogue regularly and otherwise prosper without running afoul of the government—an amazing prospect for someone used to the czar's tender mercies. My mother's father was also terribly exploited. Robert Green drove a horse and wagon through the streets of Malden, Massachusetts, picking up used mattresses that he could recondition and sell at a profit without having to pay bribes to the czar's men. My grandparents were able to build a better material life for their children, and they for their children.

I was a material beneficiary of all that hard work. The spiritual side was to be taken care of by Hebrew school, which I attended after public school for seven years. I learned Jewish customs, ceremonies and history, and read the Hebrew Scriptures and a little Talmud. But by the time I was fourteen, the rituals that were at the heart of my family's practice seemed inadequate. It puzzled me that the sacrificial system designed to cover over sins could simply end two thousand years ago without God's setting up something else to take its place. More fundamental, however, was a desire not to think about sin, or even limitations. I excelled in school and became used to receiving praise for "creative thinking . . . independent analysis . . . questioning dogmas." There were no moral boundaries, and the intellectual arrogance that won praise from liberal teachers prepared me to win scholarships and enter Yale, where I was ripe for further training by professors and graduate students who relished the radical.

What I remember most about college is that I could do and write the silliest things and receive plaudits, as long as my lunacy was leftward. I received honors grades for, among other things, cutting out pictures from old Red Sox yearbooks and interspersing them with commentary about baseball racism; describing my own atheism and then claiming that such belief was at the core of the American tradition; taking a black cat in a bag to a course in the art museum, letting him out on the floor and explaining that I had just created a work of art that showed how the Black Panthers were freeing themselves from the container in which American society placed members of their race. (The cat ran away and hid among some expensive canvases, prompting a frenzied search.)

In 1969 I convinced a college council to make one of the janitors an honorary Yale fellow. *Life* ran an affectionate article about the bemused proletarian and me. In 1970, when students such as I wanted to travel around protesting the Vietnam War, the college called off the last month of classes. In 1971, when I participated in a five-day hunger strike outside the administration building, the college president offered us his sympathies. Once, when my roommates and I went to Washington to educate members of Congress about their deceitfulness, Speaker John McCormick took us into the House chamber and let each of us spin around in his big chair.

Journalism also fanned my pride. As a twenty-year-old intern on the *Boston Globe*, I could go into a suburban Boston community, spend a day talking to people about a complicated issue, write an article that was probably filled with gross misunderstandings but was nevertheless correctly progressive, and the *Globe* would print it without even checking to see if I had gotten it right. The day after graduation I headed west from Boston on a bicycle and pedaled to Oregon, where I became a reporter on a small-town newspaper. With some physical toughness now to go along with my intellectual superiority, I would proceed to educate the residents of Deschutes County on the way things ought to be. I wrote snotty articles and was surprised when the bourgeoisie took umbrage. My publisher tried to explain to me that I was not the center of the world. Being quick to speak and slow to listen, I grandiosely resigned and pushed further left.

I had become a casual Marxist in college and in 1972 spent six months writing a draft of the great proletarian novel and reading Marx and Lenin. I joined the Communist Party and thought I had it all figured out. Communists were the most enlightened heirs of the Enlightenment. There was no God who could change people from the inside out, and anyway, ordinary individuals were unimportant. Radical change could come only outside in, by shifting the socioeconomic environment; the only way to do so quickly and decisively was through dictatorial action by a wise collective of leaders who would act for the good of all. I, of course, would be one of those leaders.

CPUSA activities—distributing party newspapers, playing chess at parties with Paul Robeson music in the background—were uninspiring, but I joined to ride on the big bear. The Soviet Union was then on a roll, with America heading out of Vietnam and apparently ready to retreat around the world. A trip in 1972 across the Pacific on a Soviet freighter and across my new fatherland on the Trans-Siberian railroad should have disillusioned me, but Lenin had said it would be necessary to "crawl on one's belly, like a snake," for the good of the revolution, and I was ready to slither.

In 1973 I worked at the *Boston Globe* and then went on to graduate school at the University of Michigan. Professors there were so impressed by my theorizing that they wrote recommendations citing my "brilliance" and "genius." They also increased my fellowship. (Get Marx. It pays.) Each month I paid my party dues, pasting the dues stamps bearing Lenin's picture onto a genuine Communist Party card.

We were all full of ourselves and our own wisdom, and we were vindictive toward anyone who might get in our way. Once I sneered to comrades that my Russian language instructor, a morose escapee from Moscow, had said that he would cut his throat if Communists ever came to power in the United States. A sweet young CP lady replied, "That old fool won't have to cut his throat. We'll do it for him." And I wanted to be there, at least holding the coats of those who wielded long knives.

One day near the end of 1973 I was reading Lenin's famous essay "Socialism and Religion," in which he wrote, "We must combat religion—this is the ABC of all materialism, and consequently Marxism." But a small whisper made itself heard somewhere within me and it became a repeated, resounding question: "What if Lenin is wrong? What if there is a God?"

My communism was based on atheism, and when I could no longer be an atheist, I resigned from the party. In 1974, with the goal of satisfying a Ph.D. language requirement by improving my reading knowledge of Russian, I plucked from my bookcase a Russian New Testament that had been given to me as a novelty item two years before. To my surprise, what had before seemed like superstition now had the ring of truth. (It helped that I had to read it very slowly and puzzle over many words.) In 1975, when I was assigned to teach a course in early American literature, my preparation involved reading Puritan sermons. Those dead white males also made great sense to me.

During the mid-1970s I went through an intellectual change. When I was a communist I believed that humanity's problems were external and that revolution was the solution. But Bible and sermon reading pushed me to see that the problem was internal and the cure was personal. God reconfigured my psychology so that the arrogance that had previously characterized me was largely gone. I remain a sinner and still have periods of self-centeredness, but ego does not control me as it used to. I no longer exalt my wisdom above God's. Reading the whole Bible helped me to confess sin. The New Testament clearly lays out the full gravity of humankind's problem and the full opportunity for redemption. When I was baptized and joined a church in 1976, I did not agonize about leaving Judaism to accept Christ, since I had left Judaism a long time before. Joining a church seemed like a homecoming.

My political philosophy changed along with my theology. I began to see family and business as God-given aids in the pursuit of true happiness. I became a partisan of governmental decentralization, since the doctrine of original sin suggests that those who gain godlike power act like the devil. Because people are prone to sin, it is vital to create a social environment that does not foster depravity. American history is a story of striving for liberty and virtue. God can change people, no matter how self-centered, as he changed me. Transforming people one by one, not passing legislation or writing checks, leads to social transformation. We must serve one another directly, following Christ's example.

As I began to write from a nascent biblical worldview, my academic reputation began to fall. I received a Ph.D. in 1976 only through the support of the one conservative in the Michigan history department, Stephen Tonsor. He came on to chair my dissertation committee after the previous chairman, who had written glowingly about my intellect when I was spouting communist dialectic, decided that I had suddenly become stupid. Because the academic environment had grown so politically hostile toward me, I left it to join the Du Pont public affairs department in 1978.

By 1983, however, I returned to academe because I wanted more freedom to research and write on my own. During the next six years at the University of Texas, faced with a publish-or-perish mandate, I dug deep but narrow holes in the history of journalism and public relations. Since Christianity was central to my being, I began to couple implicitly biblical academic writing with writing that made the principles explicit. For example, I began editing (and writing some of) a series of sixteen books called the Turning Point Christian Worldview Series. I also wrote the first of two books on the history of abortion in America.

Following our marriage in 1976, my wife, Susan, and I had three children by birth and a fourth by adoption, between 1977 and 1990. We put our faith into action by volunteering in various ways. I came to believe that mustard-seed-sized groups can grow and change America because I have seen efforts that began at my kitchen table affect for the better a little piece of our country. For example, Susan started a crisis pregnancy center in Austin shortly after we arrived. Over the years, that center has saved hundreds of lives by helping pregnant women discover alternatives to abortion. If folk like us can do a few kind things, through God's grace, then I see no reason why many people cannot do the same.

My book *The Tragedy of American Compassion* came out of historical research that I did at the Library of Congress in 1989 and 1990. The criticism I often receive about welfare replacement proposals is that they are overly optimistic about what volunteers can accomplish. But millions of ordinary people keep this country going by building enterprises and praying to the Lord of all. These people are the ones we speak to in *World*, the weekly Christian newsmagazine that I edit. These are the people I try to keep in mind as I write because in quiet ways they do heroic things and, if challenged, can do even more. They are people like my grandparents who should not be underestimated: people whose task is to ask not what they can do for their country but what their country can encourage them to do, without impediment, for their families, neighbors and others in need.

177

18

This Calls for a Map

Philip J. Gersmehl

Geography

University of Minnesota

Whatever your hand finds to do, do it with your might.
—QOHELETH

The debate—about taxes and urban policy—threatened to go on forever. Strident voices shouted "too much" and "who needs it?" In the midst of it all a geographer quietly laid four maps on a table. The maps had been drawn by students in an inner-city high school, which gave them a certain kind of authenticity in the eyes of some. Others viewed them with suspicion, demanding to know what the data sources were and how the maps were compiled.

The first map was basically a road map with a mass of black and red lines. A cluster of small dark squares indicated the central business district of a city. Pastel colors in the upper right corner suggested that several areas differed qualitatively from the rest of the city. The map legend clarified the distinction: these were suburbs and were politically separate from the city. Americans accept this separation as "normal," but the distinction is rare in the rest of the world. Hidden inside that sentence, said the geographer, is a key point: what is "normal," "obvious" or "true" in one place may not be in another place.

The second map showed the amount of tax money spent for school crossing guards. The students got this information from city budgets and made a map of the tax as a percentage of family income—dark colors (more tax burden) in the city, lighter colors in the suburbs. Those familiar with the pattern of income in an American city are not surprised by this result. People who live in inner cities often have relatively low incomes. If they want a specific municipal service, they usually have to pay a higher share of their income to get it. This map showed that the people in this city were willing to pay the price in order to get a specific service they thought they needed, namely, school crossing guards.

The third map had about forty red dots on it. Each dot showed the location of a traffic accident where a pedestrian child was injured or killed by an automobile driver who lived in one of the suburbs. Like many truly profound statements, the map is deceptively simple. Many hours of digging through accident reports went into gathering the information. Laid on the table, this map has a starkly simple message: most of the dots were in a relatively small area between the pastel suburbs and the central business district. The first map showed that this area has no limited-access freeways. For that reason, commuters have to use "surface streets" to get through the area on their way from the suburbs to downtown.

The final map of the four adds an important dimension to the debate. This map shows the percentage of the population that the Census Bureau records as "black." Like the maps of many American cities, this one has darker colors (more African-American people) in the inner-city area and lighter colors in the suburbs.

Individually, none of the maps is particularly surprising. Together, however, they make it all but impossible for a thoughtful human being to accept the claim that suburban residents "have no moral or fiscal responsibility for the problems of the inner city." Ironically, one of the witnesses at this hearing made this very claim less than half an hour before the four maps were put on the table.

Why four maps? Couldn't the message fit on just one? Perhaps, but that is a tactical decision, and for good pedagogical reasons someone might choose to delay the "punch line." Presenting the first two maps as separate, simple and easy to digest might add to the impact of the third map. In this particular case, the maps had the desired effect: People began to consider old opinions in a new light.

It Could Be a Call, If You Believe It Is

How can I see a call from God in these maps? Because they say that by using a particular kind of talent—analyzing the world through the seemingly narrow perspective of a geographer, seeking to discern and interpret locational patterns—we can uncover information that has important ethical implications. In effect, these four maps helped some people realize that a change was needed in order to "be fair." It is impressive that even high-school-level mapmaking could have this effect.

Admittedly, the maps could support multiple interpretations. People who are inclined to conspiracy theories could cite the maps as "proof" of several "truths," ranging from racist domination to genetic inferiority. Others might assert that mapmaking is just a job and there is no reason to describe it as some kind of divine "call." So be it—those opinions make my example even more valid as a microcosm of the world I live in, a world in which unquestioning faith coexists with skeptical inquiry, and personal choices must be made in the context of incomplete knowledge.

In this world, said Martin Luther, we should sin boldly but believe more boldly still. I heard Luther's aphoristic statement often through childhood (as a son of Lutheran teachers) and adolescence (as a student in Lutheran schools and colleges).

Luther, as a leader in the Protestant Reformation, was trying to provide a "sound bite" answer to a frequently asked question: How can we live in a world where uncertainty is the norm, where some people steal or even murder to get what they want, and, perhaps most unsettling, where even well-intentioned actions by "good" people can have bad effects? In that kind of world, said Luther, we should make decisions on all types of issues—faith, marriage, vocation and the like —thoughtfully, prayerfully and then boldly, unquestioningly, confident of forgiveness.

That assurance of forgiveness in the midst of doubt is the central idea of the Christian worldview. It is not just that "God so loved the world that he gave his only Son, that whoever believes in him should not perish but have eternal life" (John 3:16 RSV). God also freely gives that faith to those who do not refuse it. The problem with these last two sentences is the implicit assumption that we all agree on what is meant by the words *God* and *faith*.

In considering the impact my faith has on my profession, I made a short list of questions. Each question, at first glance, seems to present an either-or choice. A merging of apparent opposites, however, is precisely what the Bible says about Jesus Christ—he was "both God and Man," not one or the other. For the moment, let's not look at this historic claim as a miracle of any kind—religion does not have to be miraculous or magical, though some people say it is. In fact, the Christian message does not even try to say what it means by the word *God*. The entity behind that word could be an old man with a long beard, or a vaporous spirit, or a crystallization of the life force of the universe, or something we can't even begin to imagine. Or none of the above, or all of the above. Perhaps the question of whether or not God exists cannot be answered in that either-or form. It is more useful to look at the Christian message as a way of thinking, a way of transforming "either-or" questions so that they have a "both-and" kind of answer. The rest of this short essay is an attempt to do exactly that. It describes four EOBAs (either-or/both-and) that permeate my life as a Christian teacher in a public university.

EOBA 1: Self or/and Others?

At first glance, this seems to be a real dilemma: selfish actions tend to hurt other people, whereas actions to help others may involve unpleasant sacrifices for an individual. Most people, however, outgrow such a simple-minded worldview. They realize that a person is simultaneously a unique self and a part of larger groups. This notion can fit on a bumper sticker—Think Globally, Act Locally—and at the same time be a subtle, pervasive part of both private and public morality.

At face value, the slogan implies some awareness that things are connected. For that reason, an act that is intended mainly to help others can also have beneficial results for the person who does it. Likewise, what appears to be a good deed for an individual could have consequences for a larger group. For example, one might choose to send a child to a church-sponsored school for "good" reasons, at a personal scale. That act, however, can simultaneously be part of a great injustice at a metropolitan scale if the decision to support a private school results in an erosion of support for public schools.

Awareness of adverse consequences of individual action often pushes people to support specific kinds of group activity to counteract these consequences. For example, a company that closes a factory may start an employee-retraining program to help people who lose their jobs. A more personal example: I serve on the board of a religious elementary school, and at the same time I contribute to several public schools. Does this make sense? I don't really know for sure. It seems plausible that doing these seemingly contradictory things can help to maintain some kind of balance. If pressed, however, I could probably frame a persuasive argument that private schools in urban areas are either a vital alternative or a pernicious anachronism. In short, I can think of valid-sounding reasons on many sides of this issue, but on balance (and lacking the guidance that might be provided by an irrefutable set of maps or some equally persuasive product from some other discipline!), I finally just yield to the mercy of the God that Luther was describing. In short, I make a leap of faith and just do it.

A series of shoe commercials appropriated the phrase "just do it" and robbed it of some of the glistening aptness it had in my college theology class. I cannot, however, blame them for co-opting such a resonant idea. Moreover, their ads provide a good example for my next point: Christian teaching speaks directly and repeatedly about the relationship between self and group, but the message must be at least partly rephrased by each generation to fit its own circumstances. I admit that I have great fondness for some of the music and literature of the church, but that is not the essence of my faith. Frankly, I find it hard to defend the idea that today's young people will be awed by the relevance of biblical ideas such as leaving ninety-and-nine sheep in the wilderness (Luke 15:3-7) or foolish maidens who forgot oil for their lamps (Matthew 25:1-13) or being of one substance with the Father.[1]

That language seems at best out of date, though the ideas behind the words have great relevance to present-day issues. For example, what is the value of a single child's life in a bombed-out part of northern Ireland? What kind of plans make sense if you live right over the San Andreas fault, or if your spouse tests HIV positive? Why does the world remember just one out of the thousands of people who died on Roman crosses nearly two thousand years ago?

The point of this section is that working out a balance between the concerns of individuals and the welfare of humanity is an ongoing process, not a once-and-for-all given. The power of the Christian message is its assurance of forgiveness, which sets us free to act in an uncertain world even as we seek the knowledge that will make our action more effective.

A Christian perspective helps us avoid two extremes. One is the evil that occurs when people see no connection between their personal choices and what happens to others (or worse, do not care). The other extreme is the paralysis (inaction, drug-induced withdrawal or pointless fun seeking) that occurs when people feel powerless and unable to bridge the gap between the personal and the societal scale. Those tendencies, toward self-centeredness on one extreme and fatalism on the other, are not equally prevalent in all places. That observable fact is related to the next "either-or" on my list.

EOBA 2: Culture or/and Environment

Is a given trait of human personality the result of heredity or environment? Here again, most thoughtful people reject an either-or phrasing of the issue; they see personality being caused by the interplay of heredity and environment. That observation raises intriguing questions about altruism, ingenuity, intelligence or criminal tendencies. Are some people born with a tendency to bully others? Do they learn to do it? Or does some environmental condition or event "trigger" a genetic predisposition? For example, does abuse experienced in childhood trigger an inborn tendency to abuse others? These are questions about which I plead interested ignorance, since I am a geographer, not a psychologist. Geographers, however, apply basically the same idea at a broad scale—we believe that the landscape in a place is the result of an ongoing interplay between the culture of a people (their ideas about how to behave) and the resources and limitations in their environment. The results of that interplay can be seen in the most mundane landscape features.

Consider, for example, barn painting. Most barns are painted white or red—not too exciting. A few people, however, paint elaborate murals on their barns. In the gently rolling cornfields of northern Iowa, nine barn wall murals were visible from Interstate 35 in 1984 (the year I collected this information in a systematic way in order to verify a suspicion raised by casual observation on previous trips). Seven of those nine murals had a similar theme, something like a basket of fruit under a banner that proclaimed, "Thanks be to God, the bountiful Lord of the harvest." The surrounding landscape has huge fields of tall corn, individually not much different from each other and collectively stretching to the horizon in all directions, "Bo-ring," said the New Yorker riding with me. He's right, if we're talking only about what we can see at a glance.

Even on an analytical as opposed to a casual level, it is hardly surprising to see a proclamation of thanksgiving in this place. It is obvious, even to a New Yorker's eye, that this part of Iowa is uncommonly rich land. Thanksgiving seems to be an appropriate human response. (You may have inferred that I find it impossible to defend my discipline against the accusation that most of geography is the science of the rather obvious. So what if it is? What is rather obvious in one place may be subtle, questionable or even dead wrong in another. That is where geography acquires much of its ethical component and where my call comes in. Let's continue south on I-35 to see why.)

As the road curves west around Des Moines and turns south again, the landscape changes. There are more trees and hills. From here to the Missouri border we see eight more barns sporting murals. Six of those eight have a judgment theme, such as "Are YOU prepared to meet your maker?"

Seven thanksgiving themes out of nine barn paintings north of Des Moines; six judgment themes out of eight murals to the south. This is hardly the stuff of which statistical certainty is made, but the difference is still striking. It is hard to escape the feeling that something changed profoundly near Des Moines. That something is evident on a variety of measures—terrain, crop yield, land values, house sizes, teacher salaries, religious denominations and so on. When we try to arrange these ideas in some kind of causal order, it seems plausible to put a recent glacier near the head of the list. That glacier came south just as far as Des Moines (which is why it is called the Des Moines lobe, another typical bit of rather-obviousness). The glacier flattened the land, scraping the tops off the hills and depositing soil from Minnesota and Canada in the low areas of Iowa. A census map shows that yields of corn are about 20 percent higher on the recently glaciated land north of Des Moines. Another map says that the glaciated land is "worth" more per acre than the hillier land south of Des Moines. Other maps show that property taxes north of Des Moines are higher; roads are better maintained; school districts (before equalization) have more money per pupil; test scores are noticeably higher and so on.

Taken together, a dozen maps suggest that a simple geologic fact has some disturbing ethical overtones. These can be expressed as a single messy question: In a humane society, should a child who happens to be raised in the recently glaciated part of Iowa be therefore entitled to better schools, a better chance of going to college and a better chance of getting a good, high-paying job? Should other children be penalized just because they were born south of the glacier's terminal moraine? At the scale of a state, perhaps some transfer of tax dollars from the fertile counties north of Des Moines to the less productive counties to the south is justifiable.

Of course, this brief explanation is far too cut-and-dried. I have artificially restricted the discussion to barn paintings and soil quality when we should be considering many other variables: population growth and immigration, highway construction and factory location, tornadoes and regional history, philanthropy and work ethic and prejudice and so on. The bottom line is that the "right" course of action is not easy to see. This is not just an Iowa issue. For a variety of reasons, practically every state is wrestling with the question of how much transfer of tax dollars from one school district to another is "fair."

As a geographer, I beg forgiveness if I seem perhaps too eager to underscore that this is a profoundly geographical question. Answers should be informed by geographical data. Moreover, the question cannot be answered fairly as long as it is phrased as either-or rather than both-and and how-much.

For a Christian teacher, another conclusion from this story is even more important. What seems at first glance to be an abstract, other-worldly topic—religious belief, as inferred from church denominations and barn paintings—also seems to be linked in some way to the kind of soil in the place where a person grew up. If growing up on land covered by an old glacier can have that kind of effect, what about growing up in a high-rise housing project, where drug dealers settle their scores with Uzis and sirens scream through the night?

As we try to understand how environment and personality interact, it is worth noting that the biblical story of the Tower of Babel was about much more than mere words (Genesis 11:1-9). That story suggests that people are divided from each other, and from God, by gulfs of language and meaning that cannot be bridged without great concern (which makes us want to bridge the gaps), aided by considerable knowledge. The need for knowledge is evident when we realize that human cultures are influenced by environments and, increasingly, environments are altered by the people living there. The complex mutual influence of culture and environment leads to the next big "either-or" on my list.

EOBA 3: Saint or/and Sinner?

Simul justus et peccatur is a Latin phrase from the far reaches of church history. Roughly translated, it says that a person is at once a forgiven saint and a condemned sinner. Christians believe that the law of God condemns, whereas the gospel gives life, and both come from the same God. This apparent contradiction arises even when the law is viewed in its simple forms—the Ten Commandments (Exodus 20:1-14) or the single commandment known as the Golden Rule: "Do to others as you would have them do to you" (Luke 6:31 RSV). The contradiction is even more pronounced if you look at the law in its full complexity, as the inevitable workings of a world in which "right" answers are hard to discern and even harder to implement. (The third chapter of the book of Genesis in the Bible is quite insightful on this point. It was not just the people who were condemned for their error, but their children, the land, the entire world.)

The power of the gospel message is not that Christian faith automatically makes people good. One glance at a newspaper clearly shows that it does not! No, the power of the gospel is in the assurance of forgiveness and the continual repointing in the right direction. By faith Christians become reconciled to the fact that as long as we live in this world we have to act in the midst of uncertainty, and even the most well-intentioned action can have adverse effects. If Christians can live with that profound ambiguity in their personal life, shouldn't they also accept a similar ambiguity in their relations with others and their public policies? As suggested in the four-map example at the beginning of this essay, maps can be used to identify seeming "bad guys"—suburbanites who accept no responsibility for city problems, fertile-land farmers who congratulate themselves too heartily on the fine schools they helped build, Israeli settlements that divert water from nearby Palestinian villages, oil companies that use directional drilling to extract oil from beneath nearby Indian reservations, and so on.

As a Christian teaching in a secular university, I see two problems with publicly identifying powerful people as "bad guys." First, individuals often act out of ignorance, not malice. In any case, Christians should start from the premise that all people are capable of changing when they become aware of the consequences of their actions (in other words, when the law speaks to them). Second, when backed into a corner, powerful people usually have the resources to defend their positions well. Thunderous preaching of moral absolutes in a classroom may feel oh so righteous and at the same time be ethically inferior to less confrontational approaches.

A Christian teacher sees all human beings as "God's little sheep gone astray" (Luke 15:3-7). That awareness makes it harder to come up with valid generalizations about preferred courses of action. I'm not saying that a well-aimed whip isn't occasionally needed to drive the moneychangers from the temple, but I am saying that we should learn something from the fact that Jesus apparently resorted to that tactic only once (Matthew 21:12)!

In the case of the traffic fatalities "caused" by suburban drivers on city streets, there is a temptation to make angry speeches at council meetings, denouncing the accidents as "murder" (which, in one sense, is exactly what they are—preventable if not premeditated taking of human life). A more promising approach, however, might be to design educational units that lead students to "discover" some facts about cities on their own. One of those facts is that most attempts to identify "livable cities" tend to award high rankings to urban areas where cities and suburbs are forced to cooperate under fairly strong metropolitan governments.

What is needed in this arena (among other things, such as sound history and economics and political action) is more good geographic study to gather the information needed by those who want to do the right thing but may not know what it is in a specific situation. The same information, of course, can also help expose those who are doing the wrong thing for the wrong reasons.

This conclusion about the need for information fits well with the concept of a vocational "call" that I mentioned earlier. That concept is outlined in many places in the Bible, most notably in Jesus' parable of the talents (Matthew 25:14-30) and in Paul's letters to the Corinthians, Ephesians and Romans. Here's a sentence from the book of Romans: "Having gifts that differ . . . let us use them [to do good]: if prophecy, in proportion to our faith; if service, in our serving; he who teaches, in his teaching [and so on through a long list of occupations]" (Romans 12:6-7 RSV). My suggestion that it is possible to feel a divine "call" to make maps brings me to the last either-or dilemma on my list.

EOBA 4: Thought or/and Action?

Personal philosophy should be both profoundly reflective and ruthlessly parsimonious. In other words, think about things but not more than you need to! I come to that conclusion on many paths: urban tax policy, physical exercise, public welfare, banjo practice, civil rights, endangered species, child abuse—the list is long.

In all cases, the ethical issues can be intriguing, and knowledge is needed to help us make good decisions. In that context, my call seems to be to focus my talent on doing research and teaching within an arbitrarily narrow academic discipline in order to provide part of the answer as quickly as possible. That focus means that I cannot go to many of the well-intentioned and widely advertised forums for ethical discussion at my university, although the organizers of those forums may interpret my nonparticipation as disinterest or antipathy.

The dilemma I am describing is easy to express but very difficult to solve. Each of us has been given stewardship of twenty-four hours each day, for an unknown number of days. Let's see how that abstract idea works in the real world. The Library of Congress logs more than a million new books a year, about two per minute. No one can read them all! By extension, no one can support every cause, pursue every research question or address every problem. We can only try to reflect enough to find a reasonable balance, and then, in the words of Luther, sin (act) confidently but believe even more confidently.

The God who speaks to me through the Bible has placed at the center of his message a Redeemer who spent much of his public ministry doing precisely that: ministering to the public, feeding the hungry, counseling the disturbed, consoling those who mourn. His spoken message was direct, not complex: "Love one another" (John 13:34; 15:12, 17).

In this world, however, that command is made difficult by both our human fallibility and the nature of the world around us—in short, by the same "either-or/both-ands" I have been discussing. The relevance of the Christian message is not just in the simple but profound command to love one another. It is also in the equally simple but profound central phrase of the Lord's Prayer: "Forgive us, . . . As we also have forgiven" (Matthew 6:12 RSV).

Those two short phrases provide a perspective on all of the either-or/both-and dilemmas. An important part of that perspective is the realization that we dare not let philosophical debates take too much of our lives. A person can always expand a discussion about belief by adding examples and refinements, but each minute devoted to clarifying how we express our belief is a minute that is not available for anything else. As with the other items on my list, some kind of balance is needed. In this spirit, therefore, I should perhaps concede that this article is long enough.

Having an Answer for Questions About Our Faith

The Bible says that Christians should have a ready answer for those who ask about our faith (1 Peter 3:15). My answer is at once abstract and concrete.

Abstractly, much of life seems to consist of apparently irreconcilable either-or dilemmas. In that situation, the Christian gospel suggests a both-and kind of reconciliation—one of inclusion rather than rejection, of forgiveness in spite of uncertainty and error. In this way our faith sets us free to search for better ways to put love in action.

Concretely, I have become persuaded that individuals and society would be better off if we had more maps of mundane topics such as schoolchildren injured by commuter-driven automobiles. That kind of knowledge would help us "do the right thing." And, in keeping with the notion that philosophizing (by those called to some vocation other than philosophy!) should be parsimonious, I should now probably go back to finishing a map of farmers who collect government payments not to grow crops on erosion-prone land. That's my research topic this year, and I was rather careful not to say anything about it in this article, because, like most disciplined research, it is resolutely (perhaps even gloriously) both-and.

It is far too narrow to be interesting for long (unless you are sustained by both its nitty-gritty scientific questions and its broad ethical implications). At the same time, it is far too complex for a short article. In short, it's just a big, bold "I believe"—the kind of life commitment that is easy if we heed the words about vocation in the Old Testament book of Ecclesiastes: "Whatever your hand finds to do, do it with your might" (Ecclesiates 9:10 RSV).

That is precisely the kind of Bible quotation that some people can find enormously comforting, whereas others see it as irrelevant. So be it. Nowhere in this article did I suggest that the gift of faith was anything other than an affirmation in the midst of doubt and uncertainty. Indeed, the second "both-and" on my list suggested that different people might find different phrasings of the Christian message more convincing than others. For example, my college theology teacher wondered whether the book of Ecclesiastes should even be in the Bible. I, however, find it the most interesting and insightful book in the canon. It shows clearly that these either-or questions have been puzzling people for a very long time.

Perhaps the best way for a Christian teacher to teach how to deal with such questions is by just doing it and having an answer ready if someone asks. Over the years, I have weighed ideas thoughtfully and I find that accepting the gift of a Christian worldview is not just a plausible option at the close of the twentieth century. It is a leap of faith that can make the world much better than it is, both for individuals and for all humankind. And that, as we say in Minnesota, would be a pretty good deal.

Note

[1]From the Nicene Creed, in *The Lutheran Hymnal* (St. Louis: Concordia Publishing House, 1941), p. 22.

19

An Ancient Historian's View of Christianity

EDWIN M. YAMAUCHI

History

Miami University

If we had ancient sources like those in the Gospels
for the history of Alexander the Great or Julius Caesar,
for example, we should not cast any doubt
upon them whatsoever.
—JOSEPH KLAUSNER

I was born in Hawaii in 1937. My father, who was an immigrant from Okinawa, died just before the 1941 surprise attack of the Japanese on Pearl Harbor. My mother's parents were also immigrants from Okinawa. Like about 150,000 other people, they had left Japan to work on Hawaiian sugar plantations. Though my mother was born in Hawaii, she spent her childhood in Okinawa, an island that was considered a backwater by other Japanese.

After my father died, my mother worked as a maid in wealthy Caucasian houses. She had no education, but she valued books and learning. The beautifully illustrated books she gave me instilled in me a love of reading. Somehow she was able to send me in the seventh grade to Iolani, a private Episcopalian school for boys. In the nineteenth century Sun Yat-Sen, the father of the Chinese Republic, had attended this school.

My father had been active in a Buddhist temple, and I was a nominal Buddhist. Occasionally my mother and I went to the temple to pay respect to my father's *hotoke*, or spirit. While attending Iolani, I became an Episcopalian and an acolyte at St. Andrew's Cathedral. So I became a nominal Christian, but I had no personal understanding of Christianity.

A high school friend invited me to an evangelical Congregational church, where I first heard the gospel from a visiting basketball player from Indiana. Though I raised my hand at the invitation, I still had no concept of a relationship to Jesus Christ. It was through the patient explanation of a retired English educator, Robert Hambrook, that I came to understand that Christ had died for me personally and that I needed to commit my life to him. This I did in the fall of 1952.

My mother remarried and moved to Los Angeles, where I attended Los Angeles Polytechnic High School. After a year I returned to Hawaii to work at a missionary farm, the Christian Youth Center, which was run by Claude Curtis, an ex-marine. As I had no prior farming experience, I was rather incompetent at feeding chickens, milking goats and killing rabbits. But this trying experience allowed me to draw closer to God, as I had time to memorize books of the New Testament while doing my chores.

I also found a book at the center, J. B. Lightfoot's commentary on Paul's letters, which first aroused my interest in Greek. Prior to my conversion I had been primarily interested in science, math and fiction. Now I became especially interested in languages. At this time I wrote my first published article, "The Blessings of Trials," an exposition on the first chapter of the book of James. It was published in *His* magazine.

I worked on the Youth Center farm for a year after graduating from a rural high school. In 1956-1957 I attended Columbia Bible College in South Carolina. Coming from such a small island, I was unprepared for the seventy-two-hour coast-to-coast bus trip. At CBC I was exposed to what God was doing on many mission fields, since many of the school's graduates served as missionaries overseas.

After spending another year working at the Youth Center, I entered the University of Hawaii, ostensibly as an anthropology major. But what I studied was languages, five at a time, which is not the best strategy for learning any language well. Much of my time was taken up by my work as a reporter, a feature editor and a columnist for the student newspaper. In a column entitled "He That Hath Ears" I tried to present the Christian message.

In 1958-1960 I attended Shelton College, a small Christian school in Ringwood, New Jersey. I was attracted to it by an outdated catalog that listed several scholars who taught a unique major in Hebrew and Greek. But when the Bible Presbyterian denomination split, many of the professors I had read about left Shelton for Covenant College and Seminary in St. Louis.

I did get to study Greek, Hebrew and Arabic in a magnificent setting, as the campus had been the estate of a millionaire. My instructor in Hebrew, Melvin Dahl, had been a student of the renowned Jewish Old Testament scholar Cyrus H. Gordon of Brandeis University, and I attended a summer session at Brandeis in 1960. I studied under S. N. Kramer of the University of Pennsylvania, a noted authority on the Sumerians, who produced the world's first literate civilization. In 1960-1961 I served as an instructor in Greek at Shelton College.

In graduate school at Brandeis (M.A. 1962, Ph.D. 1964) I studied such ancient languages as Akkadian, Egyptian, Ugaritic, Linear A and B, Coptic, Syriac and Arabic. My dissertation was a study of magic bowls written in Mandaic, a dialect of Aramaic. It is the language of a unique Gnostic community, the Mandaeans, who live in Iraq and Iran. Their texts had been used by the influential German New Testament scholar Rudolf Bultmann to develop his thesis of a pre-Christian Gnosticism that he believed influenced the New Testament.[1]

Whereas most of my fellow classmates from Brandeis became Old Testament specialists, I was given an opportunity to teach ancient history at Rutgers, the State University of New Jersey (1964-1969). One of the joys I had there was to serve as the faculty adviser for InterVarsity Christian Fellowship, a role that I have also served at Miami University in Oxford, Ohio, where I have been teaching since 1969. The name of our university, which was founded in 1809 (ten years before the University of Virginia), was derived from the Miami Indians of Indiana and Ohio. It was an Ohioan who gave the name "Miami" to that famous beachfront in Florida.

As a member of the history department, I have taught graduate students at both the doctoral and the master's level, as well as undergraduates. I periodically teach a large Western civilization survey course. For a textbook I require the Bible, which I consider the most important book in Western history. I have found that few students know much about it. From time to time I also teach a senior seminar that investigates the Jewish background of Christianity.

I spent five months in Israel in 1968 after receiving a fellowship from the National Endowment for the Humanities. I participated in the first season of excavations at the temple area in Jerusalem under the direction of Benjamin Mazar, the former president of Hebrew University, with whom I had taken a course at Brandeis. The excavations revealed parts of the Herodian temple that had been covered by debris and yielded evidence of the destruction of the temple by Titus in A.D. 70.[2]

Archaeology is a relatively new field. Egypt was brought to European attention by Napoleon's invasion of 1798 and the deciphering of Egyptian hieroglyphics by Champollion in 1822. Initial excavations took place in Mesopotamia in 1840 under Paul Émile Botta, in 1870 at Troy and in 1876 at Mycenae under Heinrich Schliemann, and in Palestine in 1890 under Flinders Petrie. In general, archaeology has corrected the negative tendencies in the literary critical study not only of the Bible but also of Greek classics like Homer and Herodotus. Some Old Testament scholars have recently reverted to a highly skeptical posture, which in my opinion is not justified.[3] One must bear in mind the extremely fragmentary nature of the archaeological evidence before assuming that the Bible is erroneous on the basis of arguments from silence, that is, because we lack at present external corroboration of biblical events or persons.[4]

The discovery and excavation of sites, as well as the translation of ancient texts, have helped to illuminate the backgrounds of the patriarchs, the exodus, the conquest, the united monarchy, the divided kingdoms and the exile.[5] The life of Jesus has been illuminated especially by the study of many Herodian monuments in Israel.[6] The missionary journeys of Paul have been made more vivid by excavations at many of the sites he evangelized, in both Asia Minor (Turkey) and Greece.[7]

The Dead Sea Scrolls were found at Qumran in 1947. At Brandeis I had the privilege of studying these texts under Shemaryahu Talmon, a renowned scrolls scholar from Israel. Unfortunately, the scrolls have been misused in extravagant claims made by such scholars as A. Dupont-Sommer, E. Wilson, John Marco Allegro and more recently Barbara Thiering.[8]

Equally important for the study of the early church was the discovery of the Coptic Nag Hammadi codices in Egypt in 1945. One of the languages I studied at Brandeis was Coptic, a form of the Egyptian language written in Greek letters (plus seven additional letters derived from the Demotic script), used by the early Christians. The Nag Hammadi texts are the most important documents relating to a movement called Gnosticism, a heresy that troubled the early church. Some scholars, following the lead of Rudolf Bultmann, have assumed that Gnosticism was an independent movement that predated and also influenced Christianity, a position that I have criticized.[9]

Though I was born into a Buddhist background, it was not until college and graduate school that I studied the teachings of various religious leaders, including Buddha, Zoroaster, Socrates and Muhammad. Brandeis University, which has long enjoyed the support of the Jewish community, afforded me opportunities to learn from outstanding Jewish scholars.

Among the courses I took at Brandeis were Arabic courses in the Qur'an and the Hadith (traditions about Muhammad) taught by Joseph de Somogyi, an eminent Hungarian Islamicist who also taught at Harvard. One of my fellow classmates, Gordon Newby, is now one of the leading scholars on Muhammad and the Jews in Arabia.

Though there are several parallels in the lives and teachings of these great religious leaders, there are also distinctive features both about the available sources we have for them and about their teachings.[10] Sources about Buddha and Zoroaster[11] are largely late and legendary, whereas sources about Socrates, Jesus and Muhammad are contemporary or come from a generation after their lifetimes.

196

Distinctive features about Jesus are claims made for his miracles, the saving significance of his crucifixion, his resurrection and his identification with God.[12] Although the earliest and best sources are the canonical Gospels (Matthew, Mark, Luke and John) and other writings of the New Testament, some skeptical critics dismiss these sources as biased. But we also have non-Christian sources such as Josephus, a Jewish historian,[13] and Tacitus, a Roman historian, which confirm some of the basic facts about Jesus.[14] More dubious sources are numerous apocryphal gospels such as the recently discovered *Gospel of Thomas,* which has been hailed by some scholars as the Fifth Gospel.[15]

Even without the New Testament we can establish that Jesus was probably born in Judea before the death of Herod the Great in 4 B.C. and that he was crucified under Pontius Pilate[16] in the reign of Tiberius, either in A.D. 30 or more probably in A.D. 33.[17] Crucifixion was so shameful a death that Christian artists did not depict the crucified Christ until the fifth century A.D.[18] Despite this most horrific death,[19] his followers did not disappear but increased in number and spread throughout the Roman Empire. Though despised by many and persecuted by some Roman rulers, the movement continued to expand until it "triumphed" with the conversion of the Roman emperor himself, Constantine, in A.D. 312.[20]

How can we explain this? As a Christian historian, I maintain that the most persuasive explanation lies in an event that was historical but transcended history in its uniqueness and significance, not in myth or hallucination.[21] Even a Jewish scholar has acknowledged that the evidence for the resurrection of Jesus is persuasive.[22] I believe that Jesus, who was crucified, did rise from the dead on Easter morning and manifested himself to his followers. This so transformed them that they joyfully shared this good news despite opposition and obstacles, convincing more and more people that God is revealed in Jesus Christ.

This revelation was mediated in a particular culture. The interpretation of the Bible involves two horizons: the ancient horizon and our contemporary horizon. It is, therefore, an error to attempt a literal transfer of biblical passages to our own situations without understanding their contexts. An understanding of ancient history, cultures and languages helps us to appreciate the original significance of these texts and to appreciate more fully their abiding values. The history of the early church offers us inspiring lessons from the expansion of Christianity[23] and also warns us of some of the problems of the misapplication of the Bible through the ages.[24] A knowledge of history also helps us to understand the need for contextualization in conveying this message to other cultures today.[25]

Notes

[1]See Edwin M. Yamauchi, *Gnostic Ethics and Mandaean Origins* (Cambridge, Mass.: Harvard University Press, 1970).

[2]See Benjamin Mazar, *The Mountain of the Lord* (Garden City, N.Y.: Doubleday, 1975).

[3]See Edwin M. Yamauchi, "The Present Status of Old Testament Historiography," in *Faith, Tradition and History: Old Testament Historiography in Its Near Eastern Context*, ed. D. Baker, J. Hoffmeier and A. Millard (Winona Lake, Ind.: Eisenbrauns, 1994), pp. 1-36.

[4]See Edwin M. Yamauchi, *The Stones and the Scriptures* (Grand Rapids: Baker , 1981).

[5]See Alfred J. Hoerth, Gerald L. Mattingly and Edwin M. Yamauchi, eds., *Peoples of the Old Testament World* (Grand Rapids: Baker, 1994).

[6]See D. J. Wiseman and Edwin M. Yamauchi, *Archaeology and the Bible* (Grand Rapids: Zondervan, 1979); John McRay, *Archaeology and the New Testament* (Grand Rapids: Baker, 1991); Jack Finegan, *The Archeology of the New Testament: The Life of Jesus and the Beginning of the Early Church*, rev. ed. (Princeton, N.J.: Princeton University Press, 1992).

[7]See Edwin M. Yamauchi, *Harper's World of the New Testament* (San Francisco: Harper & Row, 1981), and Yamauchi, *New Testament Cities in Western Asia Minor* (Grand Rapids: Baker, 1987).

[8]See Edwin M. Yamauchi, "The Teacher of Righteousness from Qumran and Jesus of Nazareth," *Christianity Today*, May 13, 1966, pp. 816-18; Timothy Jones, "Scrolls Hype," *Christianity Today*, October 4, 1993, pp. 28-31. See also Edward M. Cook, *Solving the Mysteries of the Dead Sea Scrolls* (Grand Rapids: Zondervan, 1994).

[9]See Edwin M. Yamauchi, *Pre-Christian Gnosticism*, 2nd ed. (Grand Rapids: Baker, 1983).

[10]See Edwin M. Yamauchi, "Historical Notes on the (In)comparable Christ," *Christianity Today*, October 22, 1971, pp. 7-11.

[11]On Zoroaster and Zoroastrianism, see Edwin M. Yamauchi, *Persia and the Bible* (Grand Rapids: Baker, 1990).

[12]See Murray J. Harris, *Jesus as God* (Grand Rapids: Baker, 1992).

[13]See Edwin M. Yamauchi, "Josephus and the Scriptures," *Fides et Historia* 13 (1980): 42-63.

[14]See Edwin M. Yamauchi, "Jesus Outside the New Testament: What Is the Evidence?" in *Jesus Under Fire*, ed. Michael J. Wilkins and J. P. Moreland (Grand Rapids:

Zondervan, 1995), pp. 207-29. See also F. F. Bruce, *Jesus and Christian Origins Outside the New Testament* (Grand Rapids: Eerdmans, 1974); Gary R. Habermas, *The Historical Jesus: Ancient Evidence for the Life of Christ* (Joplin, Mo.: College Press, 1996).

[15]See Edwin M. Yamauchi, "Agrapha" and "Apocryphal Gospels," in *The International Standard Bible Encyclopedia*, rev. ed. (Grand Rapids: Eerdmans, 1979), 1:69-71, 181-88; "Logia," in *International Standard Bible Encyclopedia*, 3:152-54. For a criticism of the Jesus Seminar's well-publicized volume *The Five Gospels*, see Luke Timothy Johnson, *The Real Jesus* (San Francisco: HarperCollins, 1996); for a detailed critique of revisionist lives of Jesus, see Ben Witherington III, *The Jesus Quest* (Downers Grove, Ill.: InterVarsity Press, 1995).

[16]On the trial narratives, see Edwin M. Yamauchi, "Historical Notes on the Trial and Crucifixion of Jesus Christ," *Christianity Today*, April 9, 1971, pp. 6-11. For more detailed studies, see David Catchpole, *The Trial of Jesus* (Leiden: Brill, 1971); Raymond E. Brown, *The Death of the Messiah*, 2 vols. (Garden City, N.Y.: Doubleday, 1994).

[17]See the articles by Harold W. Hoehner and Paul L. Maier in *Chronos, Kairos, Christos*, ed. Jerry Vardaman and Edwin M. Yamauchi (Winona Lake, Ind.: Eisenbrauns, 1989). Alternative chronologies are proposed by Vardaman and Ernest Martin.

[18]Graydon F. Snyder, *Ante Pacem: Archaeological Evidence of Church Life Before Constantine* (Macon, Ga.: Mercer University Press, 1985), p. 27.

[19]See Edwin M. Yamauchi, "The Crucifixion and Docetic Christology," *Concordia Theological Quarterly* 46 (1982): 1-20; Martin Hengel, *Crucifixion* (London: SCM Press, 1977).

[20]See Robert G. Clouse, Richard V. Pierard and Edwin M. Yamauchi, *The Two Kingdoms: The Church and Culture Throughout the Ages* (Chicago: Moody Press, 1993).

[21]See Edwin M. Yamauchi, "Easter: Myth, Hallucination or History?" *Christianity Today*, March 15, 1974, pp. 4-7, and March 29, 1974, pp. 12-14, 16. The material in these articles forms the basis of a presentation that I have given at a number of universities, including Cornell, Yale and Princeton. This talk, along with testimonies from Christian faculty at Princeton, is included on a videotape entitled *The Princeton Chronicles*, which is available from Tom Woodward (1957 Sourwood Blvd., Dunedin, FL 34698). See also William Lane Craig, "Did Jesus Rise from the Dead?" in *Jesus Under Fire*, pp. 141-76, as well as his more detailed studies *The Historical Argument for the Resurrection of Jesus* (Lewiston, Maine: Edwin Mellen, 1985), and *Assessing the New Testament Evidence for the Historicity of the Resurrection of Jesus* (Lewiston, Maine: Edwin Mellen, 1989).

[22]Pinchas Lapide, *The Resurrection of Jesus: A Jewish Perspective* (Minneapolis: Augsburg, 1983).

[23]See Edwin M. Yamauchi, "How the Early Church Responded to Social Problems," *Christianity Today*, November 24, 1972, pp. 6-8.

[24]See Clouse, Pierard and Yamauchi, *The Two Kingdoms*.

[25]Edwin M. Yamauchi, "Christianity and Cultural Differences," *Christianity Today*, June 23, 1972, pp. 5-8.

20

We Worship the Same God You Do

MICHAEL W. MCCONNELL

Law

University of Utah

Now when the adversaries of Judah and Benjamin heard
that the returned exiles were building a temple to the LORD,
the God of Israel, they approached Zerubbabel and
the heads of fathers' houses and said to them,
"Let us build with you; for we worship your God as you do,
and we have been sacrificing to him ever since the days of
Esarhaddon king of Assyria who brought us here."
But Zerubbabel, Jeshua, and the rest of the heads of
fathers' houses in Israel said to them, "You have nothing
to do with us in building a house to our God; but we
alone will build to the LORD, the God of Israel. . . . "
Then the people of the land discouraged the people
of Judah, and made them afraid to build, and
hired counselors against them to frustrate their purpose.
—EZRA 4:1-4 RSV

*T*here is a strangely postmodern cast to this old story. The
"adversaries" of Judah and Benjamin did not undertake a
frontal challenge to the returning exiles. They did not question
the exiles' understanding of God or argue with them about proper
religious practice. That might even have been welcome. Open and
honest opponents can be the best of friends. They force us to justify our
premises, clarify our conclusions and defend the ground for our

beliefs. Instead, seemingly in the interest of peace, the adversaries of Judah and Benjamin set aside discussion of concepts like "truth" and "falsehood" and substituted claims of equivalence and perspective. Does that sound familiar? "We live our lives our way, and you live your lives your way," they seemed to say. "These are just different ways of attaining the same end. We all worship the same God." The only absolute in such a world is the absolute that no one is permitted to claim: A particular perspective is Truth.

The world the returning exiles faced, like the academy of today, was filled with people with different, often antagonistic visions of the good. And like the struggles in the academy today, the controversies faced by these men and women were essentially ideological in nature —fought with the weapons of words, law and public opinion. Finally, like the obstacles we face in the academy today, the opposition to the reconstruction of Jerusalem proceeded not so much by frontal assault as by sticks and carrots, threats and temptations.

The "adversaries of Judah and Benjamin" came to the people of God with an offer and a threat. The offer was to "build with them." The threat was to "frustrate their purpose" by intimidation and legal action. What did the "adversaries" hope to gain from their offer of assistance? Precisely this: that the people of God would accept their claim that "we worship God as you do." In other words, they sought to induce the faithful remnant to abandon the claim that their understanding of God is fundamentally distinct from competing understandings. From the perspective of the modern secular world, similarly, it is Christianity's claim to the status of Truth that gives offense. No one would care that Christians worship in their own way, if only they would agree that alternative creeds (including secular creeds) are morally equivalent. The exiles were not asked to declare their religion false but to admit that it is not much different from anybody else's.

The offer to help build the temple thus presented the Jews a temptation and a danger. The temptation was joining forces with their adversaries and the danger was losing their distinctive understanding of God. The promise was peace (even alliance) with the powers of the world; the price was accepting the world's ideas of truth as being equal to—nay, identical to—the claims of the Lord, the God of Israel.

The unlucky ones among us (or are they the lucky ones?) will face open hostility and will be driven to an ultimatum: deny God or be crushed. In a sense, we are all prepared for that. More often, however, we will face a more subtle temptation: not to deny our faith but to relegate it to a private world of subjectivity, where no one can challenge us because "it's just my personal belief." A "personal" faith means a faith that makes no claim on the intelligence of anyone else, a faith that offers no challenge to the world. If religion is nothing more than personal preference, it will not be threatened because it will not be threatening. The easiest way for believers to escape conflict is to wrap themselves in subjectivity.

All of us face this temptation, in small ways and large. I recall a lunchtime conversation with my colleagues about euthanasia. I attempted to explain traditional Christian teaching on the subject and was immediately countered by an aggressively rationalist soul, who opined that superstition and dogma had no place in serious conversation. One of my colleagues, bless his heart, stepped in to protect me. "Hey, watch your language. That's his religion you are attacking." I was relieved and off the hook. Only later did I realize what I had done. I had acquiesced in the idea (convenient but deadly) that "religion" is a personal thing that should be treated with kid gloves rather than a claim of truth that must be argued and defended. I should have said, "No, friend, let me respond. My position should be subjected to the same searching inquiry that any philosophy or worldview receives. I am not telling you about my religion. I am telling you what I think is true. I have an obligation to explain why."

Unfortunately, the flip side of the temptation is the threat. It was only when the Jews rejected their adversaries' offer that things turned nasty. Only then did the "people of the land" attempt to "make them afraid." Only then did they hire "counselors" to go to Babylon to appeal to the king to stop the newcomers from proceeding with their project.

As a specialist in the constitutional law of church and state, I find the aftermath of the story intriguing. The "counselors" ask the king to conduct a "search" in "the book of the records of your fathers" (Ezra 4:15 RSV), which they say will show that the Jews' reconstruction efforts are unlawful. In response to this one-sided account of the facts, Babylon issues a decree telling the Jews to cease and desist. The Jews respond, as described in the fifth chapter of Ezra, with a fuller account of the record in the royal archive, which confirms their right to restore the walls and temple of Jerusalem. The king then changes the decree and instructs his officials to "let the work on this house of God alone" (Ezra 6:7 RSV). This is more than vaguely reminiscent of recent constitutional history, in which the Supreme Court, responding to one-sided accounts of the purposes of the First Amendment, issued decrees that were often hostile or uncomprehending toward the exercise of religion in America. In more recent years, responding in part to a more balanced account of the history of "the book of the record of [our] fathers"—the Constitution—the Supreme Court has come a great distance toward recognizing that the Constitution does not compel the government to be hostile toward religion but permits full and equal participation by religious citizens in the public life of the nation.

The approach taken by the "adversaries of Judah and Benjamin" in the old story is much like the postmodern ideology of much of today's academy. Postmodernism is, in essence, philosophical paganism: there are many gods (understandings of the good), and there is no way to choose between them. It is permissible, within the pagan worldview, for peoples to give special attention to their particular "god" (the god of the city). Indeed, the gods of one's own city (identity politics) assume particular importance when the possibility of a coherent monotheism is dismissed. This produces a kind of tolerance. You can worship pretty much the way you choose, and anything you choose, without running afoul of the logic of paganism. There is only one heresy within the pagan understanding: the insistence that one's own "god" is God.

No one entering a secular university in the United States today should underestimate the power of postmodern ideology, which is pervasive, self-righteous and armed with power. The temptation, the easy way out, is to buy peace on the terms rejected in the Ezra story— by accepting the understanding of religious conviction as a matter of subjective commitment rather than truth. Reduce religion to "faith" (meaning private intuition, untestable by objective standards) and religion will get along just fine in the modern world, even in the academy. Religious preference, like sexual preference, is then properly protected as a matter of "privacy." To believe that the claims of God are in any objective sense "true," however, is a form of intolerance, which cannot be tolerated.

The charge of "intolerance," not an attempted refutation of truth claims, is the principal line of attack on Christianity in modern America. Just imagine the reaction of most moderns to the story from Ezra. Surely the Jews should have allowed the inhabitants of the land to help. Who were they to say that their understanding of God was better than anyone else's? The Jews were being narrow-minded, exclusive and intolerant. Their adversaries were being broad-minded, inclusive and loving. Which group do you think played the role of good liberal citizens in a pluralistic republic?

Yet who makes the appeal to power to prevent others from living according to their convictions? The doubters and the scoffers—the good liberal citizens—turned out to be the truly intolerant. For much of my professional life I have tried to make one point: that the only tolerance worth having is tolerance for different understandings of the truth. A toleration based on skepticism, indifference or relativism is no tolerance at all.

Our task as exiles in this post-Christian land is to rebuild the temple. It is not to fight a holy war. The temple we are building is in the hearts and minds of men and women. We must reach their hearts through love and their minds through intelligence and persuasion. We must not be distracted from our task by the efforts of the world to discourage us and to make us afraid. But to show love and understanding and respect for contrary ideas does not require us to retreat from the truth. My advice to young men and women entering the academy is this: Stick to what is true, respect the efforts of others to find the truth even if they are still far from it, and never, never give in to the proposition that it is just a matter of personal "faith."

21

Christianity and a Conceptual Orientation

KEITH E. YANDELL

Philosophy

University of Wisconsin

This century is not the first to invite Christianity
before the judgment bar of philosophy, to dispute the
presuppositions upon which so much of its solidarity and
potency turns. Nor has the Christian theistic view, when so
pressed, hesitated to appear. For, from the very first,
Christianity appealed to the intellect. Revelational theism
has never offered itself as an escape from rationality.
—CARL F. H. HENRY, *REMAKING THE MODERN MIND*

What follows is an informal description of my own religious belief. I do not have any new religious doctrines to propound. While I was in college, Prophet Jones was active in Detroit. Wearing an ermine coat, he would step from his Cadillac and throw money to his supporters. As poor students, a friend and I playfully wondered one day if there was anything in our beliefs that we could shape into a religion that would make us wealthy. We decided that since what we believed, as far as religion went, was just plain old Christian doctrine, our prospects for wealth along such lines were not bright.

In spite of the heavy weather sometimes made about trying to figure out what Christianity teaches, the rather plain fact is that Roman Catholicism, Eastern Orthodoxy, the Reformed and the Anabaptist traditions, and the mainline Protestant denominations have all accepted a set of core doctrines that C. S. Lewis properly called "mere Christianity." As Carl Henry once remarked, novelty in doctrine at this point in church history is suspect. In any case, I have no doctrinal novelty to add to mere Christianity.

Thanks to my parents, I was raised in Methodist churches that preached mere Christianity, which in some sense I believed. I read the New Testament as a teenager one summer, attended a Billy Graham crusade and began to go to a Baptist church, all of which led to a conversion or a rededication. Beyond that, I have little in the way of religious roots to describe—no rich tradition of Baptist family piety or Free Church Scandinavian religious ethnicity or nurturing Dutch Reformed cultural and scholarly tradition. Only later did I learn that there are such things in the world.

Without any claims to being a very good member of the type, I am a Christian. I believe that God—an omnipotent, omniscient, morally perfect Creator and Providence—exists in such a way that there is nothing on which God depends for existence. I believe that God is trinitarian, that the Second Person of the Trinity became incarnate, becoming human, living a perfect life, dying on a cross for our sins and rising from the dead. To this God, insofar as I am able, I have offered repentance and trust. I take these to be reasonable beliefs and reject the idea that by virtue of having them I have somehow abandoned myself to a blind leap of faith, denied the worth and power of rational reflection, or otherwise become intellectually objectionable. Hence by *confession* I mean "statement of belief," not "report of something I am guilty of."[1]

For good or ill, I am a conceptually oriented person. I love my wife, children and grandchildren, and I hold my golden retriever in the high affection he deserves. But I have no sympathy with "heart versus head," let alone "heart over head." Biblically, the heart is the locus of both thought and feeling. Without suggesting that everyone ought to be like me in this respect and being fully aware that most people are not, the fact remains that I am conceptually oriented. I think of beliefs that matter to me in terms of clarity, consistency, coherence and evidence. What do such beliefs mean? Are they true? How I would feel were I to change significant beliefs or what I would like to be true is irrelevant. Many people will think that this is a mere pose and that I (like everyone else) believe what I do because it is what I like to believe. I do not think that *anyone* is like this about everything or that *everyone* is like this about significant beliefs. Anyone who claims that all people believe what they want or simply embrace the significant beliefs they prefer should not be taken seriously on their own terms. Such a person merely reports that she happens to prefer the belief that people embrace the significant beliefs that they prefer. Such preference gives no support to her thesis.

After graduating from Cooley High School in Detroit, I went downtown to Wayne University because it had a good reputation and I could afford it. I began as a psychology major, but the deeply behaviorist orientation of the department hardly encouraged my interests in personality theory. I switched to intellectual history, which I loved, but when I asked whether the people whose ideas we studied ever got anything right, I was told to go ask the philosophers. I did, and I earned a B.A. in history and philosophy. Knowing I hadn't the faintest idea of what philosophy was really all about, I stayed for an M.A., and by the end of that time I was hooked, good and proper, on philosophy.

During my time there, Wayne University became Wayne State University. The philosophy department came to be chaired by George Nakhnikian, and he brought in Hector Castaneda, Edmund Gettier, Robert C. Sleigh, Alvin Plantinga and David Falk. Hardly household names in American culture, these philosophers were in the process of gaining a deserved reputation for being among the profession's best. Even before Keith Lehrer and Richard Cartwright joined them, for a few years they made the department one of the strongest in the world. Through no fault of mine, I was there during those years and thus got a first-class education.

I spent a dismal year in a seminary that was about as prepared for a philosophy student as a bird's nest is for a golden retriever and two years teaching all of the philosophy courses at a small college. Then I was offered a teaching assistant position (and later a lectureship) at Ohio State, got my Ph.D. and accepted a position at the University of Wisconsin-Madison, where I have been ever since. Given the invaluable training I got at Wayne State and the reading I did while teaching for two years, graduate school was a thoroughly enjoyable experience. Marvin Fox, an orthodox Jewish rabbi, and Richard Severens, an amiable agnostic or atheist, provided the same high quality of teaching at Ohio State that I had received at Wayne, and Julius Weinberg, a distinguished expert on medieval philosophy, became my informal mentor in Madison. Talking with him (we shared an office) was the equivalent of a postdoctoral education.

Integrating my Christianity and my education was up to me. My teachers, on the whole, have been atheists and agnostics. Alvin Plantinga, whose sheer presence (let alone lectures) was highly encouraging, was just getting his teaching feet wet. Marvin Fox and I talked a good deal about philosophy and monotheism, but of course did not entirely agree about Christianity. The idea that a Christian or the Christian church has nothing to learn from agnostics and atheists is absurd. Most of what I learned in my own field came from agnostic and atheist teachers, many of whom became close friends. Both Scripture and experience confirm the doctrine of common grace; reason is God's good gift to all.

My undergraduate and M.A. years were a matter of intellectually coming to life for me. During my time at Wayne State the writings of Carl Henry especially but also Gordon Clark and Bernard Ramm started me on the task of trying to make sense of what I believed as a Christian and what I was learning as a budding philosopher. An Episcopal cathedral near campus had a bookstore, and there I learned about William Temple and F. R. Tennant, Anglican philosophers of considerable ability. My Baptist pastor, Roy McBeth, introduced me to C. S. Lewis. The InterVarsity Christian Fellowship chapter on campus held Tuesday meetings at which Vernon Grounds talked about Christianity and psychology, Gordon Clark discussed Emil Brunner's theory of revelation, and the group's academic adviser, David Gillespie, lectured on Christian social theory and Christian social practice. These lectures were as good as any in my university classes. In those days, *Christianity Today*, edited by Carl Henry, carried articles dealing with intellectual issues. A group of some seven or eight InterVarsity members met in Bill Brown's campus apartment a couple of times a week for no-holds-barred discussions of matters theological, historical, psychological and philosophical. I read the New Testament thoroughly, and thus gained an ability to distinguish what Christianity teaches from various perversions of it. From such invaluable if unstructured sources as these I learned about what Christian colleges these days like to describe as "the integration of faith and learning."[2]

Whatever else I did or didn't learn during this period, two things became clear. The campus ministries (InterVarsity aside) seemed impressed by the various perspectives newly available within very broadly construed Christian thought. Paul Tillich's *God Beyond God* and Rudolf Bultmann's demythologizing, for example, were considered to be better than anything mere Christianity might offer. Later the "death of God" movement took pride of place. So I felt obligated to read Tillich, Bultmann and the "death of God" writers. Doing so convinced me that whether or not mere Christianity was true, Tillich's version of the apersonal absolute, Bultmann's Christianity filtered through Heidegger, and Van Buren's or Altizer's "God-is-dead" views could not withstand anything like a careful rational assessment. Viewed under the sort of scrutiny that philosophers on both sides of the fence gave to Christian belief, these substitutes fell apart.

At the theological dining table, trading mere Christianity for these perspectives was a matter of giving up bone china and getting paper plates instead. A more recent example is provided by John Hick's critique of the incarnation and Tom Morris's defense of the doctrine in *The Logic of God Incarnate*[3]; the former is water and the latter is wine. After this extensive reading I drew a moral that I continue to accept: *Secularized versions of mere Christianity are uniformly very less reasonable to accept than is mere Christianity itself.* Atheism I can respect; it has some impressive representatives and formulations. Christianity filtered through some sort of secularism is not something that I, as a philosopher, can take seriously.

The other thing that became clear was this. I read a lot of works arguing that Christianity is true—books of "Christian apologetics." Most of them were depressing, typically claiming to prove everything while proving nothing at all. The few decent ones concluded that Christianity was true from premises that at best supported monotheism. So I read apologetics for the other side, books like Bertrand Russell's *Why I Am Not a Christian*. Russell's work in logic was brilliant; his work in metaphysics and epistemology was deep, probing and fascinating. But I found that he neither understood Christianity very well nor had any powerful things to say against what he did understand. Like his writings in ethics, his book on religion seemed (and seems) to me sloppy, poorly argued and richly unpersuasive. So, I concluded, writing about the justification of religious belief, or the lack thereof, is extremely difficult. *Rational assessment of anything worth assessing is hard, and bad arguments can be given for a view that in fact is entirely defensible.*

I later discovered much more interesting arguments on both sides of the fence, but it is very easy to write badly about such matters, and most of what is written on these topics is poor stuff. It is, of course, crucial to read arguments on both sides of the issue in order to obtain a real understanding of either side.[4]

The sorts of views that I have confessed are very paradigms of what many academics regard as irrational psychological crutches at best. Others view them as private matters, the way that some people feel about really big things and others do not. Some even grant that there might be reasons for accepting them, and then go on to distinguish between truth-supporting reasons and pragmatic reasons. If I open a box that I am carrying and show you the turtle inside it, I give you a truth-supporting reason for believing that there is a turtle in the box. If I show you the box and offer you a hundred dollars if you will believe that there is a turtle in it, I give you a pragmatic but not truth-supporting reason for coming to believe that the box contains a turtle. So, we are kindly told, there may be pragmatic reasons for having religious beliefs, but there cannot be any truth-supporting reasons.

These sorts of views about reasons for belief seem to me patently false. They come largely from the privatization of religion and morals. On this popular perspective, what one believes about politicians, planets and football can be objective, reasonable, supported by evidence and true. But if one believes that God exists or that child abuse is wrong, that is just one's opinion—feelings about things and nothing more. Thought through and made consistent, this privatization would have disastrous consequences, making law arbitrary and any preference for science over superstition or democracy over tyranny merely arbitrary. So the privatization line is appealed to when convenient and left aside otherwise. Neither right-to-life nor right-to-choice proponents are likely to think their views are mere private sentiments on the level of liking or not liking anchovies, and they are right not to do so. Similarly, members of the Evangelical Theology Society and of the Freedom from Religion Foundation are unlikely to think of their differences as simply a difference in taste, comparable with their feelings about eating cooked cabbage, and they too are right not to do so.

Taking a cold, hard look at the reasons offered for thinking that the sorts of beliefs I began by confessing cannot be reasonably held, cannot be supported by anything better than pragmatic reasons or should be privatized reveals that the case is not very impressive. There are theories of meaning that cannot bear their own weight; the most famous is one that says *Whatever is true or false is true or false by definition or can be confirmed or disconfirmed by sensory experience,* which of course is itself neither true nor false by definition nor anything that sensory experience can confirm or disconfirm. There are theories of confirmation that are as hard as religious doctrines to decide between and require defense by similar sorts of arguments; the more restrictive of such theories—the ones whose truth would entail that we cannot make any rational decisions regarding religious doctrines—turn out to be false even on their own terms. There is no truth-supporting reason to accept the view that only pragmatic reasons can be given for accepting religious beliefs. The idea that we can reliably believe only what science tells us is not itself something science tells us, so we cannot reliably believe it. Whatever may be the source of the view that religious doctrines are beyond all possibility of rational assessment, it isn't reason.

I discovered early on that interest in the rationality of Christian belief may well not be welcomed in American churches that embrace mere Christianity. One reason for this is the impact of the privatization view within the church, which in many ways reflects the general culture. Another is a misunderstanding of biblical texts. "Eye has not seen, neither has ear heard, nor has it entered into the heart of man, what God has prepared for those who love Him" is quoted and the rest of the passage, "but God has revealed them unto us," is quietly ignored. "My ways are not your ways, neither are my thoughts your thoughts, saith the Lord of Hosts; for as high as the heavens are above the earth, so are my thoughts above your thoughts" is quoted, but the context is ignored. The context is that the people of Israel have again turned to idolatry, which they know full well to be wrong; their problem is not that they do not know what God's view of idolatry is, but that, knowing this, they practice idolatry anyway. The problem is disobedience, not ignorance or impenetrable mystery.

Another reason for this lack of interest is a slide that scholars and nonscholars easily make from (i) *not everything about God can be known* to (ii) *God is incomprehensible* to (iii) *nothing can be known about God*. Unfortunately, (ii) can be read as identical to either (i) or (iii), and having accepted (i) it is easy to confuse it with (iii). Making such distinctions is not much prized either in the general culture or in the church. Still another reason is the diminution that has occurred in much of American Christianity, for which conversion and evangelism, sometimes supplemented by social action, exhaust Christianity. The idea that Christianity can redeem and enrich culture plays little role in pulpit or pew outside of some Reformed churches. Paul's remarks about a particular philosophy that viewed itself as a means of salvation are not infrequently—but entirely mistakenly—taken to have unkind consequences for contemporary philosophy. No doubt there are other sources as well.

Paul's writings, when they come to his hopes and expectations for Christian believers, are liberally sprinkled with cognitive verbs and moral adjectives. He sees Christian maturity in terms of knowledge and understanding, mature virtue and principled, self-giving love. His emphasis, in my experience, has largely been lost in American Christianity. I take it as obvious that the cognitive verbs are not part of a mandate for all Christians to earn at least one degree in philosophy. What they do sanction is the sort of integration of faith and learning that such an education (among a variety of other things) can facilitate.

My professional life is divided between teaching and research (with the inevitable pound of flesh for administration—administrators who have power can do good; administration as it comes into the average faculty member's experience involves no power and centers on paperwork). I have done almost all of my teaching in a very secular state university. This context has been excellent for me. At times Christians, usually associated with one or another campus-oriented group, have suggested that the classroom is a good place for evangelism. They have found me utterly lacking in appreciation for this perspective. My students expect to be taught philosophy. Once they sign up and start attending, they are a captive audience. My job is to teach them some philosophy. It has always seemed to me that to proselytize, in this context, would be wrong. I do not do it.

Two arguments have been advanced in an effort to change my view. The first is that since atheist professors make their atheism plain in their classrooms, why should I not make my Christian convictions plain? *Do two wrongs make a right?* The other argument is more subtle: We cannot be objective anyway, so we owe it to our students to tell them where we are coming from. *Let's see now. The idea is that we can objectively tell that we cannot be objective, and objectively tell that we therefore owe our students a list of our assumptions, about which we cannot be objective in the first place.* I find it hard to see, on this view, why getting an education would be worth the effort, save as a union card for certain sorts of employment. In any case, I reject the reasoning, such as it is.

Earlier I alluded to the typical, though not universal, inadequacy of books on apologetics. The most nourishing works by Christian scholars are typically excellent work in their field, done in accord with the highest academic standards (which does not include being conformed to whatever dogmas happen to dominate the discipline at the moment), done on topics related to Christian thought. There are topics in philosophy (as in other areas) where a materialist will write differently from a dualist, a utilitarian differently from a respect-for-persons ethicist, a confirmationist differently from a falsificationist, and so on, in ways that do not mean that either party is guilty of simply imposing her basic commitments on the data under discussion. Neither writer need be cheating. Such work, at its best, reveals something of the degree to which different basic perspectives do or do not illumine evidence, data, experience and theory. There are topics in philosophy (and in other areas) on which a theist will write differently from an atheist or an agnostic, and a few where a Christian will write differently from a non-Christian monotheist. I suggest that it is in such work, in whatever field, that the most helpful, nourishing, informative and insightful work is done for those who wish to see Christian scholarship at work. In such work, the views of the writer will come out in the process of work that is well done, publicly accessible (at least within the field), and without misuse of the mild authority a professor possesses in a classroom.[5]

It is not for nothing that Paul wrote of our seeing "in a glass darkly." The problem of evil has two aspects. One is evidential: Does the existence of evil provide evidence that God does not exist? The other is behavioral: How does one deal with the evils that afflict those one loves? I take the answer to the former question to be no. The answer to the second question is enormously harder. Christianity affirms the worth of the people we love, viewing them as created in God's own image. On this view, the suffering they undergo is objectively evil and rightly deplored. Hence, from a Christian view, the behavioral problem is genuine. It arises from how things are, not merely from how we feel about how things are. Hard thinking is relevant to, and sufficient for, the evidential problem of evil. It may be relevant to, but it is certainly not sufficient for, the behavioral problem.

Distinct though they are, there is a bridge between the problems. One wants to understand particular evils—why did my mother suffer from Parkinson's disease, my mother-in-law from cancer. Hard thought about the problem of evil can give some understanding of why there is evil. It will not tell you why there is this particular evil or that. Clear-headed reasoning is the only remedy for the evidential problem. As far as I can see, trust in God is the main element in constructing the bridge between the problems.

214

What little there is to say about my own religious beliefs (other than the far more interesting question as to why anyone might think them true[6]) has been said. People obviously differ. So do universities and colleges, local understandings of what is appropriate and desirable, and social and political contexts. My comments apply to myself and my understanding of my own university. I have excellent reason to be grateful to God's common grace, having been extremely fortunate in my teachers, colleagues and students, most of whom have not embraced mere Christianity.

The issues discussed in this essay are easier to talk about than the mustard seed of trust, the slow business of maturing, dealing with the pain and death of loved ones, the sobering recognition that there is just so much one can do and no more, and the fact that one's ability to see what meaning events have is slight indeed, all of which partly constitute one's life.

People seem to assume that the big questions are unanswerable and the little questions are easy by comparison. I come close to taking the opposite view. The arguments in favor of monotheism seem to me much clearer and more forceful than any reasons I have for thinking that this rather than that is the solution to a problem relating to family or friends. Mere Christianity is much harder in the living than in the thinking.

Notes

[1]Some theologians have suggested that by "confession" the church has meant something incompatible with, or at least independent of, anyone claiming that anything is true. I take it that this seems preposterous because it is preposterous.

[2]Anyone wanting accessible, good examples of such integration should look up books by Arthur Holmes. His *All Truth Is God's Truth* (Grand Rapids: Eerdmans, 1977) is a good place to begin. For high-quality presentations of apologetics-relevant issues, see Basil Mitchell, *The Justification of Religious Belief* (New York: Macmillan, 1973) and *Morality: Religious and Secular* (Oxford, U.K.: Clarendon Press, 1980); Richard Purtill, *Reason to Believe* (Grand Rapids, Mich.: Eerdmans, 1974) and *Thinking About Religion*

(Englewood Cliffs, N.J.: Prentice Hall, 1978). InterVarsity Press (Downers Grove, Ill.) has a Contours of Christian Philosophy Series with volumes by C. Stephen Evans (philosophy of religion), William Hasker (metaphysics), Arthur Holmes (ethics), Del Ratzsch (philosophy of science) and W. Jay Wood (epistemology).

[3]Tom Morris, *The Logic of God Incarnate* (Ithaca, N.Y.: Cornell University Press, 1987).

[4]A recent interesting book in this regard is J. J. C. Smart and J. J. Haldane, *Atheism and Theism* (Oxford, U.K.: Blackwell, 1996).

[5]Any list of examples leaves out lots of worthy examples. With trepidation, I mention a few names: Herbert Butterfield and Robert Frykenberg in history; Paul Vitz in psychology; Brian Hebblethwaite, Ronald Feenstra, Alister McGrath and Neil Plantinga in theology; N. T. Wright in biblical studies; William Alston, Alan Donagan, George Mavrodes, Alvin Plantinga and William Wainwright in philosophy; David Lyle Jeffrey in literature. Lamin Sanneh is less easy to classify. Apologies to the many left unmentioned!

[6]For anyone who is interested, I have discussed such matters in *Basic Issues in the Philosophy of Religion* (Boston: Allyn & Bacon, 1971), *Christianity and Philosophy* (Grand Rapids, Mich.: Eerdmans, 1984), *Hume's "Inexplicable Mystery": His Views on Religion* (Philadelphia: Temple University Press, 1990), *The Epistemology of Religious Experience* (Cambridge: Cambridge University Press, 1993) and *The Philosophy of Religion* (New York: Routledge, 1998).

22

On Being a Slow Learner

DAVID LYLE JEFFREY

English Literature
(Emeritus)

University of Ottawa

Often God seems to work out his purposes for us slowly,
indirectly, and despite ourselves.
—DAVID LYLE JEFFREY

Recently I experienced a ceremonial induction as guest professor of Peking University. I was called on to show modest warrant for the honor my distinguished hosts were conferring on me in the form of an induction lecture. From among possible topics I had suggested speaking on they had chosen "Foundations of Western Literary Theory from the Bible to St. Augustine." In the presence of a delegation of faculty and university officials, about forty graduate students followed my four-page handout of biblical passages (Genesis 1; Proverbs 8; John 1; Romans and 1—2 Corinthians) and quotations from Augustine's *On Christian Doctrine* as I tracked basic early Western connections between God's Word and human utterance, God's verbal fiat and human creativity, revelation and the Word made flesh.

The hour was followed by a lively discussion period, which was somewhat unusual in my experience of Chinese universities. Ten minutes into it, a hand went up in the middle of the room. Someone whose eyes were only just visible above the sofa in front of her asked me an astonishingly direct question: "You have been showing us how early Western literary theories locate meaning not primarily in the sign or the signified, but in the person. You say that this is because human language is seen by the Bible writers as an analogue of the way God speaks—or has spoken. But if you do not mind answering this question, do you yourself, a modern Western professor, actually believe in God?" The room was suddenly quiet and tense. I smiled directly at her and said simply, "Sure!" There were a few chuckles and some murmuring in the crowd. "Yes," I said, repeating myself to be sure everyone understood. "I most certainly do believe in God."

"Of course," said an emphatic professorial voice behind me, "he is a Christian."

"Yes," I replied without taking my own gaze off the pair of eyes still fixed on me from behind the sofa, "but would you like to ask a supplementary question?" And she did.

But before I get to that supplementary question, allow me to make a couple of observations about her first question. To begin with, it will be clear that a blunt inquiry can mask a diversity of questions behind the question—often the most needful interrogative for us to discern. Her motive might have been anything from a desire for confirmation of spiritual empathy from a fellow believer to a desire for forcible exposure by one entirely antipathetic to Christianity. Or it might, as I suspect in this case, simply express an incredulous curiosity that a Western intellectual of the late twentieth century should believe in anything at all. Each of these motives calls for a distinct and attuned response to the person of the questioner—even where the short answer might be verbally almost identical. But any of them will serve to show that such a question is getting at both a popular myth and a discordant fact about the contemporary university. The myth is that serious intellectual life and Christian faith are incompatible. The discordant fact—in our own time as in others—is that some of the most vigorous, productive and learned intellectuals in many fields are Christians. Not only that, but the very vigor and courage of their intellectual life is often visibly prompted by their gratitude to God and their love of God's truth, wherever it is to be found. Yet I confess that it took me some time to appreciate this fact for myself.

When I was growing up in the rural Ottawa Valley among folk and family of quasi-Baptist fundamentalist persuasions, it was normative for my people to suspect intellectuals—for their intellectualism. These people thought (with some reason) that intellectual pride was one of the most dangerous forms of pride and that proud "intellectuals" were often the most threatening and abusive enemies of faith. Moreover, they thought them inclined to be disdainful of ordinary people and of community values and Christian virtues. They did not need to have read Rousseau, Gibbon, Nietzsche, Marx, Darwin or Freud to have come to this conclusion; newspaper columns, magazine articles and school board meetings were sufficiently instructive. Accordingly, the temptation to idolize higher education was not very widespread in my community. No one before me in my father's family had gone to university for perhaps hundreds of years; in my mother's family only the youngest of twelve children, an aunt nine years my senior, had ventured into the dangerous corridors of a public university.

But Aunt Mabel happened to have a very special place in my life. First, to keep me from driving my mother crazy, she had taught me to read at three years of age, thereby setting me well down the path to a bookish thoughtfulness before any of us knew what that might lead to. She was herself a superb student and an accomplished pianist. In her teenage years she and a friend would take me into rural Wesleyan churches where I, as a boy soprano, sang hymns to her accompaniment (and encouragement). She was in many ways my first important teacher. After she graduated from nursing school, she left to go to Bible school, and I missed her a great deal.

My young aunt collapsed with polio during her first term at Moody Bible Institute. She returned home a full paraplegic, and it seemed to me that everything I thought lovely had been irreparably stricken. As she lay in the hospital, breathing with difficulty, able to move only the little finger of her left hand, I wanted to know why God had ever let her go away to study. I can remember asking her that day if she would ever be able to play the piano again. She answered graciously, more graciously than I could then understand. "I don't know. We'll have to see. It's not too likely." Seeing me crestfallen, she added quickly, "But I can still read. And that's more important." It was. In tandem with her great courage and absence of self-pity, it provided her the means to degrees from Western (Ontario) and the University of Toronto and then a fruitful career as a medical librarian.

While Aunt Mabel was still an undergraduate at Toronto, I finished high school with no plans to go on to university. She objected and went so far as to arrange through a friend of hers at Wheaton College for me to fly down in late August and take an SAT test. I found time to catch a pickup workout with the ball team, and Coach Richard (Hooker) Gross kindly drove me back to Midway airport to go home, negotiate with my parents and, as it turned out, pack my bags.

Often God seems to work out his purposes for us slowly, indirectly and despite ourselves. My eventual academic career was not at all apparent in the chain of events that finally led me to it. I arrived at Wheaton College as a seventeen-year-old, worked my way through two years of part-time jobs, sports and economics classes ("If I am going to contribute part of this, make it practical!" my father had said) and then returned home to help for three years with our family business. After a year at home and despite deep last-minute misgivings, I married. A year and six months later I succumbed under extreme stress to what the doctors thought at first was leukemia. Obliged to rest, I read books, taking a special deep interest in Russian novels—Pushkin, Gogol, Andreev, Dostoevsky, Tolstoy, Pasternak. Deep yearnings welled up within me, yearnings for meaning, for truth, for love, for God. I prayed, promising God that if I should be spared I would leave behind my life in business and give my life instead to serving others for his sake, in whatever way I should be led to do that. In time my symptoms lessened (which the doctors attributed either to misdiagnosis or to remission), and I wrote to Wheaton College asking if they would take me back. They did, and I enrolled in courses in literature, philosophy and science. It was not until the end of my new program that I decided to take up the scholarships that I had been awarded and invest them toward a Ph.D. in English literature.

Much of my academic life has been preoccupied with devising

strategies for overcoming shyness and the indecision that often is part of it. I finally chose Princeton University over Harvard University because it was small. Later, when my mentors arranged a first job for me at Yale, I agreed to the visit but declined Yale's offer, returning instead to one of the smallest of Canadian universities at that time (University of Victoria). For the first twenty years of my career I had to combat stage fright during the opening ten minutes of my lectures. I avoided professional association meetings. Bluffing my way through public situations became much more possible, however, than coping with the stresses of a failed marriage. I became ill again, was misdiagnosed, had major surgery and was unhelpfully rediagnosed. At this time my marriage was at last dissolved altogether. For six years I lived alone, buried in a largely unproductive workaholism, more candidly withdrawn now than ever.

In retrospect I can see that in some ways my tendency to withdraw helped me to avoid at least some of the prideful miscreance my parents' church had felt sure would overtake me in the university. My indecisiveness has probably been the more costly failing. But I have known God's merciful reclamation, too, in both these measures of my own inadequacy. Some of this reclamation has been going on for a long time. At Wheaton I learned to see past the overbearing personalities of popular moment and into the fuller, richer tapestry of God's redeeming love in the life of the church. With two of my friends, one a Catholic Cuban who had escaped from Cuba during the early sixties in a rowboat, the other a skeptical midwestern evangelical (equally addicted to coffee), I would marvel at the luxuriousness and painful beauty of the traces of God's truth to be found in the annals of poetry and philosophy. I came to see for the first time that the body of Christ was not just a local and boisterously present community but a community both universal and timeless in its witness through the ages to the cross. And this made me yearn to know my deeper identity, to enter into the eternal communion of the saints with the Lord of all history. And so I found a new and vital focus, and I began to explore it eagerly.

All my subsequent scholarly life has been devoted to this exploration, through foul weather and fair. It has drawn me into a pursuit of the life of the Holy Spirit in the life of God's people, especially as that gets so variously and resonantly witnessed to not merely in words but in changed lives. My formal subject has been literature in the widest sense, particularly those expressions of literature that both track and give expression to the true "grand narrative" of our civilization. This study has taken me back to the languages and literatures of the Middle Ages and the early church, forward from great scholar saints such as Ambrose, Augustine, Jerome, John Chrysostom and Gregory to modern poets and fiction makers who swim in their wake, for example, G. M. Hopkins, T. S. Eliot, Flannery O'Connor and Wendell Berry.

It has been for me, as for many, an immensely rewarding field of inquiry. For one thing, in both teaching and research I am called on to respond to transparent echoes and reiterations of the Word of God. The primary materials in my field often render explicit what in some fields typically remains only implicit, making it more possible to share new life with others. And this makes possible vigorous and focused interlocution with those who are not open to the witness of faith as well as with those who have rejected it, sometimes for very principled reasons.

Being part of a larger academic community has allowed me to discover committed, biblically literate and Christ-centered colleagues from many disciplines and many denominational backgrounds. One of the principal joys of my professional life (and the highlight of my workweek) is our Tuesday-morning fellowship and study breakfast here at the University of Ottawa. For two hours about twenty faculty and doctoral students meet together over a text, bringing one another's disciplinary and life experiences to bear on our common quest for understanding and faithfulness. We have discovered just how much we need our membership in the body of Christ and how wonderfully germinal this is to our participation in the work of the university. We draw as fully as possible on our collective gifts and wisdom to come to that deeper knowledge of the truth and the more effective teaching we all seek. As a community of believers we are far less prone to try to survive on a pretense of solitary genius.

Now as I promised, allow me to return to the supplementary question of the Peking University graduate student: "How does your belief in God relate to your academic work?" Clearly the questioner was asking unambiguously for a standard by which to discern the true meaning of the answer I had given to her first question. So I immediately turned to the issue most basic for understanding Christian thought and Christian obedience alike. I made the point that the "literary theory" propounded by the Bible was absolutely dependent on the acceptance of two things: first, that the Bible was not merely human invention or creativity but in some fundamental sense God's revelation of himself to humankind; second, that the definitive "last word" or full expression was his word made flesh in Jesus, making the concrete, historical incarnation the cornerstone of the foundation. Many people present seemed genuinely surprised that a Western intellectual would say this. More discussion of the point followed, especially about inspiration. I referred to the prophets (Isaiah, Jeremiah, Amos) to show how the biblical writer was not at all like the "original genius" or self-styled literary prophet of Romantic literature (Blake et al.), speaking novelties on his own authority. The biblical cases make clear that biblical writers were given the words that they said; they were "mouthpieces" or a "voice" for a word too great for them to have brought into being. Accordingly, their own personalities were incidental, even irrelevant as a context for what they said. They were servants, not masters. As we finished and I was meeting some professors, a young teacher of postmodern literary theory said to me in evident conviction, "You have cast into doubt for me the value of all that I teach."

Well, I thought to myself, *fair enough.* Yet, in truth, what I have been attempting to explain determines the value of all that *I* teach. And I have been myself such a slow learner.

Nothing as desirable as an integration of Christian thought and Christian obedience comes cheaply. The *via crucis* is a path of both mortification and perseverance. I think of my Aunt Mabel as a moving instance of this. But she would be the first to agree that the one who is determined to walk on this path will meet also with unexpected joy, peace and strength to endure in times of trial. And still more—blessings beyond any reasonable expectation.

Academic success and the pleasures of the intellectual life are most certainly not the chief end of humankind. To glorify God and enjoy him forever vastly eclipses any merely instrumental goals. Further, the gifts of family—especially, for me, my magnificent wife Katherine and each of my five wonderful children—and of cherished friends in faith come far, far ahead of any academic accomplishments in my scale of affections and sources of gratitude. But I have also found increasingly over the years that the love of learning and the desire for God are not by any stretch of mind and heart incompatible with these prior affections. Indeed, it can be, in the mercy of God, that the love of learning is one of the most powerful of promptings to the love of God himself and of others for his sake.

About the Authors

Paul M. Anderson is professor of biochemistry and molecular biology in the School of Medicine at the University of Minnesota, Duluth. He received his Ph.D. in biochemistry from the University of Minnesota in 1964. After postdoctoral training at Tufts School of Medicine in Boston, he served on the faculty in the department of chemistry and biochemistry at Southern Illinois University for four years and as a research investigator at Miles Laboratories for a year before joining the faculty in the new School of Medicine at the University of Minnesota, Duluth, in 1971; he served as head of the department of biochemistry at UM Duluth for fourteen years. His research work, funded by grants from the National Science Foundation and the National Institutes of Health, has focused on enzyme mechanisms, nitrogen metabolism in fish, and more recently regulation of gene expression in fish. Professor Anderson serves on the editorial board of the *Journal of Biological Chemistry*, has published over eighty papers and review articles in journals and books, and has received a Fulbright scholarship to India. He and his wife, Carol, are members of First Lutheran Church in Duluth and have three grown children, Todd, Scott and Catherine.

Ronald D. Anderson is professor of education at the University of Colorado in Boulder, where he has been a faculty member for thirty-three years. His distinguished leadership career in science education is reflected in the titles of his numerous scholarly publications and in the many papers he has presented at conferences and as reports. Professor Anderson has served as a program director in the Directorate for Science and Engineering Education of the National Science

Foundation, as associate dean for research and science in the School of Education at the University of Colorado, as director of many science education improvement projects at the state and national levels, and as a consultant for many education programs. He received a Fulbright Senior Research Award and conducted research for a year in Germany. He and his wife, Sandra J. Anderson, have three grown children and are members of First Presbyterian Church in Boulder, Colorado.

E. C. "Gene" Ashby is Regents' Professor Emeritus at the Georgia Institute of Technology. He received the Ph.D. degree from the University of Notre Dame and worked with the Ethyl Corporation in Baton Rouge, Louisiana, for seven years before joining the Georgia Institute of Technology in 1963. Professor Ashby has published over 280 papers in leading chemical journals, has lectured at more than eighty universities in the United States and other countries, has been a plenary lecturer at meetings of the American, British and French Chemical Societies, the Congress of Pure and Applied Chemistry, and has chaired numerous national and international conferences. He has served on the editorial boards of the *Journal of Organic Chemistry* and *Organometallics,* has been a Sloan Fellow and a Guggenheim Fellow, was awarded the Lavoisier Medal by the French Chemical Society (1971) and the Herty Medal by the American Chemical Society (1984), and was the recipient of the Distinguished Professor Award at the Georgia Institute of Technology (1988). Two chemical plants have been built as a result of research carried out in his laboratory. He served as project director of the Hanford Project (nuclear waste) at Georgia Tech from its inception in 1990 until September 1993.

Ashby and his wife, Carolyn, have seven grown children and eleven grandchildren and are members of Landmark Church in Atlanta, Georgia.

James N. BeMiller has been director of the Whistler Center for Carbohydrate Research at Purdue University since its inception in 1986. He earned his Ph.D. degree in biochemistry from Purdue University in 1959 and then spent two years pursuing postdoctoral studies. He served on the faculty in various teaching, research and administrative capacities at Southern Illinois University in the department of chemistry and biochemistry and in the School of Medicine. Professor BeMiller has received several teaching and research awards and honors, including the Melville L. Wolfrom Award of the Division of Carbohydrate Chemistry, American Chemical Society, and the Medal of the Japanese Society of Applied Glycoscience. He has published over two hundred papers, book chapters and book reviews, has authored or edited twenty-two books and has presented over 160 talks or papers related to the work of his students and himself in the area of carbohydrate chemistry.

BeMiller and his wife, Pari, have two grown sons and two grandchildren and are members of Our Savior Lutheran Church in West Lafayette, Indiana.

Verna Benner Carson was a member of the faculty of the School of Nursing at the University of Maryland for over twenty-one years until 1995. She received the Ph.D. degree in human development from the University of Maryland and is certified as a clinical specialist in adult psychiatric nursing. Carson began her work in the area of spiritual care as part of nursing practice in the early 1970s. In 1989 she published a book entitled *Spiritual Dimensions of Nursing Care*, which won two *American Journal of Nursing* Book of the Year Awards and is currently being revised for a second edition. Carson has coauthored four other books, including *Mental Health Nursing: The Nurse-Patient Journey*. She has also published over fifty articles and has completed five major research projects on the importance of spirituality to patient care. Carson was recently recognized by the American Psychiatric Nurses Association for her pioneering work in the field of psychiatric home care.

Carson has three sons, Adam, Johnny and Robbie. She and her husband, Adam, are members of St. Thomas More Catholic Church in Baltimore, Maryland.

Mark T. Clark is professor of political science, chair of the political science department and director of the National Security Study Program at California State University, San Bernardino. He has also taught at the University of Southern California (USC), has served as a consultant to the U.S. government on National Security Affairs at the U.S. Naval Postgraduate School in Monterey, California, and has been a visiting scholar at the Hoover Institution on War, Revolution and Peace. Clark received his Ph.D. degree from the School of International Relations at USC in 1989. He served in the U.S. Marine Corps from 1973 to 1977. Clark has published papers on arms control, nuclear strategy, military ethics, Soviet/Russian and U.S. foreign and defense policy, nuclear proliferation and collective security/peacekeeping operations.

Clark and his wife, Mara, are members of Sierra Vista Community Church in Claremont, California.

J. Gary Eden is professor of electrical and computer engineering at the University of Illinois, Urbana. Upon receiving the Ph.D. degree from the University of Illinois in 1976, he was awarded a National Research Council Postdoctoral Research Associateship at the Naval Research Laboratory (Washington, D.C.). Subsequently, he joined the optical sciences division of NRL and made several contributions to the area of visible and ultraviolet lasers and laser spectroscopy. He received a Research Publication Award from NRL for work in which he codiscovered the proton beam-pumped laser. Eden joined the faculty of the University of Illinois in 1979. He and his students have focused their research efforts on the laser spectroscopy of small molecules and the demonstration and application of short wavelength lasers. Eden has published extensively (more than 150 publications, including a book) and has been awarded twelve patents. He is a Fellow of the Optical Society of America, the American Physical Society and the IEEE. He is also a member of four honorary organizations and was recently named the James F. Towey University Scholar at Illinois. Eden is editor in chief of the IEEE *Journal of Quantum Electronics* and has served as associate dean of the Graduate School at the University of Illinois and assistant dean of the College of Engineering. He has directed the theses of twenty-six Ph.D. students.

Eden, his wife, Carolyn, and their three children, Rob, Laura, and Kate, live in Mahomet, Illinois, and attend Grace Baptist Church.

Kenneth G. Elzinga is professor of economics at the University of Virginia, where he has been a faculty member since 1967. Elzinga earned his Ph.D. degree at Michigan State University. He has been a Fellow in Law and Economics at the University of Chicago and was the Thomas Jefferson Visiting Scholar at Downing College, Cambridge University. He is the recipient of the Cavaliers' Distinguished Teaching Professorship, the Thomas Jefferson Award, the Commonwealth of Virginia Outstanding Faculty Award, the Raven Society Faculty Honor Award and the UVA Alumni Association Distinguished Professor Award. His major research interest is antitrust economics. The author of more than seventy publications, Elzinga is best known for *The Antitrust Penalties* and *The Antitrust Casebook* along with three mystery novels coauthored with William Briet—*Murder at the Margin, The Fatal Equilibrium* and *A Deadly Indifference*—that employ economic analysis in solving crimes. In addition to membership in economics associations, Elzinga is a member of Mystery Writers of America and serves on the board of directors of InterVarsity Christian Fellowship/USA.

Elzinga and his wife, Terry, are members of Trinity Presbyterian Church in Charlottesville, Virginia.

Philip J. Gersmehl is professor of geography and adjunct professor of American studies and education at the University of Minnesota. After receiving his Ph.D. degree from the University of Georgia, Gersmehl was a member of the faculty at Concordia Teachers College, where he had received his B.A. degree, until joining the faculty at the University of Minnesota in 1975. He has published numerous articles in major academic journals in the general area of agricultural resources and education as related to geography. Gersmehl's accomplishments in and commitment to education and the field of geography have been recognized by outstanding teaching awards from the University of Minnesota and the National Council for Geographic Education, participation as an invited consultant in numerous workshops, review panels and United States-Russia and United States-Japan curriculum development teams, and service on the editorial board of *The Professional Geographer.*

Gersmehl and his wife, Carol Ahlschwede, are members of St. Stephanus Lutheran Church in St. Paul, Minnesota.

Louisa (Sue) Hulett is professor and chair of political science at Knox College, and advises the campus chapters of InterVarsity Christian Fellowship and Fellowship of Christian Athletes. She received the Distinguished Teaching Award in 1994. In addition to her teaching career at Knox College, she has taught at the University of Illinois, University of Nebraska and California State University (Long Beach). She also taught as an Associated Colleges of the Midwest Exchange Professor in Russia in 1995. Hulett received the Ph.D. degree in International Relations at the University of Southern California. She has received fellowships from the Earhart, Ford and Lilly Foundations, the Illinois Humanities Council, Exxon and the University of Michigan. Recently she has participated in the Association of Religion and Intellectual Life Summer Seminar, the C. S. Lewis Summer Institute on Science and Faith in Cambridge, U.K., the European Association for the Advancement of Social Sciences Euroconference in Vienna, and faculty development seminars in international relations in Maine and Russia. Hulett has published three books and ten articles on the topic of international relations.

Hulett attends Bethel Baptist Church (Midwest Baptist Conference) and is a member of the Cursillo and Chrysalis renewal/retreat ministries.

David Lyle Jeffrey is professor emeritus of English literature at the University of Ottawa, where he has served for twenty years, including three years as chair of the department of English. Professor Jeffrey earned his Ph.D. degree from Princeton University. Before accepting his appointment to Ottawa, the Canadian-born scholar had been an associate professor and chair of the department of English at the University of Victoria, visiting professor at Regent College, visiting professor of English literature at the University of Hull (England) and assistant professor, then associate professor, of English at the University of Rochester (New York). He has also been a visiting professor at the Graduate School of Notre Dame University and is guest professor at Peking University in China. Most recently he has helped to found Augustine College, a one-year foundation program in Christianity and the liberal arts located in Ottawa, Canada. Jeffrey's primary areas of professional interest are medieval studies (including the history of the English language), the Bible and literature, and modern English literature. He has been the recipient of numerous academic awards, among them Woodrow Wilson and Canada Council Doctoral Awards and several book-of-the-year awards. He was named University of Ottawa Faculty of Arts Professor of the Year (1995) and Fellow of the Royal Society of Canada in 1996. Professor Jeffrey is a member of numerous literary societies and is general editor and coauthor of the monumental reference work *A Dictionary of Biblical Tradition in English Literature*. He is the author of numerous books, including *People of the Book: Christian Identity and Literary Culture*.

Jeffrey has five children: Bruce, Kirsten, Adrienne, Gideon and Joshua. Jeffrey and his wife, Katherine, are members of St. James Anglican Church in Crystal Rock, Ontario.

James P. Keener is professor of mathematics at the University of Utah, where he has served on the faculty for nineteen years, following six years at the University of Arizona. During his academic career Keener has been a visiting scholar of the University of Heidelberg (West Germany), Oxford University (England), National Institutes of Health and Stanford University. Professor Keener received the Ph.D. degree from the California Institute of Technology. His research interests are in applied mathematics, specifically chemical and biological dynamics, and electrocardiology. Keener authored the textbook *Principles of Applied Mathematics*, and he has authored or coauthored more than eighty papers in major journals. He is coauthor of the recently published book *Mathematical Physiology*.

Keener and his wife, Kristine, and their two children, Samantha and Justin, are members of First Presbyterian Church of Salt Lake City.

Michael W. McConnell assumed the Presidential Professorship at the University of Utah College of Law in January 1997, prior to which he was on the faculty of the Law School at the University of Chicago (since 1985). He served as William B. Graham Professor of Law and Senior Fellow, John M. Olin Center for Inquiry into the Theory and Practice of Democracy, from 1992 to 1996, and as assistant to the solicitor general, Department of Justice, from 1983 to 1985. Other positions held include visiting and research professor at the University of Utah, President's Intelligence Oversight Board member, assistant general counsel to the Office of Management and Budget, law clerk to Justice William J. Brennan Jr., U.S. Supreme Court, and special consultant to Mayer, Brown, and Platt (constitutional and other appellate litigation). He received his J.D. degree from the University of Chicago in 1979. McConnell has argued nine cases in the U.S. Supreme Court, has filed many briefs in the U.S. Supreme Court, lower federal courts and state courts, has published extensively on the subjects of First Amendment, constitutional and interpretive theory, allocation of powers, economic rights and regulation and the Fourteenth Amendment. He is a Fellow of the American Academy of Arts and Sciences, and is a member of the Christian Legal Society and numerous other academic, professional and civic organizations. He presently serves as chair of the Constitutional Law section of the Association of American Law Schools.

McConnell and his wife, Mary, and their three children, Harriet, Emily and Samuel, are members of the Evangelical Free Church of Salt Lake City.

Marvin Olasky, professor of journalism at the University of Texas at Austin, is also editor of *World*, a weekly newsmagazine from a Christian perspective, and an elder of Redeemer Presbyterian Church (PCA). He is the author of eleven books of history and cultural analysis, including *The Tragedy of American Compassion, Fighting for Liberty and Virtue,* and *Abortion Rites,* and is coauthor of six more. He has written 350 articles for publications such as *World, Policy Review, The Weekly Standard, National Review* and *The Wall Street Journal.* Olasky received an A.B. from Yale University in 1971 and a Ph.D. in American culture from the University of Michigan in 1976. In recent years he has been general editor of the Turning Point Christian Worldview series, chairman of a crisis pregnancy center and president of a PTA. He has also served as Bradley Scholar of the Heritage Foundation, Americans United for Life Scholar and Senior Fellow of the Progress and Freedom Foundation. Before becoming a University of Texas professor in 1983, he was a reporter on the *Bulletin* (Bend, Oregon) and the *Boston Globe*, a speaker for the Christian Anti-Communism Crusade and a speechwriter and program coordinator at the DuPont Company in Wilmington, Delaware.

Olasky and his wife, Susan, an author of children's novels, have four sons: Pete, David, Daniel and Benjamin.

John Patrick is associate professor of clinical nutrition in the departments of biochemistry and pediatrics at the University of Ottawa. He received his M.B., B.S., M.R.C.P. and M.D. degrees from the University of London and the Royal College of Physicians (England). He served in a number of clinical positions before obtaining MRC and Wellcome Research Fellowships to study cell physiology in London and then at the MRC Tropical Metabolism Research Unit at the University of the West Indies in Jamaica. He joined the faculty at the University of Ottawa in 1980. Patrick's research interests have included sodium transport, especially its derangements in malnourished children, and the clinical treatment of affected children. Recently he has been concerned with the failure of nutrition education in Africa and is involved in the development of more culturally effective programs. His summers are usually spent teaching nutrition and theology and conducting research in Zaire with his wife, family and students. He has published over seventy articles in professional journals, has lectured at numerous universities and society meetings and has participated in policy formulating committees in Ontario and Canada.

Patrick and his wife, Sally, have four children and three grandchildren. They currently worship in an Anglican community and meet weekly with a number of Christian professors from the University of Ottawa. They have been involved in starting a pre-university year for university-bound students, called Augustine College, for the purpose of providing an introduction to the history of ideas within a Christian context.

Patricia Raybon is associate professor in the School of Journalism and Mass Communication at the University of Colorado. She received journalism degrees from Ohio State University (B.A.) and the University of Colorado (M.A.) and worked for more than a dozen years in print journalism, first at the *Denver Post* and also at the *Rocky Mountain News* in Denver. In the late 1980s she was editor of the *Denver Post's Sunday Contemporary Magazine* and then worked a year as media relations officer at the Piton Foundation in Denver before joining the faculty at the University of Colorado in 1991. Patricia Raybon is an award-winning journalist whose essays on race, family and culture have been published in the *New York Times Magazine, Newsweek, USA Weekend, USA Today, Guideposts*, the *Chicago Tribune*, the *Denver Post*, the *Rocky Mountain News* and many other newspapers, and in college writing texts and other publications. She is a contributor to National Public Radio's *Weekend Edition*. Raybon's recent book *My First White Friend: Confessions on Race, Love and Forgiveness* (1996) has been awarded a Christopher Award for "artistic excellence affirming the highest values of the human spirit" and a first-place Books for a Better Life Award.

Raybon and her husband, J. Daniel, and their two daughters are members of the Shorter Community African Methodist Episcopal Church in Denver, Colorado.

Patricia H. Reiff is professor and department chairman of space physics and astronomy at Rice University, where she received her Ph.D. degree. Reiff was involved in plasma data analysis for the Apollo and atmosphere explorer missions and was a co-investigator on the dynamics explorer mission. She is a coinvestigator with the magnetic field experiment on the "polar" spacecraft (launched February 24, 1996), part of the global geospace science mission. She is involved in the planning of grand tour cluster and the magnetosphere imager mission and is a coinvestigator on the IMAGE mission to be launched in 2000. Reiff is also involved in public outreach. She has served as project director for teacher enhancement programs and is now working on a project funded by NASA to create interactive real-time exhibits of space science data for museums and schools, with real-time weather, space weather and solar image data obtained from the Internet. She has over sixty refereed publications in journals and book sections, and has served as editor or associate editor for EOS, *Journal of Geophysical Research* and *Reviews of Geophysics*. She has served on advisory committees for the National Science Foundation, NASA, the National Academy of Science and the Association of American Universities. She is presently a member of NASA's Space Science Advisory Committee (strategic planning for all of the Office of Space Science), a member of the space science working group, and is the Rice institutional representative for the Universities Space Research Association. She has received numerous awards, was elected to the Cosmos Club in 1992 and has guided numerous scientific tours. Reiff is also active in the environmental community and has served on the board of trustees of the Citizens' Environmental Coalition for the past seventeen years, including two terms as president.

Reiff and her husband, Thomas Hill, have three children: Andrea and twins Adam and Amelia ("Amy") Hill. She and Andrea are members of Macedonia United Methodist Church in Hockley, Texas.

John Suppe is Blair Professor of Geology at Princeton University and has been a visiting professor at National Taiwan University, California Institute of Technology and Universidad de Barcelona. He served as chair of the Department of Geosciences at Princeton from 1991 to 1994. In 1995 he was elected to the National Academy of Sciences. His Ph.D. is from Yale University. Professor Suppe's research is in structural geology and tectonics, emphasizing the fundamental processes of deformation in the upper crust and the mechanics of mountain building. Professor Suppe has authored or coauthored with his students five books (including a widely used textbook) and seventy articles in major scholarly journals. He was a Guggenheim Fellow and a guest investigator of the NASA Magellan mission to Venus, and has served as associate editor of the *American Journal of Science*.

Suppe and his wife, Barbara, are members of Westerly Road Church, which is attended by many Princeton students and faculty. They have two grown children living in California: Ben, a financial analyst, and Ann, a psychologist who works with abused children

Glenn Tinder is professor emeritus of political science at the University of Massachusetts at Boston, where he has served on the faculty since 1965. He received the Ph.D. degree from the University of California at Berkeley and did postdoctoral work at Harvard University before joining the faculty at the University of Massachusetts at Amherst in 1952. Tinder served on the board of editors for *Polity* and is a member of the editorial advisory board for the *Review of Politics*. Tinder has authored six books, including a major textbook (*Political Thinking*, now in its sixth edition) and *The Political Meaning of Christianity*, as well as numerous articles in major scholarly or literary journals and journals of opinion such as *The Yale Review* and *Atlantic Monthly*.

Tinder and his wife, Gloria, have two grown sons, Galen and Evan, and are members of St. Anne's-in-the-Fields, an Episcopalian church in Lincoln, Massachusetts.

John F. Walkup has been a Paul W. Horn Professor of Electrical Engineering and director of the optical systems laboratory at Texas Tech University, where he was a faculty member from 1971 to 1998. He is currently a national faculty representative with Christian Leadership Ministries, the faculty ministry of Campus Crusade for Christ, International. Walkup received the B.A. degree in engineering science (magna cum laude) from Dartmouth in 1962 and the Ph.D. degree in electrical engineering from Stanford University in 1971. He has been a visiting scholar at the University of Arizona's Optical Sciences Center, a visiting professor at Stanford University and a National Research Council senior associate at NASA's Ames Research Center. Walkup has served as chair of the Education Council of the Optical Society of America, as a member of OSA's board of directors and as chair of the Gordon Research Conference on Holography and Optical Information Processing. He has served as an associate editor for both the *Journal of the Optical Society of America-A* and *Applied Optics-Information Processing*. Walkup is a Fellow of the Institute of Electrical and Electronics Engineers, the International Society for Optical Engineering and the Optical Society of America. His awards include the AT&T Foundation Award for Excellence in the Instruction of Engineering Students (1985) and Texas Tech's President's Academic Achievement Award for teaching, research and service (1994).

Walkup and his wife, Pat, have three grown daughters, Mary, Amy and Becky. They are members of Melonie Park Baptist Church in Lubbock, Texas, where he serves as an elder.

Edwin Yamauchi is professor of history at Miami University. Prior to joining the faculty there in 1964, Yamauchi was assistant professor of history at Rutgers University. He received a Ph.D. degree in Mediterranean studies from Brandeis University. He has studied twenty-two different languages. Yamauchi's scholarly interests are broad but focus on the titles of two of the fifteen books he has authored, coauthored or edited (*The World of the First Christians* and *Peoples of the Old Testament World*). He has presented nearly two hundred papers and lectures at learned society meetings, universities, colleges and seminaries. He has written chapters for twenty-four books, 158 articles in thirty reference works, eighty articles in thirty-seven journals, and ninety-seven reviews in twenty-four journals. Professor Yamauchi has also served in various editorial capacities for several journals, including senior editor for *Christianity Today*.

Yamauchi has two grown children, Brian and Gail. The Oxford Bible Fellowship, which he and his wife, Kimie, helped to found in 1970, ministers each week to about three hundred students from Miami University.

Keith E. Yandell is professor of philosophy and professor of South Asian studies at the University of Wisconsin. He joined the faculty at Wisconsin after receiving the Ph.D. degree in philosophy from Ohio State University in 1966. The results of Yandell's academic career are highlighted in the fifteen books authored or edited, fifty-one scholarly articles authored, numerous entries authored and over 150 papers presented. His academic interests are reflected by the following representative book titles: *Christianity and Philosophy*; *Hume's "Inexplicable Mystery": His Views on Religion*; *Ockham, Descartes and Hume*; *Ethics in Business*; and *Introduction to Ethics*. Yandell has served as Distinguished

237

Visiting Professor at Hope College and Wheaton College.

Yandell is a member of the IFACS (Institute for Advanced Christian Studies) board and is an elder in the Reformed Church of America. He and his wife, Sharon, have four children, Karen, David, Eric, and Merritt, and two grandsons, Steven and Patrick.